The Book of Herbs And Magic

Other Books by Heather Eaton:

The Encyclopedia of the Divine, Spiritual, and Occult Volume I
The Encyclopedia of the Divine, Spiritual, and Occult Volume I I
The Encyclopedia of the Divine, Spiritual, and Occult Volume III

The Book of Herbs And Magic

by

Heather Eaton

One Spirit Press
Portland, Oregon

Copyright © 2013,2014 by Heather Eaton

ISBN: 978-1-893075-32-0
LCCN: 2013954978

Art work by Carolina Ferdanez
Chapter 6 art by Spirit Press

No part of this publication may be reproduced, stored in a retrieval system, or transmitted in any form or by any means, electronic, mechanical, photocopying, recording, scanning, or otherwise, except as permitted under Section 107 or 108 of the 1976 United States Copyright Act, without either the prior written permission of the author, or authorization through payment of the appropriate per-copy fee to the Copyright Clearance Center, 222 Rosewood Drive, Danvers, MA 01923, (978) 750-8400, fax 978-646-8600 or on the web at www.copyright.com.

Limit of Liability/Disclaimer of Warranty: While the publisher and the author have used their best efforts in preparing this book, they make no representations or warranties with respect to the accuracy or completeness of the contents of this book and specifically disclaim any implied warranties of merchantability or fitness for a particular purpose. No warranty may be created or extended by sales representatives or written sales materials. The advice and strategies contained herein may not be suitable for your situation. You should consult with a professional where appropriate. Neither the publisher nor the author shall be liable for any loss of profit or any other commercial damages, including but not limited to special, incidental, consequential, or other damages.

One Spirit Press
Portland, Oregon
www.onespiritpress.com

Color Version Available on Kindle

Table of Contents

Chapter	I	What is Magic	page 2
Chapter	II	Incense	page 12
Chapter	III	Spiritual Baths	page 26
Chapter	IV	Oil Essences	page 40
Chapter	V	Astrology and Incense	page 52
Chapter	VI	Color and Magic	page 66
Chapter	VII	Magical & Spiritual Use of Candles	page 80
Chapter	VIII	Gems and Minerals	page 88
Chapter	IX	Preparation of Rituals	Page 108
Chapter	X	Herbs and Spices	
Plant Index			page 257
Bibliography			page 279
Webliography			page 285
Glossary			page 295
Spell Book			page 333
Colophon			page 335

Chapter I

What is Magic?

Magic Circle (1880) by John William Waterhouse

Introduction

Magic is a form of spiritual expression, the desire to help, to produce positive changes for others and ourselves, the outcome of the mental energy that we project. A blessing is a form of white magic because it is positive spiritual energy *intentionally directed* towards someone; it's something that is not physically tangible but is real. The development of the magical abilities is the result of the spiritualization of the human soul and its capacity for love, concentration, and learning.

Magic is only good or bad depending on how we use it; if in our hearts we desire good things for others, we are projecting good vibrations towards them and by extension, ourselves. If, by contrast, we desire evil, we are sending out negative vibrations, that by the mere fact of feeling them (and emanating them) hurt others and ourselves as well. Thoughts are real things.

The word *Magic* comes from the Greek word magus which means wise. It was defined by Dion Fortune as "The art of producing changes of consciousness in accordance with the Will." MacGregor Mathers said that magic is the "science of the control of the secret force of nature." Both of these statements are generally accepted by Occultists. Magic is the process of rousing, harnessing and projecting the natural energies and releasing this energy accompanied with other methods such prayer or rituals to create the desired change.

Positive and Negative

There are two major forces in this physical Universe. These opposing forces are the positive and the negative that together are in equilibrium. The words *positive and negative* do not mean good or evil, just or erroneous, but simply two opposing forces. In the Orient the positive force is considered active and masculine; and the negative passive and feminine. The equilibrium of the Universe depends on these two forces; the day, positive, could not exist without the night, negative, man without woman, heat without cold, light without dark, and good without evil. These two antagonistic forces, that are at the same time united, are called *yang*, positive and *yin*, negative. All that exists in nature is subject to the laws of yin-yang, the active and the passive.

Yin and Yang

In Chinese philosophy, Yin and Yang are the two complementary principals of the Universe that make up all aspects and phenomena of life. Yin is female, negative, passive, dark and wet. Yang is male, positive, active, light, active and dry. In harmony they are described as the light and dark halves of a circle and the process of the Universe depends on the interaction between them, as one increases the other decreases in a continual process of balance. The origins of Yin/Yang go back to the 3rd Century B.C.E. in China where it formed the bases of the school of cosmology, which has throughout the centuries influenced almost every aspect of Chinese thought including, government, medicine, art and even the occult sciences of astrology and divination.

Karma

From Sanskrit, meaning *action* or *deed*, in Hinduism, Buddhism and Occultism, karma is the spiritual law of cause and effect that plays itself out in the psychic, moral, and physical aspects of life. The law of karma says that every action reaps a like reaction and that the influence of an individual's past incarnations affects his present and future incarnations. Thus, neither unmerited pleasure nor undeserved suffering exists, but rather a Universal justice that works through a natural moral law rather than through divine judgment. Good and bad karma have their effect through many lifetimes, as the soul evolves slowly learning from its mistakes and growing wiser, reaping the rewards of good karma and paying off the dept of bad karma until a state of grace is reached and incarnation is no longer needed.

White Magic

Positive magic conceived and performed with good intentions for positive purposes. White magic includes thoughts and actions that promote the spiritual evolution of the soul.

Black Magic

Negative or harmful magic performed with evil intentions. Actions and thoughts perpetuated against the spiritual evolution of the soul. Any form, act or intervention against a person's free will.

The Evil Eye

The universal belief that negative energy is usually brought on by envy or greed that is projected through the eyes when these are looking intently at someone or something, with or without evil intentions at heart. The Evil Eye has also been described as the Power of Fascination and the Envious Eye. Shown here is the *Hand of Miriam*, a Jewish amulet for protection against the Evil Eye.

Every time we stare at someone and think bad thoughts towards them we are generating what is known as the *Evil Eye*. What does this mean? In mystical and magical traditions people believed that energy was produced by the eyes, which could send out good or bad energy. In modern times we know that our visual system behaves as a projection machine and therefore we do project energy through our eyes. The expression *Evil Eye* refers to the projection harmful negative energy through our eyes.

Spiritual Energy

The human being possesses spiritual energy and by his/her free will, decides to use it for good or evil. This energy is also employed mentally; whereby we can have positive or negative thoughts towards others and the world that surrounds us, and by not understanding ourselves and these energies, we can be sending out negative vibrations without the intention to do so.

Mental energy exists; on many planes of existence, on the astral planes, a thought is as real as a wall. Every time that we think in a negative way about someone, we are sending out negative energy. Our thoughts become energy that is deposited in the places where we spend our time, i.e. our homes our work places, etc. When, among a family there are fights and/or conflicting relationships, you can literally feel the tension in the air. Sensitive persons can feel these vibrations or thought forms to the point of feeling visibly uncomfortable or becoming ill.

Human Spirituality

Although spirituality has traditionally been associated with religion, deities and afterlife, it actually relates to the nature of the spirit including existentialism and introspection developed through spiritual practices such as contemplation, meditation and prayer.

The world has changed a lot in the last century, especially in the scientific area; one result of this, is that the Spiritual Cleansing traditions that were passed from generation to generation in the old days have nearly been lost in this modern time and were mostly considered to be superstitions"or old wives tales.

In past centuries life was very calm and people or family groups usually stayed in the same place all their life. In these times people were more familiar with nature, wildlife and their environment. They respected the environment and kept it physically and spiritually clean. Each home had protective talismans and each family had their domestic rituals. The talismans (tools or means of physical and spiritual protection) kept the environment clean from bad vibrations or countered the effects of evil if and when it occurred.

Every culture around the world has had (and still has in most cases) their wise men, shamans, priests, and/or mystics. Magical traditions and beliefs have been found all over the world. In the European continent it was the Druids who had the richest history in magical rituals and knowledge of herbs, followed later by the Wicca religion, from which the term "Witchcraft" originated".

A few centuries ago the religion of a person determined his/her life style. Today our established religions seem to be only a philosophy in name. Some people may understand the external meaning of the rituals of the religion that they inherited, but rarely do they understand the symbolic meaning on a spiritual level.

Most religions still use amulets and talismans. Christians wear a cross around their necks for protection as do Jews the star of David.

Spiritual Cleansing and Protection

The concept of spiritual cleansing is an integral part of religious rituals. The rituals affect our emotions and we feel better after participating in them. Spiritual cleansing is the process of removing negative vibrations from an object, person or place using positive psychic energy and natural magic.

Spiritual rituals are roads to cleanse and protect oneself from unwanted negative energy. We have all met someone who seemed to be surrounded by negativity. After spending a while with this person we might feel tired or even dirty. In occultism, these persons are called "Psychic Vampires". It may happen that upon entering a house or apartment, we feel the desire to leave immediately because we feel uncomfortable. What is making us uncomfortable are overwhelming thought forms and the vibrations that are present.

Spiritual cleansing is about how to rid ourselves of these negative vibrations and prevent and protect ourselves from them. Through rituals we become knowledgeable and adept at improving the spiritual atmosphere in our home, work place or anywhere we desire.

Magical Energy

Magical energy is the power of nature, the same energy that emanates from us as living beings. It is natural, divine and spiritual and present in every natural thing in this world, as much in ourselves as in herbs, gems, water, mountains, the earth itself and everything that surrounds us. To practice magic is simply to harness these energies through prayer, concentration and in some cases through more elaborate rituals.

The base of all magical acts is the force or energy of the Universe; that which gave us life, which makes the herbs grow, that which makes the world exist as we think we understand it. It doesn't matter what term we use to describe it, except to recognize its existence. Those of us who work with magic use this energy for our magical purposes.

Purposes of Magic

From the time that we discovered magical energy we have used it by ritual inheritance for the same reasons. In our human condition, we desire love, healing, protection, and fortune among other needs and desires.

When we lived in caves our psychic senses were more developed than today because we counted on them for survival. Over time we discovered that certain herbs or gems gave us more courage when we hunted or protected us in battles with other tribes. We learned that certain herbs had sympathetic vibrations towards us and other did not. By trial and error we found that some herbs helped cure wounds and that others alleviated internal pains and still others could kill us. Later, we discovered that some herbs helped us spiritually in baths, others in incenses and so forth.

Magic of Herbs

Herbs contain energies that connect and function both on the physical level and on the spiritual level. The magical use of herbs is to take advantage of their properties, by themselves or by combining them with other herbs and/or substances with the same properties, for the desired effect. Herbs, as living beings respond to the vibrations of the person that handles them and cares for them. The best way to receive their cooperation, so to speak, is to respect them and try to empathize with their vibrations. In the same way that we give and receive love of people, we can receive the same from herbs that we grow and care for.

Principles of White Magic

Cause No Harm

If we project negative energy or thoughts in rituals with the purpose of harming someone, we may get what we want, but, we will receive the same energies with more force bounced back and, we would be operating completely against the principals of the universal plan of spiritual evolution. For students of occultism and almost all the religions in the world, the rule is that one receives what one gives, be this good or bad, in this life or the next. As true Christians would say "do unto others as thou would have others do unto thee".

Effort

The results obtained from rituals are in direct proportion to the dedication, personal effort and concentration, reflected in the time dedicated to the preparation of the ritual and to the energy generated by the concentration and the desire to obtain the objective. The greater the need the more possibilities that the ritual, charm or prayer will be successful.

Patience

When we perform rituals or pray for something the energy generated may take time to produce tangible results. To produce results in anything that we do we need knowledge (on how to do what ever it is that we need), concentration, practice and a lot of patience. Everything requires time and things happen when they should. Notwithstanding, when we do obtain results and realize that we can have positive effects over situations or states of mind, we may feel the joy of having helped to produce these results.

Energy

The energy is generated by our own mind through concentration. This energy, together with the vibrations of nature, the Universe, God (or whatever word you wish to use) makes magic reality. The tools that may be used, such as herbs, incenses, gems, etc., must be chosen carefully and always of the best quality. We can make most of the implements that will be required. It is always better to use something made by oneself then to buy it. The act of preparing and making something takes time and concentration and in this process we are already charging the implement with our vibrations, energy and intentions. For these same reasons, we should not participate in rituals when we are ill, bleeding (from an open wound or menstruation) or are in an unhappy, fearful or stressful state of mind.

Magic is a Spiritual Creative Art

From the light, purity emerges. Whoever desires to perform magic rituals should be clean, in body, spirit and soul. If we do not manage the required concentration and the spiritual force required or our desires are not completely pure and disinterested, the desired effects can be dispersed, losing effectiveness or not producing any effect at all. When, on the contrary we desire from the bottom of our hearts to help ourselves or others (with their knowledge and consent), and we perform rituals we are also growing spiritually ourselves.

It Should be Joyful

Much of the positive energy that we radiate is more potent when we are happy, in good spirits, in a good mood and laughing from our hearts. Rituals should be a happy event and we should be happy in mind and spirit. If we feel that to facilitate these positive energies, we should laugh, dance and/or sing during a ritual, then go ahead, spontaneity is very beneficial because it is generated from our spiritual selves.

Concentration and Visualization

To be capable of concentrating our minds and our thoughts on the objective and to clearly *see* what we wish to accomplish is absolutely fundamental for positive results in magic. From the moment that we commence the design and preparation of a ritual, we should know exactly what it is that we desire and focus our efforts and all our energy to that objective. Clear visualization of the desired result is crucial, therefore we need to know very clearly what it is that we desire before we begin our preparations. All of us are capable of directing and concentrating our natural energies and vibrations and, as in all other activities that we undertake "practice makes perfect".

Chapter I — What is Magic?

Faith

Whoever does not trust their own motives and intentions in the practice of magic or is not optimistic about the results, should not bother with them. Faith is one of the most import elements in magic. When we trust in ourselves and our motives, we project vibrations of success in the astral world which are then generated onto the physical world, but if by contrast we do not trust in ourselves we will only generate uncertain vibrations and those will not help us succeed. All the knowledge that we need is already in our minds and it is always convenient to listen to that little internal voice that tells us what to do or not to do. The more we trust ourselves and our natural latent powers the more probabilities of success we have. Our most powerful natural energy is the power of our will, concentrated on achieving our objective and our faith in the fact that we *will* achieve our objective.

Chapter II

Incenses

Photograph by Heather Eaton

The Book of Herbs and Magic — Heather Eaton

Introduction

From the Latin *incendere*, meaning "to burn", incense is a mixture of aromatic herbs, spices and other biological materials that release a fragrant smoke when burned. Incense has been used all around the world for thousand of years in religious and spiritual ceremonies and rituals for purification, spiritual cleansing, inducing meditation and aromatherapy.

Incense is an element practically indispensable in any ritual, as a means to have our prayers heard and/or to purify and protect the area. The aromas and vibrations of incenses predispose the tranquility and help obtain the desired state of mind and correct spiritual attitude. Rituals with incense provide us with the adequate vibrations for the success of the rituals. Incense mixtures are burned prior to a ritual to purify the altar and immediate surroundings and to rid the environment of negative vibrations. During a ritual other incense recipes may be burned to assist in the release the magical energies of the spells or prayers.

Incense and its Uses

From the time that we discovered that incense is a favorable offering, we have used it mainly for the following purposes:

Consecration to the Gods

That the scents and fragrances of incense are favorable to the Gods and the petitions we ask of them is something that we have believed for many, many years. Almost every religion throughout history has and still uses incense in their temples, churches and other places of worship. The scented smoke transports the prayers of those who concentrate on their wishes or prayers while burning incense. It is also good for charging oneself with good energy and personal power for rituals.

Neutralization

In various ancient civilizations incense was used to cover up smells in sacrifices and burials. In our times it is also burned to neutralize or cover up bad smells as well as to neutralize negative vibrations.

Alter States of Consciousness

Aromatherapy tells us that the aromas and vibrations of incense predispose the state of mind of those who burn incense. The odors and vibrations awaken sensations of the body, soul and spirit. The scents and smells of the burning incense can alter our states of conscience and assist us in obtaining the state of mind necessary for the success of the ritual.

Preparation of Incenses

When using herbs to prepare incenses, the ingredients must be completely dry and pulverized. Most of the herbs and other ingredients can be bought as dry herbs or incenses that have already been prepared. Nevertheless, from an energetic point of view, it is much more productive, satisfying and powerful (preparing incenses impregnates personal vibrations in the ingredients), to collect and process the ingredients oneself. Incenses prepared by ourselves have three or four times the potency of those that you can buy.

Technologically less advanced societies tend to respect life, *all life*, more than our advanced societies do. They have a special care and even reverence towards the plant and animal world. Native American tribes even ask permission from the herbs before they harvest or trim them.

To have, grow and care for herbs makes them more receptive towards us. Herbs are living beings that share our same environment (they also have auras), and it has been demonstrated that they react to our vibrations and moods. They also show sympathies or empathies towards different people. To grow our own herbs (for medicinal or magical purposes or just to have them) empowers them with more powerful energetic vibrations for our purposes than to buy them or harvest them from other places.

Harvesting

Herbs are made of energy the same way as we are, they receive energy from the Earth and Sun and are subject to effects of the same forces of nature, such as the tides and lunar and solar cycles. Centuries of experience have taught us the advantages in harvesting procedures that allow us to harness the maximum natural energies for optimum results.

The Moon passes through a waning and a waxing phase, its constant rhythmic movements attract our seas as we see in the movement of the tides. This attractive force affects all living beings, including herbs. When the Moon is in the waxing stage all the vital energy raises. This is the best time to harvest the aerial sections of herbs; flowers, leaves, stem or bark. In the waning stage, the vital energy descends. This is the best time to harvest the subterranean parts of the herbs; roots and bulbs. Since the night is under the dominion of the Moon, after dark on a clear night is the ideal time to harvest most herbs. The best time to harvest leaves or stems is before the herb flowers, because the substances that are concentrated in the leaves are passed on to the flowers when the herb blooms.

Drying

Most herbs can be dried and stored up to a year before they lose their properties. Before setting the herbs to dry, all dead and bug eaten parts should be removed. They should be rinsed in clean water, optimally with spring water, placed on a soft cloth or paper and set to dry.

The leaves can be left in open air, placing them on absorbent paper and turning them over once a day to avoid mold. They should not be exposed to direct sunlight. The best place to dry herbs is in a dark well ventilated room. They are dry when you can pulverize them with your fingers and this is the right time to take the leaves off the stems.

To dry seeds such as Juniper or Anise seeds, however, there is a different procedure; the stems should be introduced upside down into brown paper bags with the stems at the opening and tied at the top. This procedure assures that the seed capsules will fall into the paper bag and none will be lost. These bags may be placed in direct sunlight. When they are dry the bags are shaken or the dried herb pulverized manually.

Some flowers such as Rose and Lavender flowers should also be dried differently. To dry Roses its best to take off the petals one by one and place them on paper. Lavender flowers by contrast should not be separated from the stem until they are dry.

Roots take a long time to dry because they contain high amounts of humidity. Some roots may take up to a year to be completely dry. Roots can be hung close to a chimney or stove. Drying time varies from one herb to another. The herbs must be completely dry to burn well.

Storage

It's convenient to have a good quantity of glass jars, preferably dark glass. When you place the dry herbs into the jars it is highly recommendable to label and date them. The dried contents should be used up completely or discarded before a new batch is prepared. Dried herbs should never be left in the direct sunlight or close to electronic devices, stoves, chimneys or other forms of energy generating apparatus.

Herbal Incenses

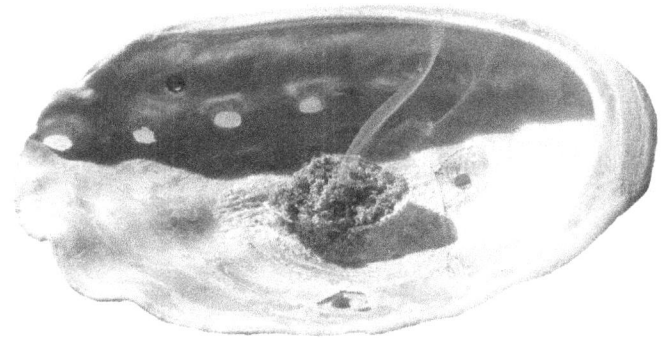

Photograph by Heather Eaton

Herbs and Their Use in Incense

Agrimony — Especially useful to eliminate fears.

Aloe Vera — Spiritual healer.

Amber — Aphrodisiac and remedy for nervous maladies.

Angelica — Protects and purifies. The seeds are burned to induce clairvoyance and visions.

Anise — Protection, clairvoyance and visions.

Asafetida — Rejects illness, misfortune and repels negative vibrations. Also used to invoke spirits.

Balsam — Burned to create a material base to invoke good spirits and for protection.

Basil — With a sweet spicy scent, basil eliminates bad vibrations, purifies wherever it is burned and protects love. Ends love discussions.

Bay — The leaves are burned to generate visions and stimulate the psychic abilities. Also used for love, purification and protection.

Benzoin — Purifies the soul and attracts success and love. Attracts good spiritual vibrations, clears the mind and eliminates bad vibrations.

Betony — Used as a component in protection and purification incenses.

Bistort — Good for predictions and divinations, works better when mixed with Frankincense.

Broom	An excellent component in purification incenses.
Calendula	Incenses made from the flowers make excellent condensers of astral forces.
California Poppy	Stimulates luck and fertility.
Camphor	Added to incenses for prediction, divination and for health protection.
Carnation	Used to increase astral energy, it can be very powerful.
Cassia	Love.
Catnip	Mixed with Rose petals it makes an excellent love incense.
Chamomile	Favors a calm spiritual attitude for meditation. Also used for relaxation since it contains sedative properties.
Cinnamon	Attracts good vibrations and fortune. Stimulates concentration and favors clairvoyance and visions. Also used for love and success.
Clove	Repels negative energy, purifies the environment and generates highly spiritual vibrations. Favors visions and luck.
Copal	Used for love, purification, spiritual cleansing and protection.
Cyclamen	For love incenses.
Eucalyptus	Used with blue candles it liberates healing vibrations. Stimulates the spirit and spirituality.
Eyebright	Helps develop the spirit and the mind. Also favors visions.
Fenugreek	Used as an offering to the Gods and for clarity of thought.
Flax	Used for protection against the Evil Eye and for purification.
Frankincense	Protects against the Evil Eye. It is a very powerful protector. Used to purify and consecrate. Attracts love, success and stimulates spirituality.
Fumitory	Protection and purification.
Gardenia	Incenses prepared with the flowers are used for love and attracting the opposite sex. Charged with lunar energy it is also used in potions for health and protection.

Garlic	The skin of the cloves is burned to conserve money at home and to eliminate negative thoughts in the environment.
Geranium	The red flowers are used in protection and healing incenses and the pink flowers in love incenses.
Ginger	Acts as a catalyzer improving the effects of other incenses as long as it is in lesser quantity than the other ingredients.
Greater Burnet	Used in protection and purification incenses.
Gum Arabic	Used to purify rooms or places for ceremonies and rituals. Stimulates clairvoyance and psychic powers.
Honeysuckle	The flowers are used in incenses destined for success in business.
Horehound	Used in incense potions to eliminate negative vibrations.
Hyacinth	Good for calming hyperactive people and for avoiding nightmares.
Hyssop	Used to eliminate negative feelings and to protect and purify the soul.
Iris	Used for visits from lovers, creating an ideal atmosphere. Induces visions and prophetic dreams.
Jasmine	Helps fight depression by providing optimism, eliminates anguish and increases self-esteem. Attracts good luck and good spirits.
Juniper	Scares away evil entities, counteracts nightmares and helps in psychic and spiritual development.
Lavender	Induces prophetic dreams. Used for love, protection and purification and for insomnia.
Lemon	The flower petals are burned to facilitate prophetic dreams.
Lemon Balm	Luck and protection.
Lotus	Used for protection, healing and spiritual development. Rejects negative influences.
Marjoram	Eliminates negative thought forms and clears the environment of bad vibrations.
Mastic	Used in fumigations to stimulate extra-sensorial energies, to invoke spirits

and to heighten personal powers.

Mate	It is an excellent astral cleanser.
Meadowsweet	Has very positive vibrations and is used for love, tranquility and peace.
Mugwort	Used in incenses for protection, purification, and to induce true dreams, clairvoyance and divinations.
Mullein	Used in protection and purification incenses.
Musk	Used for courage and valor and to stimulate love and passion.
Myrrh	Favors visions, protects against the Evil Eye, induces true dreams, and attracts love and success. Its smoke is also used to consecrate rings and amulets.
Myrtle	Aphrodisiac, increases personal charm and attracts highly positive influences and vibrations.
Nutmeg	Increases empathy, attracts love, good fortune and favors clairvoyance.
Orange	Orange flowers are used in healing incenses.
Patchouli	Burned in the morning to stimulate energy and attract good vibrations and in the evening for love, divination and clairvoyance.
Pennyroyal	Used in healing and summer incenses.
Peppermint	Aphrodisiac, against insomnia and for purifying.
Pokeweed	Has very powerful effects eliminating negative vibrations.
Rose	Rose leaves are burned to generate clairvoyant dreams. The scent of the flowers produces spiritual peace, invites love and calms accumulated tensions.
Rosemary	Protects and purifies, rejects bad vibrations. Increases and awakens mental capacities.
Rue	Burned for general protection, especially useful to drive away evil spirits. Stimulates virtue and alerts to danger.
Sage	Used in healing incenses and incenses that help finish personal projects with success.

Saint John's Wort	One of the most powerful protective herbs.
Sandalwood	It's a psychic and spiritual developer. Stimulates fantasy, love, success and attracts good vibrations. Relaxes the body and stimulates the mind.
Snapdragon	Eliminates bad vibrations.
Solomon's Seal	Attracts love, success, good psychic vibrations, relaxes the body and calms the mind. Used in incenses for protection and purification and for invoking good spirits.
Spikenard	Excellent incense for business, especially when mixed with Sandalwood. By itself it attracts good spiritual vibrations.
Sweet Flag	The root is used in healing incenses and to attract good fortune and money.
Thyme	Burned in small quantities to increase luck and to purify. Also used in love incenses.
Vervain	Eliminates heavy malicious thoughtforms. Also used in love incenses.
Violet	Creates positive energy and opens new spiritual dimensions.
Wallflower	Reveals the intentions of other people.
Wormwood	Invokes good spirits, eliminates the Evil Eye, and favors clairvoyance and predictions. Increases psychic power.
Yarrow	Used in love and purification incenses.

Love Incenses

Love is energy, the glue of the universe, going beyond space and time. Notwithstanding, love can not be forced on someone, meaning we can not make someone love us. True love is not selfish. If love is real and sincere there should be no demands or expectations. If the person that we love does not love us we should let them go because we want the best for that person that is, *their* happiness. There is a very wise saying that goes "if you love someone let them go, if they return to you it is because they have always loved you, if they don't it is because they never loved you".

When we deal with love incenses we should understand that their purpose is not to swindle someone, but to make a statement to the universe, that we are prepared to love and to receive love, without having someone in mind. The following love incense recipes are geared to announce to the world that we are available for love and want to find someone.

Musk and Patchouli Incense

The following ingredients should be mixed in equal parts on a Friday, adding 3 drops of Musk and Patchouli essences to the mixture and burn on charcoal:

Lavender + Iris Root + Rose Petals

Venus Incense

Mix a pinch of Nutmeg and burn with equal parts of:

Benzoin + Rose Petals

Charming Incense

This incense predisposes calm and interior peace. Burn a quarter of a teaspoon on charcoal:

1 Teaspoon Bay + 1 Teaspoon Sandalwood + 1 Teaspoon Myrrh + 2 Teaspoons Frankincense + 3 Drops Essence of Gardenia + 3 Drops Essence of Benzoin

Egyptian Incense

This incense possesses a soft aroma and generates an oriental atmosphere.

12 Parts Sandalwood + 4 Parts Iris Root + 4 Parts Patchouli Leaves + 4 Parts Myrrh + 4 Parts Frankincense + 1 Part Sawdust

Attraction Incense

The fragrance of this incense is a caress for senses and fills the spirit with pleasant thoughts:

10 Parts Sawdust + 8 Parts Frankincense + 4 Parts Sandalwood + 2 Parts Myrrh + 1 Part Iris Root + 4 Parts Cinnamon

Incenses for Success and Money

Most of the old religions used incenses as offerings to their God(s), when asking for success and fortune. They believed that thoughts and desires were transported by the vibrations of the incense to a superior universal force.

Incense for Luck

This recipe is a mixture to favor luck in general. It is better prepared on a Sunday with a waning moon. Moisten the mixture with a few drops of Almond Oil.

1 Part Cloves + 1 Part Nutmeg + 1 Part Lemon Balm + 1 Part California Poppy + 1 Part Cedar Wood

Incense for Success

This recipe favors success and prosperity.

1 Part Sandalwood + 2 Parts Cinnamon + 1 Part White Incense + 2 Drops Benzoin Essence + 1/2 Part Iris Root

Incense for Fortune

10 Parts Sandalwood + 2 Parts Frankincense + 2 Parts Myrrh

Incense for Fortune and Success

This recipe also favors success and prosperity. Mix in equal parts and burn a teaspoon on charcoal.

Benzoin + Cinnamon

Incense for Business

8 Parts Sawdust + 2 Parts Frankincense + 2 Parts Sandalwood + 1 Part Myrrh + 1 Part Iris Root + 2 Parts Cinnamon

Incenses for Protection and Purification

Many herbs and other forms of plant life have protective energies. When they are burned, hung or carried, they dissolve negative energy and form a protective shield. Some herbs are charged with highly energetic vibrations that reject or repel the negative energy found in the environment or generated by people.

The following are some incense potions that have been specifically designed to reject and protect from bad vibrations.

High Spirit Incense

This incense attracts superior spiritual forces and protect, blessing and clearing up the spiritual environment. Burn a quarter of a teaspoon on charcoal.

3 Teaspoons Frankincense + 2 Teaspoons Benzoin + 1 Teaspoon Myrrh

Incense for Clearing the Environment

This incense can be used to clear the environment when there are discussions or fights.

3 Parts Frankincense + 2 Parts White Incense + 1 Part Myrrh +
2 Parts Sandalwood

Purification Incense

To purify means eliminating negative influences. Purification is obtained when the environment has good vibrations and *feels* relaxed and comfortable. When you move into a new house it is convenient to purify it. The purification process is intended to rid the atmosphere of thought forms or vibrations from the previous inhabitants. The following is a good mixture for purification incense. Mix in equal parts:

Basil   Yarrow   Rosemary
Angelica   Juniper   Sawdust
Mugwort   Bay

The ingredients should be ground until a fine mix is produced. It is advisable to fumigate every room.

Simple Purification Incense

Another good simple purification incense is made by mixing equal parts of:

Frankincense   Sandalwood   Rosemary

Temple Purification Incense

This incense is used specifically to purify a temple or altar.

3 Parts Frankincense + 1 Part Myrrh + 1 Part Lavender +
5 Drops Sandalwood Oil

Chapter II — Incenses

Incenses for Prediction, Divination, and Spiritual Development

In prediction or divination conditions are generated and activated that allow the veil of the present to be lifted so the future can be seen. Some incense potions create an atmosphere that activates these forces or states, while other incenses possess vibrations and aromas that influence the powers of clairvoyance in sensitive and psychic persons.

Many incense potions that activate these faculties are best used before sleep when they tend to produce the best effects. When we are about to go to sleep, our minds relax and pass to states of conscience that we do not access when we are fully awake and conscience of our normal environment. In these states the answers may be accessible while we dream. Other incense potions may create ideal spiritual attitudes; calming the conscience and allowing us to receive messages or answers to our questions.

For optimal results certain conditions or states of mind must be obtained. Our minds and spirits must be calm. We should not be distracted, it is advisable to create an environment that eliminates or minimizes all noises and external interruptions, worries or problems. All the mental and spiritual energy must be concentrated on the objective of letting the mind go blank and allowing the reception of the messages or answers.

Incense for Psychic and Spiritual Development

The following recipe may be used with any other auxiliary method, such as cards or a crystal ball. Mix in equal parts and add a few drops of Musk Essence:

Mastic	Juniper	Sandalwood
Cinnamon	Patchouli	

Psychic Power Incense

This incense is burned specifically to develop psychic powers.

2 Parts Frankincense + 2 Parts Sandalwood + 2 Parts Cinnamon +
1 Part Nutmeg + 3 Drops Orange Flower Oil

Psychic Awareness Incense

This incense is burned to promote psychic awareness.

2 Parts Mastic + 2 Parts Juniper + 2 Parts Cinnamon +
1 Part Sandalwood + 3 Drops Patchouli Oil

Incense for Astral Projection

The following incense is used to induce prophetic dreams, divination and astral projection.

    2 Parts Sandalwood + 2 Drops Benzoin Essence + 2 Part Rose Petals

Traditional Incense for Astral Projection

This incense is burned to assist in astral projection.

    3 Parts Sandalwood + 3 Parts Benzoin + 1 Part Mugwort

Incense for Prophetic Dreams

This other incense is very effective in inducing prophetic dreams.

    1 Part Sandalwood + 2 Drops Spikenard or Jasmine oil + 1 Part Rose Petals

Incense for Dreams

This incense is used to help remember dreams.

    2 Parts Sandalwood + 2 Parts Rose Petals + 2 Parts Jasmine Flowers

Incense for Visions

This incense affects our state of mind, allowing visions to be received.

    10 Parts Sawdust + 2 Parts Frankincense + 3 Parts Sandalwood + 1 Part Myrr + 1 Part Iris Root + 2 Parts Cinnamon

Spirit Incense

This incense is used to invite good spirits and good vibrations to be present.

    2 Parts Sandalwood + 1 Part Lavender

Incense to Awaken Interior Forces

Many inhabitants and mystics of the orient believe that they awaken interior forces by placing their hands over the smoke and rubbing their eyes using the following incense. The mixture must be prepared with herbs and ingredients of the best possible quality.

    32 Parts Sawdust + 16 Parts Frankincense + 8 Parts Sandalwood +

4 Parts Myrrh + 4 Parts Iris Root + 8 Parts Cinnamon

Incense Potions for Moon Magic

Egyptian Lunar Incense

Egyptian in origin, this incense is used in honor of the Moon.

1 Part Sandalwood + 1/2 Part Jasmine + 1/5 Part Myrrh

European Lunar Incense

This European incense is also used for its lunar energies.

2 Parts Jasmin + 2 Parts Camphor + 7 Parts Cedar Wood + 2 Parts Honeysuckle Flowers

Incense for Full Moon Magic

This incense is used for rituals during the full Moon.

3 Part Gardenia Petals + 2 Parts Rose Petal + 1 Part Myrrh + 1 Part Frankincense

Incense for Moon Magic

This incense is used for rituals under the influence of the Moon.

3 Part Sandalwood + 2 Parts Eucaliptus + 2 Part Frankincense
1 Drop Jasmine Oil

Traditional Lunar Incense

This incense comes from an old tradition of lunar magic.

1 Part Frankincense + 1/4 Part Iris Roo + 1 Part Sandalwood

Incense Potions for Other Purposes

Incense to Fumigate Clothes

If you burn this incense as you dress, it charges the body and spirit with positive vibrations. It works better in the full moon because of its lunar vibrations. Add a few drops of essence of Orange Flowers.

16 Parts Sawdust + 8 Parts Frankincense + 4 Parts Sandalwood + 2 Parts Myrrh + 2 Parts Iris Root + 4 Parts Cinnamon + 1 Part Jasmine Essence

Incense for Offerings

This incense is often used as an offering by itself but it can also be combined with other ritual elements.

1 Part Rose Petals + 1 Part Vervain + 1 Part Cinnamon + 1 Part Myrrh + 1 Part Frankincense

Incense for Concentration

The following incense is good for studying; its vibrations increase spiritual energy, favor concentration and stimulate the memory.

1 Part Cinnamon + 1 Part Nutmeg Flowers + 1 Part Rosemary

Incense for Summer Solstice

This incense is generally used on the summer solstice.

1 Part Fennel + 1 Part Rue + 2 Parts Cinnamon + 6 Parts Red Sandalwood + 2 Parts Geranium + 1 Part White Incense + 2 Parts Cedar Wood

Wiccan Incense for Summer Solstice

This Wiccan recipe is also burned on the summer solstice.

2 Parts Sandalwood + 1 Part Mugwort + 1 Part Chamomile + 2 Parts Gardenia + 1 Part Yarrow + 3 Drops Lavender Oil + 3 Drops Rose Oil

Chapter III　　　　　　　　　　　　　　　　　　　　　　　　Incenses

Chapter III

Spiritual Baths

The Tepidarium (1881) by Lawrence Alma-Tadema

What is a Spiritual Bath?

When we take a bath to clean up physically, we get physically clean. A spiritual bath is used for spiritual cleansing and this cleansing extends beyond the physical planes. This concept is found in most of the spiritual practices in most religions. It is found in the Christian baptism ritual and in the Muslim act of washing before prayer; among other religious practices and shows the desire to be clean when one approaches God.

While most people accept baptisms or other religious rituals as a form of spiritual cleansing, it seems harder to accept that a bath in our own home can also be taken to cleanse oneself spiritually. Spiritual baths are taken to cleanse ourselves of negative influences or vibrations that are not beneficial to our spiritual selves. The ritual in itself indicates the desire to request from the universe or God, assistance in cleansing ourselves or changing what we feel that should be done to benefit our bodies, spirits and souls.

What it Involves

A bath that is taken to cleanse spiritually and protect is different from a bath taken to cleanse the body. A few basic principles should be applied when taking a spiritual bath. When we take a spiritual bath we do not use shampoos or commercial bath salts or soap. We use clean cool water and add herbs, oils, or other elements and calmly stir with our hands for a while. Decorate with and light candles and incenses to create the comfortable environment and mood. Once the bath is prepared we are entering into a spiritual experience. This requires us to relax, breath deeply and calmly and mentally separate our minds and spirits from a conventional bath attitude and open ourselves to another kind of experience.

How to Take a Spiritual Bath

Before a spiritual bath is taken, we should take a physical cleansing bath first, i.e.., shower or tub. After we are clean we should always clean the tub and surrounding areas. Since the purpose of a spiritual bath is of a spiritual nature the implements and environment should be clean of physical impurities. The clean atmosphere should involve the whole room. Any additional decoration such as flowers, candles, colored curtains or scarves, music, etc., should be freely applied according to our hearts and tastes; listen to your inner voice. In general spiritual baths that are taken to rid ourselves of negative influences and vibrations, should be taken with salt water or sea water.

After the bathtub is about half full, we add our preparations to the water and stir slowly (preferably with the right hand) we should relax our bodies, breathing deeply and slowly, and calm our minds. Then, naked, we should lie down and let the water cover us (even our heads) for a few seconds. The time that we should remain in a spiritual bath varies depending on the bath's recipe though, in general around 10 minutes is enough. There are certain spiritual baths that can take longer for optimal results.

Relaxation and concentration are of the utmost importance because our concentration requires a conscious effort and relaxation helps predispose our bodies and minds. Those of us who profess religious beliefs should pray accordingly for our needs. When we feel that it is time, we should let the water drain and visualize all our negative thoughts and vibrations leave with the bath water. It is important to dry in the open air as much as possible, we should not rub our bodies or hair with a towel. A towel for the hair and a robe for our body can be used when necessary, without drying off first, but whenever possible we should not even do this, but let our bodies dry naturally.

Having felt effects immediately or not we should rest, assured that the bath has and will have the desired effect. The effects are produced at spiritual levels of conscience, not on the physical plane, at least at first. After a spiritual bath we should not bathe for at least for a day.

Baths with Herbs

Many spiritual bath recipes are made with herbs or combinations of herbs. In general the preparations use a half a cup of fresh herbs or four tablespoons of dried herbs to one cup of boiling water, this mixture should be covered and allowed to seep for a few minutes. When the mixture is added to the bathtub the herbs should be should be strained unless otherwise indicated.

Herbs and Their Use in the Bath

Agrimony — Eliminates vibrations of fear and anguish from the environment.

Aloe Vera — For patience.
{Soak ¼ cup of sliced Aloe Vera in boiling water a few minutes}

Angelica — Protects against the accumulation of negative influences.

Anise — Anise seeds produce a psychological state ideal for spiritual development.
{2 tablespoons of Anise seeds in 1 cup boiling water, seep and add to a half tub of warm water.}

Basil — Protects, cleans and eliminates the bad vibrations and negativity in the environment. Also protects against the accumulation of negative influences.

Bay — Used in purification baths.
{Herbal sacks with Bay leaves are placed directly in the bath water.}

Broom — Works as an astral "broom". Eliminates negative influences from inferior astral spheres and cleanses the aura. {Use 1 cup of Broom tips to 2 cups of boiling water for the bath or seep a cup of Broom tips in alcohol for a week and use the alcohol to rub your body.}

Calendula — Helps gain respect and admiration from others.
{1 cup of Calendula petals and 1 cup of boiling water. Visualization is of utmost importance.}

Carnation — Eliminates negative influences and cleanses the aura.
{The buds of 7 white Carnations are rubbed directly on the body, from head to toe.}

Chamomile — Used to attract love.
{Use 1 cup of Chamomile flowers in 1 cup of boiling water.}

Cinnamon — Cinnamon bark is ideal for this bath which helps resolve problems. Also used to stimulate income and vital energy.
{Use 1 cup of boiling water for 2 or 3 pieces of Cinnamon bark.}

Coffee — Revitalizes physical weaknesses.
{Use 3 cups of strong Coffee, seep and add to the bathwater.}

Fenugreek — Clears the mind of negative or strange thoughts. Also used as a hair rinse, improves clarity of thought and destroys negative vibrations.
{Use 2 teaspoons Fenugreek in 1 cup of boiling water.}

Garlic — Neutralizes the Evil Eye.
{Boil 20 Garlic cloves for 20 minutes. Add to bathwater or use as final rinse.}

Hyssop — Protector and purifier. It is used for spiritual illumination and cleansing. Concentration and serenity are very important in this bath.

Iris — Powerful for love and protection. Also used to stabilize communications

	with loved ones.
Lavender	Spiritual purification; tends to calm nervous persons and helps overcome insomnia. {Herbal sacks with Lavender flowers are placed directly in the bathwater.}
Lemon	Used for purification baths. Especially effective in the full moon. {Use 1 cup of Lemon flowers to 1 cup of boiling water.}
Lemon Balm	Stimulates mental conditions and is useful for meditation. Also used to relax the body and calm the soul.
Lotus	Eliminates astral detritus and assists in spiritual growth.
Mate	Used as a cleansing bath in spiritual practices because of its powerful effect. Eliminates most of the astral detritus normally accumulated, and counteracts the Evil Eye. {Use 1 cup of Mate to 1 cup boiling water.}
Nutmeg	Makes people more willing to listen. Eliminates negative thoughts and attracts good luck. Good bath for personal stress situations and useful before interviews. {Use 1 tablespoon Nutmeg to 1 cup of boiling water.}
Orange	Orange flowers are used to attract love or to seduce a lover.
Parsley	Improves the economic situation, specially powerful when combined with Cinnamon. {A handful of fresh Parsley should be steamed with 4 cups of water for 20 minutes.}
Patchouli	Used in love and seduction baths.
Peppermint	As a hair rinse it eliminates the Evil Eye.
Pokeweed	Used to eliminate bad vibrations.
Rose	Both Rose petals and Rose essence are used for love.
Rosemary	Used to eliminate bad vibrations, to protect from physical harm and to conserve youth. Used in a hair rinse it improves the memory.
Rue	Used in spiritual cleansing baths and to help find illumination on the spiritual road, eliminating religious confusion. Pray for clarity. {Use 1 tablespoon Rue to 1 cup of boiling water.}
Sage	In powder or fresh, this herb helps to gain wisdom, protects against negativity and clears the mind. It is ideally taken on a Thursday before the sun rises.
Snapdragon	Breaks charms and eliminates vibrations caused by fear. {Use 1 cup of Snapdragon flowers to 1 cup of boiling water.}
Thyme	Good in Spring to help develop psychic abilities and to eliminate negativity.

Vervain   Used in spiritual baths for purification and protection, its effects can be very powerful.

Yarrow   Especially good for finding a lover.

Love Baths

The most popular esoteric baths sold are those related to love. Love is one of the most powerful feelings in the world and we often have difficulties in expressing it. Anything that interferes with our capacity to love or to be loved is worth eliminating.

Yarrow Love Bath

Yarrow leaves are one of the most effective herbs in love baths, best when grown locally and when harvested at the beginning of the new moon. This bath is especially effective on a Friday before noon, it provides a subtle announcement to the universe that we want to find a lover or a companion.

Use one cup of Yarrow leaves and cover them with boiling water. Place this in a clean jar with a lid. Close the lid and refrigerate for a week. Use only the water.

Enchant Lover Bath

Mix equal parts of Lemon and Patchouli oil and add six parts of alcohol. This recipe is simply to charm or enchant your lover.

Aphrodisiac Bath

Seep in a cup of boiling water for 10 minutes, after adding the recipe to the tub with warm water add 3 drops of Patchouli oil.

3   Parts Rose Petals + 3   Parts Rosemary   +   2   Parts Thyme   +   1   Part Jasmine

Love Bath

Seep in a cup of boiling water for 10 minutes, and to the tub with warm water:

3   Parts Rose Petals + 3   Parts Lavender   +   2   Parts Lemon Flowers   +
3   Part Gardenia + 1   Part Ginger

Bath to Attract a Lover

Seep in a cup of boiling water for 10 minutes, and to the tub with warm water:

4 Parts Rose   + 4 Parts Jasmine   + 2 Parts Hyacinth
4 Part Gardenia + 2 Parts Carnation + 2 Parts Lavender

Walnut Bath to End a Relationship

This bath has the property of preparing us spiritually for the breakup of a relationship. When we have been in a relationship for some time with someone, an astral link forms and bonds us on the astral and mental levels. We must be really sure that we want this relationship to end because the effects tend to be permanent. This bath effectively cuts the astral bond making us think less and less about this person and may even produce same effect for them.

Boil six unopened Walnuts in a pot full of water for three hours, adding more water if necessary. This produces a blackish liquid which is added to the bathwater. Concentrate on ending the relationship to end and visualize the person out of your life.

Psychic Development Baths

Divination Bath

This bath stimulates psychic awareness.

3 Parts Thyme   + 3 Parts Yarrow Leaves + 3 Parts Rose Petals +
1 Part Nutmeg   + 3 Drops Patchouli Oil

Psychic Development Bath

This bath promotes the development of psychic abilities.

2 Parts Thyme + 1 Part Clove + 3 Parts Orange Flowers + 1 Part Cinnamon

Spirituality Bath

This bath is used to retain the spiritual tranquility needed to meditate.

4 Parts Frankincense + 4 Part Cedar + 4 Parts Jasmine +
4 Parts Sandalwood   + 4 Part Myrrh + 4 Parts Lemon Flowers +
4 Part Lotus

Spiritual Cleansing Baths

Rid of Negativity Bath

This bath, a personal favorite, eliminates accumulated negative influences and leaves a feeling of a lighter body and elevated spirit as well. Add the ingredients to a half a tub of warm water and be sure to submerge yourself several times. Mix:

1 Teaspoon Sea Salt   +   1 Cup Apple Cider Vinegar

Spiritual Cleansing Bath

This simple bath is very efficient for spiritual cleansing. It lightens the aura and raises spirits. Add 1/4 cup of Bicarbonate to the bathwater.

Bath for Protection against Negativity

This bath cleans of negative influences and provides a protective shield for up to 10 or 12 hours. Useful when you visit someone hostile or negative. Add the ingredients to one liter of boiling water and let cool. Pray for negativity to be eliminated and to be protected from it. Submerge yourself at least three times.

7 Cloves Fresh Garlic   +   1 Teaspoon Dry Basil   +   1 Pinch Dry Thyme

Bath for Protection

This bath strengthens your psychic vibrations, protecting against negative vibrations.

2 Parts Rosemary + 2 Parts Basil + 3 Parts Bay + 4 Drops Patchouli Oil

Emotional Energy Liberating Bath

The following bath helps free internal conflicts and accumulated negative energy. Add 1 cup of Rye Flour to the bathwater.

General Astral Cleansing Bath

This bath liberates negative thought forms and astral detritus. It also realigns your electromagnetic field. It should be taken before bed since it has powerful effects on some people. Fill the bathtub with cool water and add 450 grams of Baking Soda and 450 grams of Sea Salt.

Spiritual Growth Bath

Spiritual power is related to spiritual growth. There is no shortcut to authentic spiritual growth and the ground gained depends on our efforts. This bath helps eliminate astral detritus that may stray us off the path of spiritual growth. Add 1 teaspoon of ground Egg Shells to 1 teaspoon of ground Lotus Root.

Purification Bath

This bath strengthens your psychic vibrations and eliminates astral detritus.

2 Parts Rosemary + 2 Parts Lavender + 3 Parts Hyssop +
2 Parts Thyme + 2 Parts Basil + 1 Part Peppermint

Energy Bath

This bath revitalizes the body and mind and rids of negative energy.

3 Parts Red Carnation Petals + 3 Parts Lavender + 3 Parts Rosemary +
1 Part Basil

Money Baths

This kind of bath should not be taken more than two or three times a year. When you take spiritual baths to obtain money, you should never speculate as to where the money will come from, just be sure that it will.

Money Bath

For best results this bath should be taken just after the new moon. Add the mixture to a liter of boiling water and let cool to room temperature before adding to the bathwater.

1 Teaspoon Cinnamon + 1 Teaspoon Nutmeg + 7 Teaspoons Dry Parsley
+ 1 Teaspoon Brown Sugar

Bath for Money and Success

Add the mixture to a liter of boiling water and let cool to room temperature, add 3 drops of Patchouli oil before adding to the bathwater.

3 Parts Cinnamon + 3 Parts Basil + 1 Part Parsley

Cinnamon Money Bath

Add 1/2 cup Cinnamon and four cups Parsley to five liters of boiling water and divide the mixture in five equal parts. Take five baths for five consecutive days.

Chapter IV

Oil Essences

The Love Potion (1903) by Evelyn de Morgan

Introduction

Oils made from herbs play an important part in ritual magic. Our predecessors believed that the aromas of certain oil essences could influence personal energy in people and objects and employed these oils in religious and magical ceremonies.

Many rituals that use candles prescribe anointing the candles with oil potions. Oils are also used frequently in baths as preparation for rituals or as rituals in themselves.

Oil scents can have curious effects on the mind, creating different states of mind and sensations allowing other levels of conscience to arise. The oil recipes may be used in baths, to anoint oneself (in many cases as perfume), as aromatherapy and to anoint candles.

Preparation of Oils

Distilled essences are ideal to prepare oils. Take a distilled essence, add a few drops of oil (Jojoba, Olive, Almonds or any other good quality oil), shake and let sit for three days or so and you will have great anointing oil.

Fresh herbs and flowers can be also be used to prepare oils.

The following method is for preparation of oils with herbs. These oils can also as ingredients for other recipes.

1. Dry herbs should be ground as finely as possible and fresh herbs should be washed and dried. The usual amounts are four tablespoons of dry herbs or a half a cup of fresh herbs to one cup of oil.

2. Place the mixture in a jar (ideally dark glass), cap, shake and leave in a dry, warm and dark place.

3. Let rest for a week, shaking once a day.

4. Strain through a clean cloth and repeat the process with a fresh batch of the same herbs and let rest another week. Repeat this process two or three times or until the oil has the desired scent.

5. When the oil is ready and you have strained it for last time, place it in a jar and label with the contents and date. These oils maintain their scents and properties for approximately one year, depending on the preparation and storage.

Chapter IV — Oil Essences

Herbal Oils

Herbs and Their Use as Oil

Amber — Favors comforts and luxury. Creates a good spiritual environment.

Angelica — Opens the energy fields for visions, angelic messages and our own interior voice.

Anise — Stimulates psychic abilities.

Basil — This spicy sweet scented herb helps create harmony in the environment, stimulates the mind and helps heal sorrow caused by lost loves.

Bay — Oil from Bay flowers is used to anoint green candles in rituals for luck and to promote energy and harmony.

Benzoin — Attracts clients and friends, purifies the soul and is also used to bless objects.

Camphor — Good for anointing candles for rituals against evil spells and illnesses. Placed in the corners of a room it rejects psychic intruders. It is worn to stimulate psychic powers.

Carnation — Used for spiritual healing and increasing psychic powers.

Cassia — Used as perfume before bed for prophetic dreams and to increase psychic powers.

Chamomile	This soft scented herb has a relaxing effect; it creates an internal equilibrium and calms nerves. Oil recipes are used in baths to attract love.
Cinnamon	Used in voodoo traditions to bless places for rituals. It stimulates vital, sexual and psychic energies, brings good luck and courage.
Clove	Aphrodisiac.
Cyclamen	Traditionally used for love and passion.
Dill	Promotes charm and helps develop the ability to communicate. It is useful for meetings with loved ones.
Eucalyptus	Protects and eases spiritual healing, it is a negative psychic energy absorber.
Frankincense	Recommended as a spiritual healer, for protection and purification.
Gardenia	Very powerful, it prevents others from disrupting our harmony. Also used to attract love and reject bad vibrations.
Geranium	Has stimulating effects physically and psychically, promotes a fresh social environment and attracts love. Used in protection rituals and to break spells and reject misfortune.
Ginger	Its spicy sweet scent penetrates us, giving us energy and creating harmony. Ginger oil is used to attract friends and induce passion.
Gum Arabic	Considered powerful when used to develop psychic abilities such as intuition and telepathy. Also used for meditation, its scent is said to help communication with spiritual guides.
Honeysuckle	Helps create an adequate environment to clear confusing situations. Also used to increase psychic powers.
Hyacinths	Brings peace and harmony, stimulates a tranquil state of mind.
Hyssop	Used to increase personal luck and for spiritual assistance and protection.
Iris	As a perfume it attracts the opposite sex. Also used for charging tools and crystals for charms and spells.
Jasmine	Attracts good spirits, neutralizes envy, and stimulates fantasy and inspiration. Used personal charm and for clairvoyance. Clears environments with negative vibrations.

Juniper	Love and protection. Excellent absorber of negative psychic energy.
Lavender	Used to promote peace of mind and inspire love. Also used against obsessions and insomnia. Helps see ghosts.
Lemon	Used in rituals designed to lift someone's spirits. Also used in love baths and baths to increase personal magnetism.
Lemon Balm	Recommended for sleep and meditation. Stimulates remembrances of past lives.
Lotus	Used for spiritual healing.
Marjoram	Has stimulant and calming effects simultaneously. Helps us to organize our interior power and apply it.
Mugwort	Used for protection.
Musk	After thousands of years, Musk is still used in rituals for seduction, purification ceremonies and to cure sexual impotence.
Myrrh	Powerful deterrent to evil spirits. Used as an offering and to dissipate bad vibrations. Also used to induce prophetic dreams.
Myrtle	Good luck and money.
Nutmeg	Used for meditation and personal spiritual equilibrium. Attracts luck and the opposite sex.
Orange	Helps reach goals quickly, promotes luck, favors concentration and attracts love. It helps create an atmosphere of peace and calm.
Parsley	Considered a female herb, calms the nerves and increases luck.
Patchouli	Aphrodisiac and stimulant, used in love baths. Awakens the desire to overcome limits, promotes spiritual power; creates mental peace. Used to bless or consecrate objects.
Peppermint	Used as a perfume and in rituals to increase physical force and to attract luck.
Pine	Used to cleanse the body and mind, it increases will and determination. Aids in ritual work.

Rose	Rose conveys peace and harmony. It is used to increase spiritual power and energy. Also used in rituals for artistic inspiration, beauty and love.
Rosemary	Good for protection and psychic purification, helps in overcoming fears, predisposes realism, creativity and stability. Also used to attract love.
Rue	Breaks spells and protects from them then when it's carried. Forms a protective shield against bad vibrations.
Sage	Produces relaxing effects, opens the horizons and awakens curiosity for the new and unknown.
Sandalwood	Restores equilibrium, stimulates fantasy and creative impulses. Transforms sexual energy and awakens spiritual forces. Used to invoke spirits of relatives.
Snapdragon	Eliminates personal fears.
Spikenard	Attracts high spiritual vibrations. Used as a perfume for its aphrodisiac effects and to develop and stimulate psychic powers.
Vervain	Transmits the sensation of security. Used in rituals to ward off the Evil Eye, and to avoid negative influences.
Violet	Love, peace and spiritual healing.
Yarrow	Used as perfume to attract your lover.

Love Oils

Attraction Oil

This oil is used in ritual love baths and as body oil to attract love. It also increases personal magnetism and friendship. Mix equal parts of:

    Lemon Flowers   +   Vegetable Oil

Love Oil

The soft scent of the following oil potion helps find a lover. Mix in equal parts and add enough Vegetable Oil to cover the ingredients.

    Jasmine Flowers   +   Lavender Flowers   +   Iris Root

Passion Oil

This recipe is used to attract the opposite sex. Mix in equal parts and add enough Vegetable Oil to cover the ingredients.

Rose Petals + Jasmine Flowers + Gardenia Petals + Lemon Flowers

Seduction Oil

Worn as perfume, it helps create the adequate environment to seduce someone. Mix in equal parts.

Cloves + Vervain Root + Vegetable Oil

Voodoo Love Oil

An attraction love oil to be worn as perfume. Mix in equal parts and add enough Vegetable Oil to cover the ingredients, add 2 drops of Camphor Oil.

Patchouli + Lavender Flowers + Cedar

Charming Oil

Used in baths or worn as perfume to enchant a lover. Mix in equal parts.

Lemon + Patchouli + Vegetable Oil

Oils for Protection and Spiritual Cleansing

Oil for Protecting the Home

Anoint this oil on cotton balls and leave in the corners of the rooms and windowsills for protection against nocturnal intruders. Mix equal parts of:

Gardenia + Sandalwood + Vegetable Oil

Blessing Oil

This oil is adequate to bless people and objects. Mix equal parts of:

Benzoin + Vegetable Oil

Protection Oil

This oil should be used as perfume. Mix in equal parts and add enough Vegetable Oil to cover the ingredients.

    Sandalwood + Patchouli Leaves + Gardenia Petals + A pinch of Sea Salt

Home Protection Oil

Used to anoint cotton balls to protect the house. Mix in equal parts and add enough Vegetable Oil to cover the ingredients.

    Rosemary + Vervain

Personal Protection Oil

This recipe should also be used as perfume, or carried in cottons balls. Mix in equal parts and add enough Vegetable Oil to cover the ingredients.

    Sandalwood + Frankincense + Carnation + Cinnamo + Clove

Oil to Repel Bad Vibrations

This oil recipe repels bad vibrations and negative energy. It also repels vibrations and thought forms left by others. Mix equal parts of:

    Sandalwood + Clove + Cedar Oil

Oil to Repel Negative Energy

This oil recipe also repels bad vibrations and negative energy. Mix equal parts of:

    Rose + Carnation + Bay + Clove + Olive Oil

Oils for Psychic Development

Divination Oil

Anointed cotton balls are placed in the corners of the bedroom or under the pillow to generate divinatory dreams. Cover the ingredients with Anise Oil Mix equal parts of:

    Sage + Lavender

Chapter IV — Oil Essences

Oil of the Spirit

Used for finding your guardian angel or spiritual guide. Also used for meditation and to activate the psychic abilities. Mix equal parts.

Anise Seeds + Angelica Seeds + Vegetable Oil

Purification Oil

Used for meditation and to purify. Mix in equal parts and add enough Vegetable Oil to cover the ingredients.

Frankincense + Myrrh + Sandalwood

Spirituality Oil

Used in rituals to promote spirituality. Mix in equal parts and add enough Vegetable Oil to cover the ingredients.

Frankincense + Rosemary + Bay + Sandalwood

Psychic Development Oil

Used for developing psychic abilities. Mix equal parts of:

Frankincense + Yarrow Flowers + Gardenia Oil.

Ritual Oil

Used to anoint the forehead before rituals, to increase awareness. Mix equal parts of:

Musk + Myrrh + Sandalwood + Vegetable Oil

Oil for Prophetic Dreams

When placed under the pillow at night, this oil stimulates prophetic dreams and astral projection. Mix in equal parts and add enough Vegetable Oil to cover the ingredients.

Lemon Flowers + Myrrh

Oil for Psychic Dreams

This recipe is also for prophetic and psychic dreams. Mix equal parts of:

Jasmine + Sandalwood + Vegetable Oil

Travels in Your Dreams Oil

Anointed cotton balls are placed under the pillow to stimulate travels in dreams and astral projection. Mix in equal parts and add Vegetable Oil to cover the ingredients.

Hyssop Flowers   +   Sage

Astral Projection Oil

Worn as a perfume or anointed on cotton balls to stimulate astral projection. Mix in equal parts and add enough Vegetable Oil to cover the ingredients.

Sandalwood   +   Cinnamon

Money Oils

Money Oil

Mix in equal parts and add enough Vegetable Oil to cover the ingredients. Used as perfume. Mix:

3 Teaspoons of Patchouli Essence   +   2 Teaspoons of Orange Flowers   +   12 Drops of Cedar Oil

Prosperity Oil

Used as a perfume to attract prosperity. Mix in equal parts and add enough Vegetable Oil to cover the ingredients.

Gardenia   +   Patchouli   Cinnamon

Oil to Attract Riches

This recipe is also used as a perfume to attract money. Mix equal parts of:

Ginger + Patchouli + Basil + Jojoba Oil

Oil Potions for Other Purposes

Oil for Courage

This potion is very useful for a job interview or an important meeting. To ensure best results, a bath with this oil should be taken the night before and then used as perfume. Mix in equal parts:

Rosemary + Gardenia Petals + Vegetable Oil

Healing Oil

Worn as a perfume, or anointed on cotton balls under the pillow, this oil helps speed the recovery of health. Mix in equal parts and add enough Vegetable Oil to cover the ingredients. When the recipe is ready add 2 drops of Eucalyptus Oil:

Rosemary + Juniper + Sandalwood

Oil for Health

Anointed on the forehead of someone ill, this oil helps restore health and strength. Mix in equal parts and add enough Vegetable Oil to cover the ingredients.

Rose Essence + Gardenia Essence + Lemon Flowers

Oil for Studying

Anointed on the forehead and wrists, this oil enhances academic skills. Mix in equal parts and add enough Vegetable Oil to cover the ingredients.

Sandalwood + Lavender + Musk + Cinnamon

Lunar Oil

Worn as a perfume for lunar rituals. Mix in equal parts:

Sandalwood + Camphor Oil + Lemon

Chapter V

Astrology and Incenses

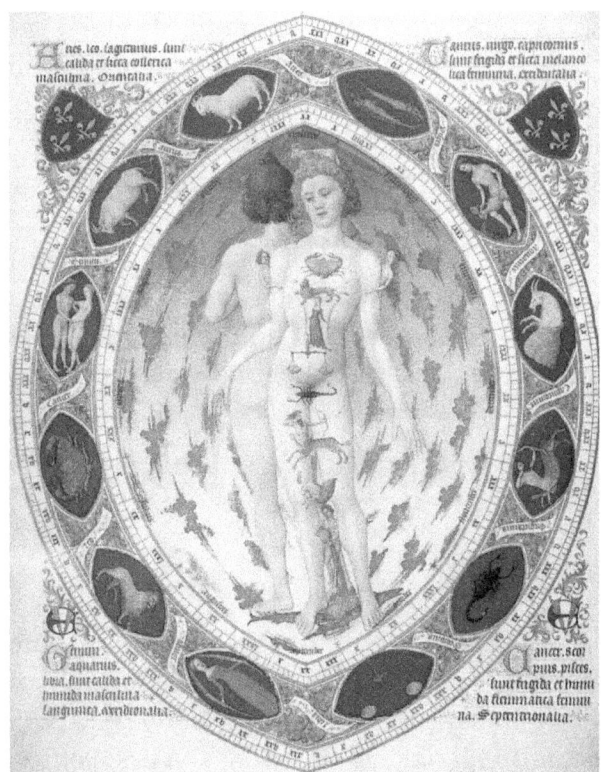

Astrological Man (1416) by Limbourg

Introduction

Astrology is one of the oldest forms of esoteric arts, traced back to ancient Mesopotamia. It is the study of the influence of the planets and astronomical bodies on human affairs, or the study of the action of the celestial bodies on living beings. Astrology uses the position of the astronomical bodies at the exact moment of a person's birth to map out a birth chart or horoscope which reflects that person's character, personality and destiny. The horoscope is illustrated by a circle or ecliptic which is divided into the twelve signs of the Zodiac.

Herbs, symbols of the Zodiac, days of the week and colors have been associated for centuries with special incense potions. Colors, days of the week, planets, signs, and herbs, among others, possess specific energies that can be channeled. The following -correspondences- may help in the selection of ingredients for incenses.

Planets, Signs and Houses

In the old days, astrologists knew seven planets: Mercury, Venus, Mars, Jupiter, Saturn and two "celestial lights", which of course are not planets but our Sun and Moon. Most of the incense recipes and almost all traditional ritual magic have their roots far behind the XVIII century. This is why the three planets discovered later, so important to modern astrology (Uranus, Neptune and Pluto,) play a small part in old traditional magic.

Each of the "seven planets" dominates a certain phase of human existence, therefore when you wish to obtain something concrete such as to favor or lessen something, it is better to choose that which represents the planet that dominates that facet or activity. Every planet dominates certain herbs which can be chosen to make incense potions for a certain purpose.

Action Fields of The Planets

Sun

Masculinity; ambition, career, honor, patrimony, fame, luck, gold and wealth; rank and high position, royalty (together with Jupiter), sovereign, father or captain of a group or organization. The human body as a whole, health and healing; children; speculation, risk; diamonds; lovers; entertainers, entertainment, theater and stage, movie and theater actors, amusement parks; authority, tyrant, pride and fall from pride; arrogance and the law.

Chapter V — Astrology and Incenses

Moon

☾ Femininity and maternity; procreation and fertility; development of psychic abilities, sensibility, public and relations; change, rhythms; indecision; family, intimacy in the home; mother, maternity, babies and children, care, maturity of seeds, feeding, food, stomach; chest; emotions and weakness; the tides, water, the sea, ships and crews; ""home"; all that holds and protects; lost objects, candles.

Mercury

☿ Intellect, spirit, entertainment, skill, writing, manuscripts, language, typewriters, etc.; mental processes and perceptions, communication, mail, newspapers and magazines, telecommunication, telephone, etc.; rumors, reports, reporters; acquisition of knowledge, books, documents; brothers, sisters, relatives, direct environment, visits; youth in general; news and messages, professors; gossip; tenants; illnesses.

Venus

♀ Love, marriage, personal relations; beauty, art, artists, artistic spirit, music; social events, sociability; romances and courtships, wedding celebrations; elegance, harmony, pleasure, peace; unbalance; money, investors and investments, property, furniture, contracts, agreements; nieces and nephews.

Mars

♂ Valor, courage; deviation from the norm; protection against physical and spiritual danger; machines, adventure, energy; cars; war and weapons, struggles, war scenarios and battlefields (domestic battlefields as well); pain, fever; management, ambition; energy or power to overcome obstacles; fighting spirit; sharp words, accidents, particularly fire and cuts or lacerations; personal gain, stubbornness, decision, violence, tantrums.

Jupiter

♃ Finances, banks, bankers; prestige and reputation; bets or wagers, horses and horse races; luck in general; religions and philosophies; lawyers and judges, the law, universities and higher education; benefits and expansion; riches, royal courts; wisdom; editorials; foreigners and foreign relations; discovery voyages; insurances; small children; dreams; ceremonies, rituals and parades; liver, blood and all that relates to them.

Saturn

♄ Houses, property and buildings; old people and old things, stability, wisdom through age, antiques; karma; mines; time, watches; patience, decision; self discipline, promises, responsibilities; depression, loneliness; economy, savings; routine; history; sadness, melancholy; all that impairs or impedes; sarcasms; career, position in the outside world, fame, reputation (name or fame); destiny; managers and workers; the government.

Uranus

⛢ Magical powers; the new and modern; liberty, paradoxes; space and nuclear technology; chaos and crisis, divorce; science; nonconformity, rebellion, unpredictability, insurrections, anarchy; desires and expectations; humanitarian endeavors, friends, club members, fraternities, associations; daughters and sons, abortions, deaths in the family.

Neptune

♆ The sea; clairvoyance; mediums; astral reality, crystal balls, that which is mystical and sensitive, mystery or mysterious; secrets; the unknown and inexplicable; prophets and prophecies; inspiration, idealism; addictions; that which is artificial or synthetic; illusions; ambushes; meetings, businesses and illegal activities; hermits, informants; sacrifices, banishments, incarcerations, hospitals, asylums and jails; bribery and corruption; worries and hidden sorrows, suicide.

Pluto

♇ The sub world, life after death; the hidden or buried (oil, gems or minerals); death and the dead, illumination, metamorphosis, evolution and revolution; fanatics; funerary professions; debts and creditors, taxes and inheritances, wills and legacies; bankrupts and losses; investigations of life after death.

Chapter V — Astrology and Incenses

Signs of the Zodiac

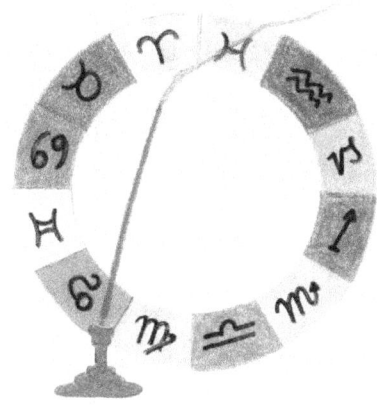

Aries (21 March - 19 April)

Aries is ruled by Mars and its symbol is the Goat. Those born under Aries, a fire sign, are impulsive and energetic. This is the first sign of the zodiac and it represents new beginnings. People born under this sign tend to have a lot of creative energy, enthusiasm and a very noticeable internal strength. They may seem to be shy, but they may have difficulty handling their aggressiveness and not be very diplomatic in their treatment of others. They are not afraid of risks and may at times go through with something without measuring the consequences. When they manage to control their impulses they can become great leaders. They always want to be best and prefer fame to riches. They desire independence and usually seek professions where they can be figures of authority. They are optimistic in general and nothing will make them change their minds. They are also famous for not finishing what they start. As friends they are cheerful and generous but sometimes too competitive.

Taurus (20 April – 20 May)

Taurus is ruled by Venus and its symbol is the Bull. Those born under Taurus, an earth sign, are usually materialist, determined and trustworthy. Their power is in their tenacity and ambition. They can be very practical hearted persons who want to feel in charge of their material positions. The key to their personality is their necessity of emotional and material security. They will feel very comfortable with familiar things and uncomfortable about change. They usually need to feel secure with a new person or situation before they feel comfortable; once convinced, they will be unconditionally loyal. The may have problems with jealousness or possessiveness. Because of their pleasure with material things they will feel best when they are at home, surrounded by their possessions and loved ones. They will like good food and good clothes and have a great appreciation for beauty and esthetics. Under a stubborn appearance, a gentler softer personality can be found. They may be very passionate and sentimental, and like to pamper the people they love. They are romantics at heart.

Gemini (21 May – 21 June)

Gemini is ruled by Mercury and its symbol is the Twins. Those born under Gemini, an air sign, are analytical and moody. They are usually intelligent, talkative and nonconformists. The influence of Mercury gives them a thirst for knowledge that they always want to communicate with everyone else. Their vivid imagination helps them change from one subject to another and maintain an audience charmed with their grace, originality and mental agility. They are constantly looking for variety and new stimuli. Their energy and quickness of thought send them in new directions all the time. A happy Gemini is a Gemini with four or five interests going at the same time. Restless by nature, they can find themselves with more than one job, career and/or lover. Their more negative side is their constant rebellion with the "status quo" and authority; they love to break the rules. With so many activities and objectives they do not always finish all their projects. However, their ability for improvisation and agile mind may save the day.

Cancer (22 June – 22 July)

Cancer is ruled by the Moon and its symbol is the Crab. Those born under Cancer, a water sign, are prone to be emotional but at the same time a great support for their loved ones. They are a sign of sensitivity and sympathy, associated with domestic security and the sense of homeliness. They are known to be complex and sometimes hard to understand due to their mood changes; they may be in an evil mood one minute and the sweetest and caring beings the next. Their very developed sense of self-defense can help them overcome their own vulnerability and shyness. They project a hard exterior within which they can isolate themselves and when they feel hurt they retreat from the rest of the world. They also can be extremely stubborn, never backing down. There is also a gentler, sensitive and emotional side to Cancer and they are by nature protective and caring, and because of this sensitive nature it is almost impossible to fool or hoax them. They tend to form relationships that last a long time and are very loyal to their friends. Their purpose in life may seem to be the need to establish a secure domestic life for their family. They may desire riches but only as a means to obtain economic stability. They almost always reach their goals.

Leo   (23 July – 22 August)

♌ Leo is ruled by the Sun and its symbol is the Lion. Those born under Leo, a water sign, are usually very majestic and creative. As the sun is the center of our universe, they believe that they are the center of life. They are the proud ones, kings of their territory, be this a company, a country or a household. They tend to be affectionate and generous and will give their entire heart to the right cause, expecting always the same integrity and loyalty of others. They like to do things big and they are in their element when they are the center of attention. They are practical people with a high self-esteem, usually very good workers. Their sense of integrity and optimism makes them good leaders. Like the lion they may also be lazy and indolent, especially when their sense of authority and leadership is not to their liking. They like the good life and don't care what they spend to have the best of everything. Nothing is too good for them, from their wardrobe to their friends. They bore easily with routine and are always on the lookout for new adventures. Their weakness is their need to be admired.

Virgo (23 August – 22 September)

♍ Virgo is ruled by Mercury and its symbol is the Virgin. Those born under Leo, an earth sign, tend to be methodical and analytical. The influence of Mercury, the planet of movement inclines the Virgo to be in constant activity. They spend a lot of energy in doing things. While other signs are thinking about what to do, Virgos are out doing things. They take ethics very seriously, are very neat and appreciate efficiency in others. They tend to be perfectionists and can't stand work that is not done correctly but at the same time they concentrate so much on the details that they tend to lose the greater picture. Their interest towards excellent work may absorb their time making them forget the pleasures of life. They may need to learn to be more tolerant with others and themselves. They sometimes appear to be cold and severe but are very sweet, devoted and loyal people. They are usually very loving parents and because of their devotion to duty they are usually important and respected members in the family.

Libra (23 September – 22 October)

Libra is ruled by Venus and its symbol is the Balance. Those born under Libra, an air sign, are known to be charming and constant. They have a developed social sense that attracts others. They also have the need to be in company with others. By nature they are attracted to beautiful delicate things. They have elegant taste and tend to buy everything they can. Their fine taste in beauty tends to attract attention from others. They can become too concerned with appearances and judge others that way. They always want harmony in life and tend to look at both sides of the coin in discussions before taking sides and have knack for calming others. Because of their constant need for peace, they may sacrifice their own opinion sometimes and end up being considered insecure or indecisive. Optimistic and hard workers, they make good business partners. People tend to respect them due to their sense of justice and their charm. They make good counselors because they are very sensible to the human psyche. They can be warm and romantic, living their lives in a constant search for harmony.

Scorpio (23 October – 21 November)

Scorpio is ruled by Pluto and its symbol is the Scorpion. Those born under Scorpio, a water sign, are usually passionate and intense. Some think that this is the most powerful sign of the zodiac. Scorpios are known for their intensity and desire to get the most out of life. They may be arduous justice defenders and loyal to just causes. They tend to be idealists and work under the principal of everything or nothing. They live their life intensely and being so extreme in their emotions tend to be either very passionate or very cold. They also may be temperamental, possessive and jealous. Their intensity in emotions and unpredictable nature may keep others at a distance but when you get to know a Scorpio you will find them to be generous, passionate and very loyal.

Sagittarius (22 November – 21 December)

Sagittarius is ruled by Jupiter and its symbol is the Archer. Those born under Sagittarius, a fire sign, tend to be free and single minded. They usually are very lucky in life and always seem to be at the right place at the right time. They always seem to have good fortune in life; they are enthusiastic, intuitive and optimistic enough to not let anything stop them. They desire the new and exciting, freedom is the most important thing form. They are energetic and extroverts, by nature lovers of travel, adventure and new discoveries. For this reason they are sometimes superficial in their relationships, even so

Chapter V — Astrology and Incenses

they can be great friends when nothing is asked in return. They will always say what they think and tend to have a good sense of humor. They are charming and honest and always expect the same from everyone else.

Capricorn (22 December – 19 January)

Capricorn is ruled by Saturn and its symbol is the Ram. Those born under Capricorn, an earth sign, tend to be ambitious and conservative. Ambition seems to define them well, they dedicate their lives to something, anything that they have chosen. They feel the internal necessity of reaching their goals and will have the patience and determination to do so. They are generally very intelligent and comfortable in positions of authority. They make excellent administrators and have the knack for solving problems very easily. They seek financial security for what may come in the future and consider that the way to do so is by working hard. They have a lot if self-esteem and faith in their own abilities. On occasions they may feel that they can only depend on themselves. They tend to have an excellent sense of humor and the know how to listen and be sympathetic.

Aquarius (20 January – 18 February)

Aquarius is ruled by Uranus and its symbol is the Water Bearer. Those born under Aquarius, an air sign, are known to be independent and non-conventional. They may be brilliant and visionary. Eccentric and always changing their minds, they seem to live in the future. They are usually intellectually independent and do not have much patience with those that desire to conform. They seek intellectual discussions as mental exercise. When they have a formed opinion of something they will defend it to the end. They are usually very friendly and like the intellectual stimulation of others. Dreamers and idealists, many times they will discover how to save the world. Since they spend so much time in limbo they may be perceived as absent-minded or disagreeable and their apparent calm may deceive because underneath they may be anxious. Their debility is finding fault in others. When they are down to earth they are the sweetest people in the world, they are reasonable and never bored. They can be very entertaining and loyal partners.

Pisces (19 February – 20 March)

♓ Pisces is ruled by Neptune and its symbol the Fish. Those born under Pisces, a water sign, are usually son emotional and compassionate. This is the last sign of the zodiac and represents eternity, reincarnation and spiritual rebirth. They tend to be very intuitive and sensitive about the environment. They are usually very spiritual beings with an elusive and seemingly indecisive personality. They tend to use their powers of perception to conform to the environment. Their charm, humor and sympathy tend to open all the doors. They may be gentle and sweet but may experience extreme mood changes. Their weak side tends to be internal conflicts, negativity, jealously and emotional confusion. They may develop an extraordinary and intense imagination because they love to live in their own dream world where they handle the situations. They may be excellent friends and partners when the control their moods. Many of the most famous poets, writers and artists are Pisces.

Chapter V — Astrology and Incenses

Incenses for Planets

The following recipes are traditional recipes for planets. Recipes of personal taste can also be used:

Sun

This incense is used in solar rituals to invoke the power of the sun, mix:

1/2 Part Sandalwood + 1/2 Part Patchouli + 5 Part Rose Petals + 1/2 Part Frankincense + 1 Part Calendula Petals + 1/4 Part Parsley

Moon

The following incense is excellent for lunar rituals, mix:

1 Part Sandalwood + 1/2 Part Powdered Ginger Root + 1/2 Part Lavender Flowers

Mercury

A traditional incense for Mercury is:

6 Parts Honeysuckle + 4 Parts Sandalwood + 2 Parts Vervain 1 Part Clove + 2 Parts Chamomile

Venus

This incense is used to invoke the powers of Venus, mix:

1 Part Benzoin + 1 Part Rose Petals + 1 Pinch Nutmeg

Mars

This Martian incense is more powerful when made on a Tuesday:

3 Parts Wormwood + 2 Parts Oak Leaves + 4 Parts Sandalwood

Jupiter

The following incense should be burned on a day consecrated to Jupiter:
2 Parts Copal + 3 Parts Iris Root + 1 Part Hyssop

Saturn

A traditional incense for Saturn is:

3 Parts Myrrh + 3 Parts Musk + 1 Part Rue + 2 Parts Cypress + 1 Part Vervain

Incenses for Astrological Talismans

The following recipes are used to consecrate astrological talismans. The talismans should be held over the smoke of the chosen incense:

Solis Dies *(Sunday)*

4 Parts Sandalwood + 2 Parts Mugwort Stems + 2 Parts of Camphor + 1 Part Aloe Vera

Martis Dies *(Tuesday)*

2 Parts Wormwood + 4 Parts Juniper + 1 Part Rue

Mercurii Dies *(Wednesday)*

4 Parts Benzoin + 1 Part Marjoram + 2 Parts Lemon Flowers

Jovis Dies *(Thursday)*

4 Parts Frankincense + 3 Parts Iris Root + 2 Parts Amber

Veneris Dies *(Friday)*

3 Parts Musk + 3 Parts Rose Petals + 3 Parts Violet Flowers + 4 Parts Cedar Wood

Saturni Dies *(Saturday)*

3 Parts Cypress + 2 Parts Sandalwood + 4 Parts Alum

Chapter V

Astrology and Incenses

Chapter VI

Colors and Magic

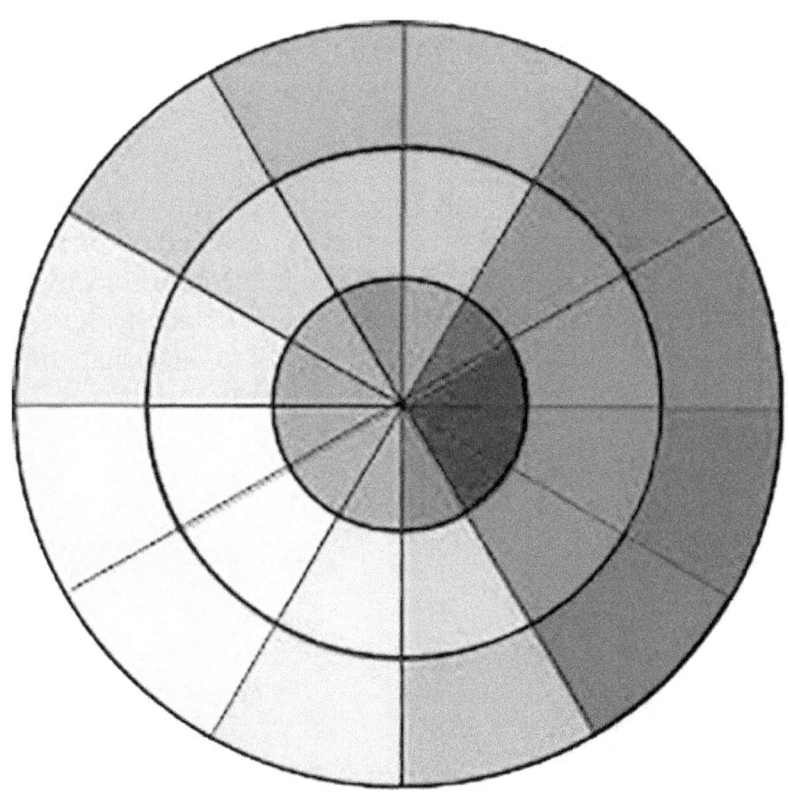

Color Wheel

Introduction

The power of colors according to the symbolic meaning of each is a fascinating study. The following chapter deals with symbolic meaning and vibrational usage of a series of important colors.

Colors

Every person has a favorite color and this choice is the result of several factors such as taste, character, the place where we live and other less rational or logical reasons. Besides our favorite colors we are also a whole set of colors and forms. The colors that we choose to dress in can reveal to others our emotional world; a person who chooses constantly to dress in black is probably different from someone who always chooses red or blue.

Colors can influence how we feel because they influence our state of mind. Every color has its own character and emits its own specific vibrations and energies. Different colors have different wave lengths. The human eye is capable of distinguishing a great scale of subtle shades. The colors that we perceive as agreeable have wave lengths that are favorable for us.

Chromotherapy

As a New Age practice of alternative medicine chromotherapy deals with healing with color. It proposes that the physical properties of light and color influence our health, be it physical, emotional, mental or spiritual. Although chromotherapy has only been seriously studied in the last few decades, color healing is an ancient system practiced in China, Egypt and India for thousands of years. Some occultists believe that the Egyptian healing techniques were based on Chromotherapy systems from Atlantis.

Blue

Color of the infinite sky and of the sea; capable of giving us a sensation of peace and calm as well as melancholy and nostalgia. Blue radiates a crystalline and radiant atmosphere easing communication with superior beings. It is the color of the archangel Miguel and of Vishnu and Krishna (Hindu Gods). The relation of this color with the gods of the air is a relation established millenniums ago. This is the color of Jupiter. The relation with the gods of the air could also explain the relationship to aristocracy and royal courts; as we say, someone from nobility has "blue blood".

Used for spiritual and physical healing due to its relaxing qualities, it can alleviate emotional tension and pain. It is used for success in businesses, work, and justice and for blessings.

Important Associations: It symbolizes peace and communication, spiritual healing, truth, inspiration, occult powers and psychic protection. It is the color of the feminine principle of nature.

Spiritual Meaning: It represents water; baptism, blessings, purity and purification, and spiritual protection, the color of the will and spiritual tranquility.

In Your Aura: Considered as the color of the spirit; symbol of contemplation and prayer. Dark and brilliant tones are more powerful and show the soul as a very spiritual being, lighter tones indicate a less deep spirituality but a soul on the right road. Deep shades are the best. Pale Blue indicates little depth.

Emotional Meaning: It represents tranquility, serenity and sweetness.

In Your Dreams: Its interpretation will depend on the tone. A vibrant deep blue represents idealism, aspirations and adventure. Sky blue calms and concentrates the mind while dark blue may indicate a state of depression.

Gems: Lapis lazuli, Opal, Sapphire and Turquoise.

We Like It: It shows the desire for a quiet life in a comfortable and harmonious environment, free from tensions, conflicts and emotional disturbances. Most tones of blue are considered beneficial both physically and psychically.

We Don't Like It: Life seems boring and changes such as stronger emotions are needed. A brilliant pink or apple green is recommended.

Positive: Spirituality, inspiration, truth, fidelity, tranquility, calm, peace, hope, deliverance, frankness, intuition, love for all creation, devotion, justice.

Negative: Coldness, depression, melancholy, tears, sadness, apathy, worries; cold where there was heat (red).

Summary: Stimulates energy, communication and comprehension of others. It is the most spiritual color of the rainbow. It gives tranquility, peace, relaxation, and harmony. Blue is considered as the primary color for spiritual and physical healing.

Pink

Like red, pink symbolizes love but its quality is more refined and delicate. It is the color of the heart and, surrounded by green the color of perfect harmony.

It symbolizes the disposition to give up oneself completely, to be nice and sweet, it is the color of platonic love. It expresses disinterested and refined love directed towards others, towards their happiness and satisfaction. It is also the color of contentment, benevolence, beauty, friendship and ethics. It is used in domestic matters for family stability and social image.

Important Associations: It represents romantic love, sense of morality, friendship, care, compassion, relaxation and success.

Spiritual Meaning: It symbolizes feminine intuitive energy, happiness and laughter.

Emotional Meaning: It represents love, compassion, friendship, peace, harmony and tranquility.

In Your Aura: Shades of pink in the aura show immaturity, a childish concern with self.

In Your Dreams: Generally represents love, happiness and harmony.

Gems: Diamond, Rose Quartz and Tourmaline.

Positive: Refined sensuality, sensitivity, and feeling of happiness, platonic love, sensibility and dreams.

Negative: Loss of the sense of reality, elevation, transfiguration, escapes from reality, sentimentalism.

Summary: It is the color of the center of the heart, of the unlimited expression of love; sensuality turned love. It has the energy to attract the love of others and self love.

Brown

Is the color of earth and is related to concepts of equilibrium, solidity, and that which is earthly. We plant and harvest from the (brown) fertile earth. Also related to contemplations about the imperfections of life; of the unavoidable, as well as with quietness, acceptation and maturity.

This color also related to the dying leaf (on one hand an ending and on the other a new beginning: the fallen leaves are food for new herbs). It is the color of wood, of Nature and the exploitation of Nature. It is useful for financial operations, especially those which have to do with mines or mining companies. To attract spirits of the earth and to favor discoveries of buried treasures.

Important Associations: Symbolizes vacillation, uncertainty, equilibrium and solidity.

In Your Dreams: Represents depression, negativity; and the earth.

In Your Aura: A dull brown color in the aura reflects avarice and greyish brown tones indicate jealousy.

We Like It: It is an indicator of the need to find a safe environment, where the body sensations are comfortable and there are no situations that affect this physical sense of well being.

Positive: Equilibrium, solidity, fertility, maturity, tranquility, new beginnings.

Negative: Lack of will.

Summary: It is the color of concentration, comforts; life tied to nature, love of the earth. It symbolizes physical and sensorial perception, but also the lack of will and penance.

Orange

Orange is the color of pure vital energy; representing the desire to live; youth and health. It is warm and stimulating and has very positive effects in almost everyone. It is a mix between active personality (red) and fully given wisdom (yellow), of soft erotism, and desire for life. Buddhist monks wear orange clothes to control their emotions and submit themselves to disciplined lives, to obtain interior happiness.

As a symbol of the Sun, orange is a "color of power"; it incites relaxation, enthusiasm, cheerfulness, vitality, dynamism, friendship and good relations. It is useful for success, luck, prosperity and to obtain self esteem, social recognition and to promote spirituality and illumination.

Important Associations: It represents dependency, co-dependency and independence, profound knowledge and ecstasy, concentration capacities, and adaptability.

Spiritual Meaning: It symbolizes energy, knowledge, individuality, and surrender.

In Your Aura: It is a good color, symbolizing vitality, and indicating a caring person. Strong or brilliant tones of orange indicate self-control while dark tones or orange indicate lack of ambition and laziness.

Emotional Meaning: Wisdom and "intuitive" feelings, spontaneous knowledge, sociability, sexual desire, excitement, extroversion, cheerfulness and profound delight.

In Your Dreams: Energy and Health.

Gems: Agate, Amber, Coral and Topaz.

We Like It: Those who like orange tend to make friends with ease, thanks to a nice smile and a talent for conversation. In general they like people a lot, and people desire their company because they radiate confidence, vitality and cheerfulness. They tend to be successful in politics and shine among groups.

We Don't Like It: Dislike of orange may be related to a dislike of superficiality, a need to find the spiritual road with seriousness. Sky blue and bright red may help these feelings.

Positive: Spiritual happiness, love of life, energy, heat, power, and pride.

Negative: Weakness, cowardice, jealousy, distrust, illness, anguish, hate and death.

Summary: Orange is the color of self-confidence; it symbolizes the will to live and the desire for happiness. It is a color of challenge, possessing an enormous spiritual energy.

Yellow

This radiant stimulating color is related to the giver of life, the Sun. It is the best color to rid oneself of bad humor; it stimulates creativity and the capacity to think. It facilitates contacts in public life and in professional and social development. It is associated with mentality and spirituality which explains its relation to Mercury, the messenger of the gods. It can also express feelings of hate and envy. It is the color that represents the Sun, it stimulates mind and promotes thought.

Important Associations: It symbolizes knowledge acquired with effort, intellect, powers of the creative imagination, communication and mental agility.

Spiritual Meaning: It represents acquired knowledge, light, will and physical energy.

Emotional Meaning: Warmth, laughter, happiness and enthusiasm.

In Your Dreams: Yellow in dreams represents the intellect. It is associated with logical processes and communication, showing intelligence and verbal abilities. As yellow represents the Sun, in our dreams it represents light, laughter and happiness. It raises our spirits, warms our hearts and alleviates the mind.

Gems: Amber, Topaz and Citrine.

We Like It: Preference towards yellow shows intelligence and desire to expand the mind and the spirit. People who prefer yellow are usually using their minds processing ideas and may seem to be distant or cold; they are always aware of what is happening around them and possess a lot of self-control. They may be idealistic and altruistic, trying to fulfill their desires.

In Your Aura: Golden yellow indicates health and well being. Those with this color in their auras are generally happy with no worries. Dark or opaque yellow indicates shyness and indecision.

Positive: Wisdom, intelligence, vivacity, high spirits, intellectual capacity, satisfaction, creativity, love for freedom.

Negative: Bad humor, false hopes, envy, low spirits, jealousy, fear, lack of self-confidence, confusion, and depression.

Summary: It is the color of contacts, of public relations; it transmits happiness. Its vibration symbolizes solutions, and sometimes even dissolution. The energy that it creates may give the base to develop love.

Grey and Silver

Considered as neutral or "bridge" color; it establishes a union between the contrast of black and white. On the positive side, it symbolizes maturity and wisdom. On the negative side it symbolizes senility. Also associated with money, which becomes commitments; money is not white nor black, good nor bad; it is what is made of it.

It is the color commitment, capacity of adaptation and discretion. It is not discarded by any color; it gives the appearance of a "grey eminence". Also associated with mourning and indifference, as with immobility. It is used in healing rituals and rituals to favor luck in business.

Important Associations: It symbolizes comprehension of suffering, astral energy and the capacity to remember past lives.

Spiritual Meaning: It represents karmic oblivion, total reflection, transparency, clarity, purity and lunar energy.

Emotional Meaning: Source of un-cried tears, suffering; comprehension of suffering, clarity and decision.

In Your Dreams: Sickness or weakness.

In Your Aura A lead colored grey indicates deep depression and/or fear.

Gems: Agate, Diamond, Moonstone, Quartz and Zircon.

We Like It: It has connotations of concealment. It shows a desire for isolation, not wanting commitment or involvement and hiding from external influences and stimuli. As a favorite color it may indicate the need to retreat from anguish.

We Don't Like It: Rejection of grey shows the desire to be actively involved in life, to activate it.

Positive: Perfect neutrality, discretion, thought.

Negative: Repression, limitation, anguish, defeat, failure.

Summary: It is the color of maturity, neutrality and the capacity for adaptation. Dark grey has a frightening or threatening effect, while silver grey has a sedative effect and can be considered as a bearer of hope. It represents the connection or "bridge" between the body and the soul.

Green

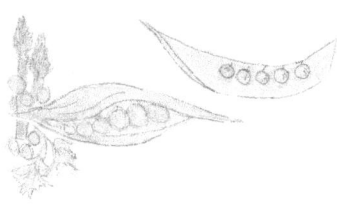

In our cultural symbolism it is one of the most important colors. In all western cultures green symbolizes nature and its abundance; the rebirth and flowering of life after winter. It radiates serenity more than any other color. This color is located between warm and stimulant colors (red, yellow and orange) and the cold colors (blue, indigo, and violet).

The herbs (green) grow producing the oxygen that we need to live, symbolizing eternal life and hope. Green and growth are intimately related. To receive a "green light" means that we may continue on our way. It is used for healing magic, agriculture, to favor fertility of the earth, women and cattle.

Important Associations: It symbolizes space, the search for truth, panoramic conscience, fertility and good crops, good luck and harmony.

Spiritual Meaning: It represents recovery, regeneration, physical and mental healing, compassion, appreciation for earth; harmony with nature and its laws.

In Your Aura Emerald green is the color of healing and shows a person with desire to help and/or heal others. Doctors and nurses often have green in their auras. If it contains traces of yellow it may indicate a weak person.

Emotional Meaning: Frankness, peace, liberty, generosity, the heart, panoramic conscience, satisfaction.

In Your Dreams: In our dreams green represents nature; regeneration and growth. It is associated with the renewal of life. As a prominent color in a dream it may represent hope, healing and the restoration of balance. On the negative side green may also represent envy or ignorance, depending on the content of the dream.

Gems: Jade, Malachite, Opal, Pyrite, Emerald, Tourmaline and Cat's Eye.

We Like It: It represents freedom, respectability and hope. When green is a favorite color usually one is very sure of oneself and inspires trust in others.

We Don't Like It: Rejection towards green may be a sign of loneliness, or anxiety, or not being recognized. Brilliant yellow, gold and navy blue may help these feelings.

Positive: Calm, healing, renovation, eternal youth, fertility, stability, happiness, tranquility, growth, abundance, well being, riches, life and nature.

Negative: Envy, illness, frugality, cowardice, animosity, malice, disharmony and jealousy.

Summary: It is the color of illumination of the heart, growth, love and desire. It liberates creative energy.

Red

Red is the color of Mars, sovereign of blood and body fluids. It has an unstable equilibrium; its energy may evolve very quickly in one direction or another. It also symbolizes purely physical energy.

In most countries red flags signal danger. It has a highly stimulant effect and symbolizes love. It is used for passion and love, to fight enemies, for success in sports, for good spirits and health; especially for tiredness or anemia.

Important Associations   It symbolizes energy, love, sexuality, force and vigor; material aspects of life, courage; the masculine principal of nature.

Spiritual Meaning: It represents a purifying force, the flame of the Holly spirit, objectivity, regeneration, sacrifice, the desire for a spiritual rebirth, spiritual energy and the power; spiritual awakening.

In Your Aura: It represents force, vigor and energy in the aura. Dark red indicates an aggressive temperament or a person who is suffering on the inside. When the tone is lighter it may indicate a nervous, very active and impulsive person.
Emotional Meaning   Passion, temperament, fire, heat, feelings, frustration, courage and daring.

In Your Dreams: Universal symbol of passion; love and anger. It activates and motivates, showing energy and vitality; heat and stimulation, desire and passion. On the negative side it may be expression of repressed anger. In also may represent possible dangers.

Gems: Agate, Jasper, Pyrite and Ruby.

We Like It: It is associated with the need for action, mood changes and the increase of blood pressure. When one prefers red, he or she will like strong emotions and intense experiences, throwing themselves into adventure without planning and assume challenges. This is the most energetic color and those who prefer it are usually courageous, optimistic, and passionate and know how to get what they want.

We Don't Like It: Rejection towards red may that that the person is overcome with their life's pace and problems. Deep blue and peppermint green can help the feelings of anguish and help promote feelings of peace, serenity and security.

Positive: Heat, force, sexuality, courage, love, health, vitality, passion, inspiration, dynamism, enthusiasm, birth and triumph.

Negative: Hate, passion, over-excitation, anarchy, rebellion, danger, war, blood, violence, cruelty, and thirst for revenge.

Summary: It is the color of the joy of living, of the vital force. It is an energy generator that stimulates the senses and can have positive or negative effects.

Violet

This color is the product of the mix between red and blue, two contrasting forces that are in harmony. It is the color of inspiration, of the mystical and enchanting sides of life. Its vibrations can initiate internal transformations. It has been traditionally related to forgiveness, passion, devotion, penance and the renouncement of mundane pleasures. It is used to resolve intellectual problems, for meditation and to recover calm and serenity when there is anguish.

Important Associations: It symbolizes spirituality, healing, service and contemplation.

Spiritual Meaning: In theosophy violet is the color of the "transmutation flame", burning the negativity to make new growth possible. It is also the color of forgiveness and of the capacity to discover the sense of life and the realization that it is not only important what we live but how we live it.

In Your Aura: When this color is present in the aura it indicates a person on a spiritual search and as the road is found it will turn to blue.

Emotional Meaning: Internal peace, union of the spirit and matter, the feeling of not wanting to be incarnated, difficulties with the material aspects of life, addictions, and the tendency to evade.

Gems: Amethyst.

Positive: Inspiration, enchantment, meditation, illumination.

Negative: Melancholy, depression, drowsiness, confusion of the conscience, enchainment to reality, introversion.

Summary: It is the color of maturity, the union of spirit and matter. It is an excellent color for profound meditation. It challenges us to recognize our imperfections.

White

White reflects all vibrations and is a perfect mirror for all the areas of life. It is a symbol of elegance, purity and innocence. It can also have negative symbolic interpretations such as cowardice and weakness due to the fact that it is associated with paleness, anemia and lack of energy.

The counter position white / black appears with numerous variants in rituals. The right hand road is white and constructive, and the left hand road is black and destructive. It is used traditionally as an offering for purity, truth, sincerity, and all moral and spiritual qualities. A white candle can be used to replace any other color

Important Associations: It represents faith, purity, truth, sincerity and the force behind spiritual awakening.

Spiritual Meaning: It symbolizes protective energy, dreams, psychic development and spiritual healing.

In Your Aura: It is the perfect color, if our souls were in perfect harmony our aura would be white.

Emotional Meaning: The divine, contact with spiritual guides.

Meaning in Dreams: It is considered a positive color in dreams, representing light, hope, purity and inspiration. When white is a predominant color in a dream, it is usually a dream of hope, that one will *see the light*.

Gems: Diamond.

We Like It: Dazzling and pure, white does not have an emotional impact. If a person prefers white in general they may appear impersonal or boring.

We Don't Like It: Rejection towards white is usually due to the sensations of boredom, innocence and sterility that are associated with it.

Positive: Purity, innocence, virginity, redemption, light, peace, humility, spirituality, sincerity and love for truth.

Negative: Weakness, vulnerability, cowardice, lack of vital force, loss of energy, impurity, falseness.

Summary: It has loving vibrations, self unity, total liberation from fears, anguish and the petty desire for power. It gives the powers of a higher force, of the regulating vital energies of the universe.

Black

In spite of its multiple negative associations, black symbolizes the initial phase of growth; as a seed is born from the dark bowels of the earth and as a child emerges from the dark womb to the light.

In magical traditions black is exclusively assigned with negative properties. It is considered to be the color that denies all other colors, in thought and fact. It is automatically associated with the night, darkness, tunnels and, consequently death. It symbolizes bad and evil, the powers of the darkness.

Important Associations: It represents all colors.

Spiritual Meaning: It symbolizes self-control and protection.

In Your Aura: Clouds of black colors showing up in the aura shows hatred and malice as well as passionate anger.

Meaning in Dreams: When black is a prominent color in dreams it is considered negative and symbolizes grief and loss of hope. If you constantly dream with black, it may mean depression or hard times. The appearance of other colors may mean hope that the bad times will pass soon. Black curtains in dreams symbolize death.

Gems: Moonstone and Black Opal.

We Like It: Eternal rebellion against destiny and also sophistication. Black can be a symbol of serenity and wisdom which helps face life with courage. When we like black we may project images to the world that are different from what we really are inside.

We Don't Like It: Rejection towards black may be a fear of death, of the unknown, of darkness and of things over which we have no control. This situation can be reverted by the use of red, green and blue green.

Positive Dignity, invincibility and prestige.

Negative Depression, desperation, mourning, panic, pessimism, and anguish.

Summary: It is the color of the unconditional disposition to absorb; colors surrounded by black give off more energy and black does not compete with any other color but by contrast helps their potency.

Chapter VII

Magical and Spiritual Use of Candles

Off to Bed (1916) by Léon Commere

Introduction

The word candle comes from the Latin verb *candere* which means "to shine". For thousands of years candles have been used in the most diverse rituals, especially religious, transcendental and magical rituals.

Magic with candles, also called Light Magic, is a means to channel the energy of our own mind to reach our goals and improve our lives. Rituals with candles are used seeking the support and light of the spiritual world, to create changes in the material or physical world.

Candles traditionally represent:

* Divine presence
* Consecration of a particular divinity
* Cosmic energy

Fire and Light

Many old traditions in many places in the world considered the hearth or chimney as a center of protection, considering fire as the purifier. The hearth symbolized the circle or family clan and the ascendant movement of the flames was the means to expel negative vibrations.

In yoga it is traditionally believed that staring into the flames of candles is a useful method for concentration and that this act helps achieve a superior spiritual level, by directing the sight towards the inside and outside simultaneously.

We ourselves in our modern times, even without being conscience of the fact, use candles for magic. We light them in our homes, especially during important dinner events (where we desire to impress with a homely environment) or to create romantic environments, without really understanding the how or why. Who of us hasn't made a wish before blowing out the candles on our birthday cake?

Ancient Beliefs about Candles

Both in the old days and today, there are three traditional occasions in which we light candles for ritual purposes:

* Births; to assure that the evil spirits stay away from the newly born.

Chapter VII — Magical and Spiritual Use of Candles

* Weddings; to impede the "Evil Eye" and envious vibrations from affecting the bride and groom.
* Deaths; as protection against demons stealing the soul of the departed and also so they may have a safe trip to the next world.

People of the Jewish persuasion traditionally light candles for a whole week in the room where a person has died. It is said that when the flame of a candle is blue or dark there is the spirit of a discarnate in the house or close to it. Blessed candles are said to protect against lightning and evil spirits.

The Nature of Candles

Old and modern occultism schools usually insist that the neophytes (students of occultism) should make all tools that they use for spells or rituals themselves. The reasons behind this are simple; while the candles and other tools are made they are being impregnated with the vibrations, personal energies and intentions of the person that is making them. This is also why it is necessary to concentrate on purpose and intention, impregnating the items with these vibrations during all phases of elaboration. The result are objects that are "impregnated" o "charged" with the thought forms, personal vibrations and energies of the person who made them and their effectiveness or energetic capacity is directly proportional to the powers of concentration used in their preparation.

The candles that are prepared in this manner and consecrated or anointed for a purpose become very personal in nature. Traditionally these manufactured candles and other objects are never shown to others or allowed to be manipulated by others less they be contaminated with negative vibrations or render them powerless.

Divination Using Candles

Many centuries have seen candles used to predict the weather. Formulas such as; "When the flame of a candle or other fire sways without visible cause, you can expect windy days; and "When candles are harder to light than usual it is a sign that wet weather is coming", were passed down through the generations.

In candle divination, the omens are simple and based on the observation of the way that the candle burns. A swaying flame indicates change. A brilliant flame tip is sign of success, unless it burns out quickly. A sparking flame means disillusion. If a flame dies out for no apparent reason this could mean a loss of a grave nature. A weak or low flame means lack of vitality or illness.

Another method of divination is to use three candles placed in a triangle; if one of the flames is higher and brighter than the others, good fortune is on its way; if all three flames are brilliant and high, and this is considered as the blessing of the light, a very good omen.

Ritual Candles

There are four main aspects in light magic; the type of candle, its function in the ritual, its color and its consecration or unction. The length of ritual candles is not important, what is important is that they burn for duration of the ritual. It is not necessary to use new candles for every ritual; alter candles, candles of the week and astrological candles may be reused many times. This is not so for offering candles which must be renewed for every ritual.

Altar Candles

The altar candles are those that are placed at the back of the altar. Traditionally two white candles are used, placed in the two corners at the back part of the altar. The altar candles are both practical and symbolical. The practical side is the illumination of the environment, these should be the first lit and the last to be put out. Symbolically they act as a "bridge" to the spiritual world.

Lighting and putting out the candles denote the beginning and the end of a ritual. Since the ritual seeks an environment of purity and peace, white candles are used to symbolize cleanliness, purity and spiritual simplicity, establishing a connection between the spiritual realm and the objective of the ritual.

Altar candles should either be the highest and least adorned or the highest and most adorned.

Offering Candles

Chapter VII — Magical and Spiritual Use of Candles

The offering candles are the most important candles in a ritual because they represent the active principle. These candles should always be placed in the center of the altar. The color of the candle symbolizes the objective. See **The Colors of Candles** below.

Astrological Candles

The astrological candles (also called Zodiac or Astral candles) represent the person or persons for whom the ritual is intended. The color is based on the birth date or the zodiac sign of the person. When you don't know someone's birth date, white or light orange candles may be used. Another option is to use a white candle and engrave the name of the person on the candle.

Candles represent the forces of the astral and earthly world; so they may be used to represent a person as well as an abstract function, such as power, justice, protection, luck, love, etc.

Candles for the Days of the Week

The candles for the days of the week are optional to any ritual. The choice of color depends of the day of the week chosen for ritual. These candles are placed on the left or right half of the altar.

Anointing or Consecrating Candles

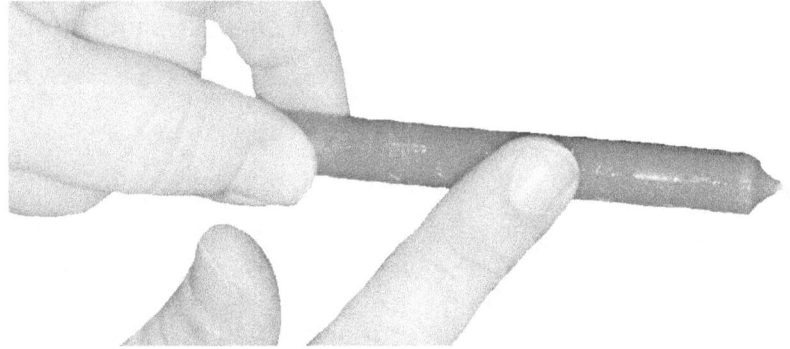

The person who will perform the ritual is the person who must anoint the candles so they will be impregnated with their own psychic, spiritual and mental vibrations. This is done to establish a psychic link between the candle and the person, empowering the candle to become a magical extension of the person. A variety of different essential oils and aromatic essences may be used. It is important to use oils or potions related to the purpose of the ritual, i.e. a ritual for luck would use and oil made from herbs that have the property to attract luck. Oils that are intense in color should be used with candles of the same color and purpose; uncolored oils may be used for any candle with the same purpose.

While anointing candles the key is to maintain the maximum concentration on the outcome of the ritual, seeing clearly in one's mind the image of the desired best possible outcome. Since these candles are now transmitters of certain vibrations, consecrated candles should not be used for any other ritual. This is also why anointing of candles is usually confined to the offering candles. Altar candles may be melted and remade or simply burned in other rituals. The anointment of candles may be done at the time of the ritual or previously. You may, for example, anoint candles to attract under the waxing moon, or to diminish under the waning moon, and then save these candles for use on another occasion. In this case, the candles should be wrapped in cloth and set aside until needed. If they are left out or handled before their use, they will lose effectiveness. You may also choose to anoint the candles at the time of the ritual to help you achieve the state of mind that will make your work more effective.

Traditional Anointing

In the traditional anointing method to consecrate candles with oil, we have the North Pole (wick), the South Pole (base) and the Equator (center). The candles are anointed starting from the center towards the wick or North Pole, followed by the reverse, anointed from the center towards the base or South Pole. Each half should be rubbed the same number of times, preferably an odd number (odd numbers have more power than even numbers).

This method is on the one hand a traditional magical method and on the other a method that favors concentration. The hands transmit energetic vibrations to the candles and empower them.

Anointing to Attract

Certain rituals are done to "attract" something, such as luck. These candles may be anointed from the wick or North Pole all the way down to the base or South Pole, with the concentration on "attracting". Anointment for attraction is best done in the waxing phase of the Moon.

Anointing to Banish

Other rituals are done to "banish" something, such as negative energy. The method is to reverse the above method and anoint the candles from the base or South Pole towards the wick or North Pole, concentrating on "banishing". Anointment for banishing is best done in the waning phase of the Moon.

Chapter VII — Magical and Spiritual Use of Candles

The Colors of Candles

Colors can be powerful forces and the correct choice of the color of the candle in a ritual is fundamental for its outcome. Days of the week, the signs of the Zodiac and the planets also have a direct relationship to the colors. All this should be considered when choosing the color of the candles.

White: Spiritual Cleansing, Clairvoyance, Healing, Search for Truth, used in rituals for Lunar Energy.

Yellow: Activity, Creativity, Energy, Assistance in the Powers of Concentration and Imagination, used in rituals for Solar Energy.

Gold: Understanding, Attracting Power and Cosmic Influences; Good for Rituals for Luck, Money and Energy, used in rituals for Solar Energy.

Pink: Promotes Romance and Friendship; Honor and Service, it is a Feminine Color.

Red: Health, Passion, Love, Fertility, Power, Courage; Increases Magnetism in Rituals.

Silver: Dissolves Negativity, Promotes Stability; Develops Psychic Powers.

Purple: Power, Success, Psychic Manifestations; Rituals for Independence, Personal Security and Contacts with the Spiritual World.

Brown: Earthly; Rituals for Material Improvement; Concentration, Telepathy, Study; Search for Lost Objects.

Sky Blue: Attracts Peace and Tranquility; it is a Spiritual Color; Rituals for Meditations and Inspiration.

Blue: Principal Spiritual Color; Rituals for Spirituality, Peace, Harmony, the Search for Inner Light; Guide for Truth.

Green: Color of Fertility, Prosperity, and Growth; Stimulates Rituals for Luck, Money and Youth.

Grey: Neutral; Useful in Complex Meditation Themes; in Ritual Magic Neutralizes Negative Influences.

Black: Opens Deep Levels of the Subconscious, Rituals for Inducing Profound States of Meditation; Rejects Evil and Negativity.

Candles for Each Day of the Week

Day of the Week	Color	Planet
Sunday	Yellow / Orange	Sun
Monday	White	Moon
Tuesday	Red	Mars
Wednesday	Blue	Mercury
Thursday	Grey / Silver	Jupiter
Friday	Green	Venus
Saturday	Black	Saturn

Chapter VII — Magical and Spiritual Use of Candles

Chapter VIII

Gems and Minerals

Introduction

All minerals and metals act as emitter-receptors of electromagnetic waves at an extremely low frequency. The energy that they emanate may be beneficial or negative depending on the molecular composition of the object, the receptivity of the person whom possesses it or wears it, and the shape and use given to it. Minerals, gems and metals may become vigorous magnetic condensers, occasionally with very powerful effects. We know that some objects generate very positive vibrations and others generate very bad vibrations. Throughout history there have been many accounts of gems and precious objects known for their very particular powers, in some cases with very positive effects on people and others, such as the Hope diamond, with very negative consequences to its owners. We have all heard the stories of the curse of Tutankhamen on all those who were to meddle with his grave and these events happened 5.000 years after he was buried.

There are many myths and stories of how gems were used. The Egyptians preferred semiprecious gems and some of their favorites were lapis lazuli, turquoise, jade and amber. Oriental civilizations in places such as Tibet and China have believed for thousands of years that certain metals and gems have spiritual and mystical properties and have used them as amulets and to promote spiritual development. They also believe that the color of the gem represents its properties. In the Renaissance travelers carried topaz to be free of fear. The Cabalists used amethyst to reverse the effects of poison. In the American continent, tribes such as the Aztecs, Incas, and Sioux among many others, used semiprecious gems to diagnose and treat physical and spiritual illnesses.

There are also special relations between the gems and the planets, and they possess very different properties which may agree or disagree with those who use them, depending on the sign they were born under and their personal energies. In nature everything is vibration and is in harmonic or non-harmonic resonance of objects upon people, which in turn depends on personal energies. Thus, the same gem may be lucky to one person and unlucky to another.

Chapter VIII — Gems and Minerals

Colors of Gems

Color plays an important role in the choosing of gems, having effects that may excite one person or calm another. We know that red excites, yellow produces a sensation of heat, green helps concentration, and blue has a calming effect. Where color is concerned all minerals and gems have very specific and individual properties.

Color of Gems Examples Properties

Color	Examples	Properties
Red	Ruby, Garnet	Healing, Protection from Fire and Storms, Energy, Courage
Pink	Rose Quartz	Calming and Relaxing, Love, Peace, Friends
Orange	Topaz, Citrine, Carnelian	Illumination, Personal Power, Self Awareness
Blue	Turquoise, Lapis Lazuli	Faith, Peace, Protection Against Nightmares, Trances, Healing, Calming
Violet	Amethyst	Virtue, Matters of the Spirit, Karma
Purple	Amethyst	Spiritual, Mysticism, Meditation, Psychic Work
Green	Emerald, Jade, Aquamarine	Fertility, Power, Luck, Money, Plants, Concentration
Yellow	Amber, Tiger Eye, Topaz	Communication, Logic, Happiness, Psychic Development
Black	Obsidian	Keeps the Feet on the Ground, Accumulates Negativity
White	Silver Diamond, White Chalcedony, Moonstone	Lunar Energy, Protection, Luck

Shapes of Gems

The shapes of gems also often reveal their powers.

Round:	Receptive Powers, Spirituality, Psychic Awareness
Triangular:	Protection
Long:	Energy, Protection
Square:	Earth, Prosperity, Stability, Abundance
Heart Shaped:	Love

Correspondences of the Planets and the Signs with the Gems and the Minerals

Astrology relates protective and fortunate gems and minerals according to the Zodiac sign under which one is born. The lunar sign and the solar ascendant are considered of equal importance.

Sign	Correspondences of Gems and Mineral	Planet
♈ Aries		Mars ♂

Red gems; blood red, and other bright red tones, in harmony with ferrous elements. Rubies especially and other gems with red tones. Amethyst, Diamond, and Topaz are also recommended when empathetic with Aries. Your metal is Iron.

| ♉ Taurus | | Venus ♀ |

Sparkling gems; light green Emeralds, sky blue Aquamarines, Zircons, Jasper, light green or pink Jade, Rose Coral, light colored Sapphires and Turquoise may be ideal for Taurus. Gold and Copper are your metals.

| ♊ Gemini | | Mercury ☿ |

Transparent gems that reflection light; Chrysolite, Cat's Eye, Agate, Amethyst, Alexandrite, Emerald, White Sapphire, Aquamarine and very soft tones of Rose Coral. Your metals are white, Mercury, Platinum, Nickel, Silver and white Gold.

| ♋ Cancer | | Moon ☾ |

Energetic gems; Moonstone, Orthoclase Quartz, Opals, especially with light tones or blue or pale green, Pearl and Emerald. Your metals are Silver and white Gold.

| ♌ Leo | | Sun ☉ |

Luminous and gold colored gems; Diamond, Topaz, Citrine, Quartz, golden Chrysolite, yellow Chalcedony and golden tones of Amber. Your metal is Gold.

Chapter VIII — Gems and Minerals

♍ Virgo   Mercury ☿

Blue and grey gems; Chalcedony, fluorescent Tourmaline, Agate, Jade, Sapphire and Turquoise. Your metals are white alloys, such as Nickel and Aluminum.

♎ Libra   Venus ♀

Green gems; blue-green Zircon, Jade, light-colored Beryl, Opal, Emerald and green Turquoise. Your metal is Copper.

♏ Scorpio   Pluto ♇

Dark red and garnet toned gems; red Hyacinths, dark red Sapphire, Ruby, Garnet, Topaz, Jasper and red Opal. Your metal is Iron.

♐ Sagittarius   Jupiter ♃

Dark blue, purple and violet gems; blue Diamond (set on Platinum), blue Sapphire, violet or purple Tourmaline, Lapis Lazuli and Turquoise. Your metals are Tin and Platinum.

♑ Capricorn   Saturn ♄

Dark gems, especially in green and black tones; Black Opal, Onyx (for some people), Malachite, dark green Chrysolite, Ruby and blue Sapphire. Your metal is Lead.

♒ Aquarius   Uranus

Fluorescent gems of all kinds; Cat's Eye, iridescent Opal, Ruby, Sapphire, Chrysolite, Amethyst, Jade, Sapphire, Zircon and Diamond. Your metal is Uranium.

♓ Pisces   Neptune

Warm gems; Aquamarine, clear tones of Sapphire, Lapis Lazuli, Chalcedony (from pale to dark blue), Turquoise, Zircon, dark green Jade and Ruby. Your metal is Tin and its alloys.

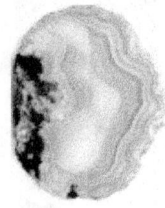

Agate

Description: Mineral composed of layers of quartz that is found in a variety of colors. The composition may vary but silica is always present. It is found in round nodules or veins; in concentric layers.

History: For the last 5.000 years agate has been used for ornamental and magical purposes. The Egyptians used it in their religious rituals. The Romans used it for fertility of their crops. In the Middle Ages it was believed that this gem protected from demons and poison. In the Orient it is carried to preserve good health. Associated with the planet Mercury.

Properties: It attracts peace, fortune and good luck. It generates emotional equilibrium and stimulates power, energy, courage and self confidence. It promotes vital energy and banishes fears. This gem has a special empathy with the plant world and is carried by gardeners as they attend their gardens. Placed in the garden with the plants it enhances the beauty of the plants and helps them grow healthy.

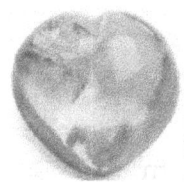

Amber

Description: Fossil resin from prehistoric trees. In general it is yellow. It is found in round and irregular forms, in grains or drops. It is fragile and gives off an agreeable aroma when rubbed. When it is burned it gives off a spicy smell and a brilliant flame.

History: The Greeks consecrated it to their God Zeus and used it as ritual incense in their temples. It has been used for centuries in China, burned in honor of the ancestors. The Chinese also believed that amber held the souls of tigers. Associated with the Sun.

Properties: It has a reputation for good luck. It emits electromagnetic waves and organic energy that are positive towards living cells. It purifies the ethereal body absorbing negative energy. It makes a powerful amulet against black magic. It is used to heal emotional disequilibrium, depressions and to calm the mind. It is also used to increase personal beauty and empowering spells.

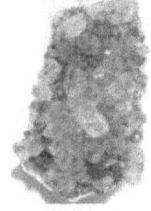

Amethyst

Description: Variety of quartz. Its violet or purple color is different from common quartz due to the presence of iron and manganese.

History: It has been used for magical purposes for last 2.000 years. The Egyptians consecrated it to their Lunar God, Toth. Greek mythology says that this gem avoided drunkenness. The Mayas and Aztecs used this gem in the decoration of their temples, probably for purposes of protection. Associated with Mars and Neptune.

Properties: This gem attracts love, promotes spiritual development and stimulates psychic powers. It has very positive vibrations, calming fears and stimulating spiritual development. Used for meditation and rituals for wisdom. Under the pillow it avoids insomnia and nightmares and stimulates intuitive and prophetic dreams. This gem also favors the beauty of herbs, the health of the animals and harmony in the home. It absorbs negative radiations and protects from the Evil Eye.

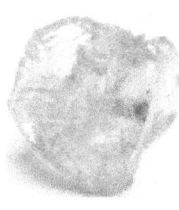

Aquamarine

Description: Semiprecious variety of beryl. Its name comes from the Latin, "aqua" water and "marina" sea. It is found in blue, blue-green and green. Blue aquamarine is the most valuable.

History: It is mentioned in the Vedas for medicinal purposes. According to the legend, this gem escaped from the coffer of the Sirens, the virgin daughters of the sea God Neptune. Associated with the Moon and Neptune.

Properties: This gem increases psychic powers when held or worn around the neck. Legend says that it is should be washed in the sea in the full moon. It is a good amulet against dangers in general and specifically against dangers in the sea. Good for job interviews. Attracts inspiration and new ideas. Rejects feelings of fear when held.

Beryl

Description: Composed of silicate of aluminum-beryl, this gem is transparent. Aquamarine and emerald are varieties of beryl.

History: In the Vedas, this gem is described as a symbol of love and purity. Alchemists used it in the Middle Ages. Used by some to call rain. In modern times it is used in crystal-therapy to stimulate the chakras. Associated with the Moon, Jupiter and Venus.

Properties: It represents idyllic and profound love. It attracts hope and reverses evil spells. It possesses very powerful protective powers. It protects against drowning and seasickness. It helps stimulate intellectual development, intuitive and psychic powers and favors concentration and meditation.

Cat's Eye

Description: Chrysoberyl cut in an oval form producing an effect that looks like the eye of a cat. It is found in, white, yellow, green and brown.

History: It has been used for centuries to avoid the Evil Eye and illnesses that affect the eyesight. Associated with Venus.

Properties: Very powerful, it promotes personal courage, produces mental clarity and calm. When used for meditation it should be placed near the area of work or study. It also purifies the area of negative thoughts. Worn to increase personal beauty.

Coral

Description: Exoskeletons of marine zoophytes that bond together. It is found in a variety of colors. Shown here is black coral.

History: The Hindus considered coral as a powerful protecting amulet. Roman women used it to attract men. Associated with Venus.

Properties: Considered to have powerful effects since it is said to eliminate evil and bad wishes sent by others. Protects from storms, floods and accidents at sea. It alleviates worries, bad thoughts and promotes mental processes. It produces a balance between the physical and psychic energies. It also has been associated with love and is recommended in combination with pink or red candles to attract love.

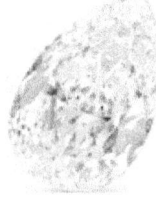

Diamond

Description: Precious gem that is formed from mineral carbon by intense heat. It is the hardest substance known to man. It can be found in several colors, white being the most common and red the most scarce (and valuable).

History: The Old Testament of the Bible describes it as an instrument of God, used by Jehovah to send the rebel angels away from paradise. The Greeks called it "Adama" which means unconquerable. There are also some old legends that see this gem as having evil effects to mankind. Associated with the Sun and Mars.

Properties: Without doubt the most powerful gem. When obtained firsthand (direct from the jeweler) it emanates extraordinary powerful vibrations. It attracts power, riches and friends, good for reconciling differences between friends. It symbolizes peace, fidelity and opulence. It eliminates emotional negativity. It protects from enemies and protects pregnant women from physical danger. Also named the Crystal of Dreams, it helps inspire prophetic and vivid dreams.

Chapter VIII — Gems and Minerals

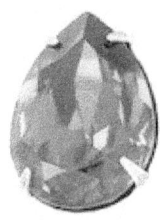

Emerald

Description: Green variety of beryl. It is green because it contains chrome and sometimes a material, called silk, in feather-like forms.

History: Probably discovered by the Egyptians, who used it for personal beauty and to conquer warriors. It was called "Pochamac", and considered as Goddess of the Sacred Light, by the Chavín and Rancuay (pre-Columbian civilizations of the Andes). It was known to them for its power to cure illnesses of the eyes. Associated with Venus and Jupiter.

Properties: Promotes spirituality, precognition and clairvoyance; favors creativity and stimulates interior perceptions; nurtures love, beauty and immortality; rejects negativity and stimulates intelligent communications. Known as the "Stone of Tranquility", it not only facilitates sleep when placed near the bed but also has the reputation of producing goodness and the instinct to nurture. It has a great affinity with the elemental spirits, especially with the Sun spirits.

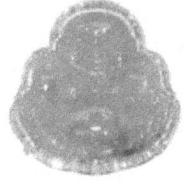

Jade

Description: Compact gem, generally opaque, found in colors from dark green to very pale green (almost white), pale lavenders, pale yellow, and other varieties. It is found in Asia, Burma and Tibet.

History: Valued in China and Japan as one of the most precious gems. It has been used in China for centuries to carve figures for magical and spiritual purposes. Especially used for love and protection. In Egypt it was used as a talisman to attract good fortune. Associated with Venus.

Properties: Considered for centuries as a sacred stone of good luck, it is also used for protection against enemies, illnesses, evil spirits and spells, and as protection during long trips. It has the fame of fomenting occult powers, representing serenity and immortality. Also used to remember past lives and for control over dreams.

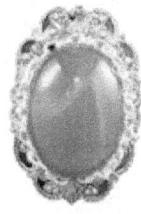

Jasper

Description: Variety of quartz. It's opaque and found in red, yellow, blue, green and brown tones. It can be found in Libya, in the Nile valley and in Arizona, USA.

History: It is mentioned in the Old Testament as an ornament used by the High Priests (Exodus 28:20) and as a stone that was placed in the foundation of the wall in New Jerusalem (Revelations 21:18). The Jews believed that this gem favored visions and also used it in rituals for rain. Associated with Saturn and Jupiter.

Properties: It protects from pain and promotes personal independence. It brings good luck and serves as protection against controlling influences of others. This gem is also considered to preserve from poisons and contagious illnesses. It increases spiritual power, acts as a defense against external dominant influences and as a shield against black magic.

Lapis Lazuli

Description: Composed of the blue mineral lazurita, it contains small quantities of calcite and pyroxene. What seem to be patches of gold are really particles of pyrite. It varies in color from intense sky blue to blue green.

History: The Egyptians have known this gem for 3.000 years, when they consecrated it to their Goddess Isis. The Greeks consecrated it to their Goddess Venus. Associated with Venus.

Properties: It is a spiritual and mental purifier, known to heal melancholy. It attracts highly evolved and powerful spirits. If used correctly this gem has powerful supernatural powers. It can increase psychic abilities and cleanse the aura. It can also empower the mind and stimulate spiritual awakening. It has also been considered to confer pure luck and is a symbol of mental power.

Malachite

Description: Carbonate of basic copper, formed by the corrosion of air and water.

History: The Romans had a high regard for this gem and believed that it would protect them from lightning and accidents. Associated with Venus.

Properties: This gem is known for its powers to promote emotional equilibrium and spiritual grown, eliminating emotional negativity. It lifts the spirit and increases hope. It is also used for success in businesses and to attract prosperity. Worn to sense danger, to protect from nightmares and to stimulate visions.

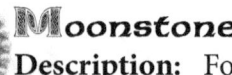

Moonstone

Description: Found in Sri Lanka and India.

History: The Greeks believed that this gem bestowed beauty to the ladies that wore it. The Wiccans dedicated it to their Moon Goddess. Associated with the Moon.

Chapter VIII — Gems and Minerals

Properties: It is considered as a gem of love and good fortune. It has the virtue of protecting love and inspiring tenderness. It is known to calm emotions and to help access ones inner self. In the full moon, placed under the pillow it may give the dreamer a vision of their true love. It also stimulates clairvoyance and telepathic powers. It protects the traveler from harm.

Opal

Description: Mineral composed of hydrated silica. Found in colors ranging from white to black and from transparent to opaque. Its most notorious characteristic is its refraction of colors.

History: Mysterious gem that the Greeks associated with love. According to a Hindu legend, it was the favorite gem of the deities; Brahma, Shiva and Vishnu. Greatly appreciated by both the Greeks and Romans as a good luck gem that protected from the dangers of bad weather. In the Middle Ages this gem had the fame of being a malefic stone. Associated with all Planets.

Properties: This gem is known for its mystical nature. It attracts good luck, love and increases personal psychic powers. It also assists in astral projection, past life recall and invisibility. It calms the nerves and the restless spirits.

Pearl

Description: The pearl is the product of a calcareous process called mother-of-pearl found in mollusks. (Bivalves such as oysters).

History: For centuries in China, the pearl has been used in medicine. According the Romans, the pearl was the ornament of their Goddess Venus. The Greeks called it "Margarita" and in Asia it was used as an amulet for female charm. The Romans dedicated it to the Goddess Isis. Associated with the Moon.

Properties: Symbol of love, the pearl equilibrates emotional energy by absorbing negative energy. It stimulates female qualities It is also used to join mental forces with spiritual forces. Good for meditation since it tends to harmonize with the spiritual body.

Quartz

Description: Composed of silicon dioxide, (silicate), it is found in veins and nodules in sedimentary rocks, especially in limestone. It crystallizes in a hexagonal system. The pure mineral has no color. It has a property called the piezo-electric effect.

History: It has had an important role in magical and esoteric rituals and has had therapeutic uses in many ancient cultures. In Japan and China it was considered to have energetic healing properties. It was used in the Middle Ages for the elaboration of magical tools. Associated with the Sun and the Moon.

Properties: It empowers communications with the cosmos. Its power synchronizes with the music of the spheres. It opens the psychic centers and attracts the energy of the light, rejecting the heavy electrical vibrations. It is very powerful when used or worn for protection against bad vibrations. Worn, it also allows the symbols and signs of the earth to be felt, amplifying their subtle vibrations. It is also used for divination.

Rose Quartz

Description: Thick crystalline that does not have independent crystals. Found in colors that range from light pink to very deep pink that loose intensity with the exposure light.

History: In Egypt it was considered a sacred gem of love. Associated with Venus.

Properties: Ideal gem for gardens since it stimulates the growth and beauty of the herbs. It relaxes the atmosphere of a house and liberates tension. It is a good stone to stimulate interior beauty and promote self-esteem. It is considered very powerful for calming a suffering heart and also for healing any type of emotional or psychic wounds. (Either under the pillow during the night or placed directly on the skin.)

Ruby

Description: Variety of corundum, the ruby is considered as one of the most precious gems. It is found in colors ranging from pink to intense bright red. The darker tones are the most appreciated and valuable. The best specimens are found in Burma. Other countries where rubies are found are Brazil, India, Thailand and China.

History: The ancient Islamics believed that the ruby conferred powers of invisibility and considered it also as a powerful protecting amulet. The Greeks consecrated it to their God Apollo. In the Middle Ages it was considered as a symbol of life and love.

Properties: The ruby is a gem of great power, generating a sense of internal security. It focuses occult energies and protects against dangers. It is used for love and passion, to develop intuition and for spiritual development. Also used to cure depressions and maintain youth. It provides energy and repels bad vibrations. It has a great affinity with the spirits of the Sun.

Chapter VIII

Gems and Minerals

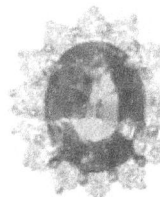
Sapphire
Description: The most valuable color is intense blue but it is also found in yellow, gold, pink and white.

History: In ancient times kings wore sapphires to prevent illnesses, avoided intrigues and ill advice. Salomon's Seal was supposed to be made of sapphire. The Persians thought that it possessed powers of immortality and eternal youth. Pope Gregory XV proclaimed it as the official gem of the Cardinals because of its powers of protection against evil influences. Associated with Saturn, Jupiter and Venus.

Properties: It is considered a powerful gem of magic and occult powers that irradiates vibrations of nobility and peace. It attracts justice and truth as well as good luck. It extends the cosmic conscience. It promotes peace, harmony and matrimonial fidelity. It increases the mental capacities and purifies the mind.

Topaz
Description: Variety of fluorosilicate of aluminum mineral. It forms crystals that are appreciated as a gem. It is found in yellow, orange, blue, red and green. The best specimens are found in Sri Lanka.

History: In occultism it has been related to the influence of the Sun and the planet Mars, with tempestuous relations. It was believed that it protected against revenge of the evil spirits. Associated with the Sun.

Properties: Topaz is considered as the protector of the warriors; it rejects evil spirits and repels spells. It protects against depression, neutralizes anguish, fear, envy and hate. It is used in divination to find water and treasures and is considered as a source of creativity. Very good when placed near the bed because it counteracts against insomnia and dissipates the vibrations of nocturnal fears.

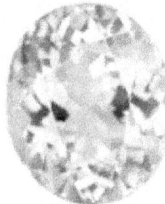
Tourmaline
Description: Found most frequently in green, pink, brown, blue black and black.

History: Dutch sailors brought it from Sri Lanka where it was known by the name of "Turmali".

Properties: It protects people and environments from negative influences and negative personalities. It is used in rituals destined to purify places such as sick rooms. It functions as a protective shield absorbing negative energy. It is recommended that it be cleansed by placing under running water or by exposing it to the light of the waning moon.

Turquoise

Description: Opaque mineral found in tones of blue, green and grey green. The sky blue tones are the most valued.

History: Used by the Egyptians in their funeral and temple decorations. The Aztecs used it in their art and magic. Associated with Venus and Neptune.

Properties: Symbol of sincerity, the turquoise preserves it owner from dangerous falls. It attracts love and courage, protects from violence of thought and fact. It repels the Evil Eye, spells and evil spirits. It purifies the psychic and physical planes and assists in the development of intuition. It harmonizes with the energetic and physical centers of the body and helps in astral projection.

Zircon

Description: Transparent mineral that crystallizes in a tetragonal system. It is composed of zirconium silicate and is found colorless and also in tones of green, grey, yellow, blue, and red. It is submitted to high temperatures to produce its shine. It is frequently found near gold and abounds in rocks that contain silica.

History: The Ayurveda (sacred book of the Hindus) mentions it with medicinal purposes. Crystal therapy today uses it to stimulate the chakras. Associated with the Sun.

Properties: It attracts fame and fortune. It is considered as the gem of wishes. It protects against accidents and natural disasters. It stimulates the vital forces, mental clarity and promotes spirituality.

Protective Metals

Aluminum
Attracts conditions necessary for an awakened state of mind, stimulating creativity and promoting rapid thought. Associated with the element Air.

Brass
Used in ritual healing and to attract love and money. Jewelry made from brass is used for protection. Associated with the element Fire.

Copper
Warm and mundane, guardian of health, it protects against arthritis and rheumatism, it also repels depression and negative thoughts and entities. It has the property of reconciling rivals and extinguishing hate. Associated with the element Air.

Gold
Whoever wears gold attracts favors, honors, riches and general estimation. It attracts success in businesses and in the theater. It is the king of metals. Associated with the element Fire.

Iron
Iron is the metal of armament, of attack and defense, of war. Talismans of iron are used for invulnerability. Associated with the element Fire.

Lead
Heavy and serious but mystical, lead is the emblem of Saturn. It is good for breaking spells and for protection against extravagant people. It preserves against illnesses and protects travelers against all dangers. It assures a natural death if worn with confidence and respect. Associated with the element Earth.

Silver
Metal of dreams and receptivity. It protects secrets and gives security in the water. It has emotional qualities and is adequate for projecting thoughts. Associated with the element Water.

Tin
Symbol of Jupiter, it concedes eloquence and success in business. It is the metal of luck and good fortune, of progress and expansion. Associated with the element Earth.

Gems According to Their Properties

The following lists of gems are given as reference to facilitate the search of certain properties or purposes.

Gems that Assist in Astral Projection
Opal and Turquoise

Gems that Rid of Bad Vibrations
Amber, Amethyst, Quartz, Ruby and Topaz

Gems for Beauty
Amber, Amethyst, Emerald and Rose Quartz

Gems for Divination
Quartz and Topaz

Gems for Overcoming Fears
Agate, Amethyst, Aquamarine, and Topaz

Gems for Love
Amethyst, Beryl, Coral, Emerald, Moonstone, Opal, Pearl, Ruby and Turquoise

Chapter VIII — Gems and Minerals

Gems for Luck and Fortune
Agate, Amber, Jade, Jasper, Lapis Lazuli, Moonstone, Opal, Sapphire and Zircon

Gems that Stimulate Prophetic Dreams
Amethyst and Diamond

Gems for Protection
Amethyst, Aquamarine, Beryl, Coral, Diamond, Jasper, Jade, Moonstone, Quartz, Ruby, Topaz, Tourmaline, Turquoise and Zircon

Gems for Psychic Powers
Amethyst, Aquamarine, Beryl, Cat's Eye, Emerald, Lapis Lazuli, Moonstone, Opal, Quartz, Ruby, Sapphire, Topaz and Turquoise

Gems for Purification
Amber, Cat's Eye, Lapis Lazuli, Sapphire, Tourmaline and Turquoise

Gems for Spiritual Development
Amethyst, Emerald, Jasper, Lapis Lazuli, Malachite, Pearl, Ruby and Zircon

Chapter IX -

Preparation of Rituals

The Sorceress (1911) by John William Waterhouse

What is a Ritual?

A ritual may be defined as a religious or magical ceremony or prescribed procedure, a formal ceremony that includes a series of physical and mental actions. Occultists describe it as "a set of external events so designed as to energize an inner set of psychic responses related to them. A practice or pattern of behavior regularly performed in a set manner. It can also be explained as an adventure between the astral plane and the mental plane due to the fact that mentally "doors" are opened between the physical and the ethereal. Its result is produced through the operator's creative imagination, meditation, concentration and visualization. All reality starts in the mind, in the thought process and the imagination before it becomes a fact. Training the mind starts with the use of creative imagination which leads to health, relaxation, peace of mind and the dominion over mental processes. Anyone can "know" something, but to "understand" it requires thought.

Ritual magic uses energy from other planes of existence (astral and mental) and knits it, so to speak, to our intentions and desired reality in the physical plane of existence. The principal purpose in any ritual is to create a change and the means for creating this change are the energies and vibrations of the astral dimension. To handle these energies and vibrations, the occultist creates a door or communication circuit through the ritual use of symbols, visualization, concentration and meditation. For this to be effective the occultist uses certain magically empowered tools such as candles, incenses, herbs, gems and others. Ritual magic opens the doors to the creative mind and the subconscious. For magic to be effective, one must "know" and "understand" that the power to make these changes that we desire comes directly from our own minds.

Chapter IX — Preparation of Rituals

Types of Rituals

Generally speaking, rituals can be divided into three main types.

Affirmation Rituals (Propitiatory Rituals)

Affirmation rituals are those that relate to the phase of the waxing moon, when we desire to grow, improve, develop; rituals to develop love, to focus energy towards success, to improve our understanding of ourselves or others, etc.

In these rituals you should always light the candles clockwise. This means that you should light the candles on the left side first and then those on the right; always the offering candles first.

Negation Rituals (Conjuration Rituals)

The negation rituals should be done when the moon is in it waning phase, when you desire to reduce, diminish, eliminate something; rituals to get rid of a bad habit, to avoid difficulties or to have less contact with certain people, for example.

In these rituals you should light the candles counterclockwise, lighting those on the right and then those on the left.

Harmonization Rituals

It is not necessary to do rituals only in times of troubles, they can be done to express thanks or satisfaction, when you desire peace of mind or want to stimulate meditation, or alter your state of consciousness.

In this category of rituals are those that relate to harmony, protection and purification. These can be done any day at any time, but with a little investigation an exceptionally good moment for the ritual may be determined. These rituals may coincide with waning or waxing phases of the moon. The most important factor is the personal choice, what ever feels right is always right.

How to Determine the Ideal Moment for a Ritual

One of the basic activities for preparation is to determine the ideal moment for a ritual. For this various conditions should be taken into account, and the first of these is the phase of the moon.

The Lunar Phases

Rituals are usually made to coincide with a determined phase of the moon. The reason for this is explained as follows:

The rituals that relate to growth, development, and expansion, should be done when the moon in its waxing phase. In this phase the moon attracts things and this is the best phase for rituals to attract love, health or success.

If the mission is to diminish something, the ritual should be in the waning phase of the moon. This is a good time to suppress a bad habit, combat illnesses and pains, overcome depressions, etc. The new moon and the following three days are known as "the dark phase of the moon", and should not be used for elaborated rituals unless you know very well what you are doing.

Chapter IX — Preparation of Rituals

The Timing

In general the best moment to do a ritual is in the late afternoon or the evening. Notwithstanding the lunar phase, the day of the week, the planetary hour or any other factor in the choice of the moment, the most important thing is still the intention and the concentration on the objective. Of all of the conditions mentioned here, only those that seem reasonable should be used. Always trust your instinct and inner voice.

The Altar

A surface or structure upon which some form of ritual worship, reverence or prayer to the gods takes place. It has deep religious and or symbolic significance and is considered a holy and revered object where communication with spirits, angels and deities is achieved. Place dedicated to the celebration of sacrifices or offerings to a deity.

The altar also may be any flat and stable surface; a coffee table, a desk, a dresser, for example. It is convenient to cover the altar with a cloth and use this cloth exclusively for rituals. The cloth acts and an "isolator" to the mundane vibrations on the altar in its everyday uses; silk is the best isolator. It is important to indicate that any area used for rituals should always be impeccably clean.

Selection of the Astrological Hour

Rituals and astrology are closely related; there is a correct time for everything. The planets rule the days of the week and the hours of the day. The hours and days are governed by each of the planets, and are useful to determine the most favorable time for rituals. The best day for a ritual is that which is ruled by the planet that best symbolizes the objective of the ritual. For example, a ritual whose objective is related with the Sun is best done on a Sunday and concretely in those hours that are ruled by the Sun.

Planetary Hours

Hour	Sunday	Monday	Tuesday	Wednesday	Thursday	Friday	Saturday
0-1 A.M.	Sun	Moon	Mars	Mercury	Jupiter	Venus	Saturn
1-2	Venus	Saturn	Sun	Moon	Mars	Mercury	Jupiter
2-3	Mercury	Jupiter	Venus	Saturn	Sun	Moon	Mars
3-4	Moon	Mars	Mercury	Jupiter	Venus	Saturn	Sun
4-5	Saturn	Sun	Moon	Mars	Mercury	Jupiter	Venus
5-6	Jupiter	Venus	Saturn	Sun	Moon	Mars	Mercury
6-7	Mars	Mercury	Jupiter	Venus	Saturn	Sun	Moon
7-8	Sun	Moon	Mars	Mercury	Jupiter	Venus	Saturn
8-9	Venus	Saturn	Sun	Moon	Mars	Mercury	Jupiter
9-10	Mercury	Jupiter	Venus	Saturn	Sun	Moon	Mars
10-11	Moon	Mars	Mercury	Jupiter	Venus	Saturn	Sun
11-12	Saturn	Sun	Moon	Mars	Mercury	Jupiter	Venus
12-01 P.M.	Jupiter	Venus	Saturn	Sun	Moon	Mars	Mercury
1-2	Mars	Mercury	Jupiter	Venus	Saturn	Sun	Moon
2-3	Sun	Moon	Mars	Mercury	Jupiter	Venus	Saturn
3-4	Venus	Saturn	Sun	Moon	Mars	Mercury	Jupiter
4-5	Mercury	Jupiter	Venus	Saturn	Sun	Moon	Mars
5-6	Moon	Mars	Mercury	Jupiter	Venus	Saturn	Sun
6-7	Saturn	Sun	Moon	Mars	Mercury	Jupiter	Venus
7-8	Jupiter	Venus	Saturn	Sun	Moon	Mars	Mercury
8-9	Mars	Mercury	Jupiter	Venus	Saturn	Sun	Moon
9-10	Sun	Moon	Mars	Mercury	Jupiter	Venus	Saturn
10-11	Venus	Saturn	Sun	Moon	Mars	Mercury	Jupiter

Chapter IX — Preparation of Rituals

| 11-12 | Mercury | Jupiter | Venus | Saturn | Sun | Moon | Mars |

Regents of the Week

Sunday
Day Of: Fortune, Family, Health
Auspicious for: Power, Riches, Honor, Glory, Friendships, Favors, Physical Healing, Prosperity, Vitality
Gems / Metal: Yellow gems and Zircon, Topaz, Diamond / Gold
Colors / Element: Yellow, Gold / Fire

Monday
Day Of: Mysticism, Dreams, Intuition
Auspicious for: Love, Receptivity, Female Fertility, Trips, Dreams, Reconciliation, Psychic Powers, Visions, Magic
Gems / Metal: White gems and Moonstone, Quartz, Pearl / Silver, Platinum
Colors / Element: White, Silver, Lavender / Water

Tuesday
Day Of: Struggle, Powerful Events
Auspicious for: Courage, Defeating Enemies, Breaking Spells, Sexual Energy, Protection from Fire and Violence, Masculinity
Gems / Metal: Red gems and Red Agate, Red Topaz, Ruby / Iron, Steel
Colors / Element: Red, Pink / Fire

Wednesday
Day Of: Knowledge, Communication
Auspicious for: Communication, Intelligence, Divination, Business, Mental Healing, Study of the Occult, Creativity, Prediction, Spells
Gems / Metal: Blue gems and Opal, Agate / Mercury
Colors / Element: Blue, Purple / Air

Thursday
Day Of: Dominion, Possessions
Auspicious for: Honors, Riches, Friendship, Masculine Fertility, Health, Legal Matters, Political Power, Luck
Gems / Metal: Purple gems and Lapis Lazuli, Amethyst, Turquoise, Sapphire / Bronze, Tin
Colors / Element: Silver, Blue / Fire

Friday
Day Of: Love, Beauty
Auspicious for: Goodness, Happiness, Trips, Beauty, Romantic Love, Music, Friendship, Spiritual Harmony, Artistic Creativity
Gems / Metal: Green gems and Amber, Malachite, Jade, Emerald, Turquoise / Copper
Colors / Element: Green, Pink, Sky Blue / Earth

Saturday
Day Of: Spirituality, Transformation
Auspicious for: Breaking Spells, Psychic Defense and Attack, Karma, Reincarnation, Protection, Communication with Spirits
Gems / Metal: Black gems and Onyx, Pearl, Sapphire / Lead
Colors / Element: Black, Grey / Earth

Elements, Elementals and Associations

Air
Elementals: Sylphs, Mountain Fairies, Zephyrs
Direction / Symbols: East / Sky, Wind, Clouds, Vibrations
Tools: Oils, Incenses. Daggers, Wands
Plane / Color: Mental / Yellow
Season / Time: Spring / Dawn
Ritual: Visualization, Concentration
Magic for: Trips, Studies, Psychic Abilities, Messages, Inspiration, Intellect, Ideas, Knowledge and Growth of Herbs

Water
Elementals: Undines, Nymphs, Mermen, Mermaids, Fairies
Direction / Symbols: West / Seas, Lakes, Rivers, Rain, Fog
Tools: Water, Perfumes, Mirrors
Plane / Color: Astral / Blue, Blue Green
Season / Time: Autumn / Dusk
Ritual: Wash, Bathe, Soak
Magic for: Love, Psychic Perception, Dreams, Intuition, Spiritual Communication, Emotions, Healing, Friendship, Plants

Earth
Elementals: Gnomes, Goblins, Hobgoblins, Dwarfs, Trolls
Direction / Symbols: North / Stones, Gems, Mountains, Earth, Mines, Caves
Tools: Salts, Powders, Pentacles, Gems, Trees, Images

Plane / Color:	Physical / Green, Brown
Season / Time:	Winter / Night
Ritual:	Bury, Plant
Magic for:	Money, Work, Prosperity, Stability, Fertility, Treasures

Fire

Elementals:	Salamanders, Fire Drakes
Direction / Symbols:	South / Fire, Lightning, Volcanoes, Sun
Tools:	Candles, Images, Fire, Incenses
Plane / Color:	Spiritual / Red, Gold
Season / Time:	Summer / Noon
Ritual:	Burn on a Low Fire
Magic for:	Protection, Courage, Energy, Energy, Spiritual Cleansing, Passion, Perception, Illumination, Purification

Development of Rituals

Preparation

How is a ritual performed? Only a little information of colors, aromas, dates, objects, herbs, etc. is required. The elements that are chosen should be according to the personal feelings and desires.

Our thought forms or psychic energies are the most important element for effectiveness of a ritual; therefore we must concentrate our energy in each step and activity of the ritual. The symbolic acts performed in the physical plane are what allow us to enter contact with the astral plane where magic happens. The steps needed to be followed to prepare a ritual are, in general, the following:

* Define the motive for ritual and the most appropriate day and time for it.
* Select the colors of candles and the decoration (flowers, gems, etc.).
* Chose the candles; either by making them or buying them.
* Select the incenses and the oils.
* Design the disposition of the altar.
* Prepare the texts.
* Gather all the materials
* Prepare ourselves, with spiritual baths, meditation, etc.

Execution

Start by purifying with incense, prepare the altar and form a circle of protection, either using a solution of water and sea salt, (or just sea salt) sprinkling it in a circle around the area to be used, including the altar, or by drawing a circle or by envisioning a circle. This should always be done clockwise. (Once the circle is formed, you should not leave it until you finish the ritual.) Next, take a few minutes to relax and breathe slowly to calm the mind and prepare yourself spiritually for task. If a ritual bath is included in your preparations it should be taken about an hour before the ritual.

Initiation

To start you should breath slowly and deeply and take as long as you feel that it is necessary to feel that the moment is right. Next:

* Light the altar candles.
* Anoint the offering candles, concentrating your thoughts on the objective.
* Light the incense.

The Mental Phase

This is the phase where the concentration and meditation on the objective is most important, and should take as much time as you feel that is right. Visualize as clearly as possible the desired outcome of the ritual. Next, read your chosen text. The text, previously chosen should be something that fills your heart with joy, it may be something written by you, a poem, a psalm, or anything that you like. When you read a text this should be done out loud in a clear and sturdy voice.

Conclusion

To conclude the ritual, first put out the candles in the reverse order in which you lit them, serenely contemplating all that has happened. There is another thing that should be taken into account and that is that even the most elemental ritual could have attracted (with or without intentions) elementals or curious spirits, and these must be gently dismissed. In a clear and firm voice you must tell them to go back to where they came from. This may be done by using a passage from the Bible, a prayer or something prepared by you. An example of something that could be used is the following:

> "To all the spirits that have graced me with your presences,
> I thank you for your company
> Go back in peace to where you belong.
> May you be blessed and loved".

Now, the circle of salt should be removed, again in the reverse, or counterclockwise. Clear the altar, clean up and put everything carefully back to order.

Sealing of the Aura

When you have completed a ritual and have cleaned everything up, the final step is to seal your aura so no negative energy can penetrate. This is done touching your forehead (or third eye), the middle of your chest (or solar plexus), your right shoulder and then your left shoulder with the fingers of your right hand. (It is very much like the Catholic ritual crossing). This represents the cross of the elements and has been used for many centuries.

Chapter X

Herbs and Spices

Gather Ye Rosebuds While Ye May (1909) by John William Waterhouse

Introduction

Herbs are living beings, vital to our survival, and they share our same environment and are exposed to the same elements; (sun, wind, water and fire), and the same climatic conditions, seasonal and lunar cycles. It was naturally supposed by our ancestors that they also emanated spiritual energies as well as produce physical nutrients. They have been used for centuries to assist us on our spiritual journey. Many native tribes all over the world even today use herbs and spices for ceremonial purposes. Even the Bible makes reference to some herbs for purification and protection.

Herbs show feelings towards the physical and psychic environment; conditions of the earth, light, humidity, and even sympathies or antipathies towards humans. This can be observed in their general state of health, when they are exposed to the presence and or care of different persons over short periods of time. The fact that herbs sympathize with some persons and not others may be due to the attitudes of the persons towards them. It has been shown that they even have musical tastes, liking in general music by Mozart and not heavy metal rock music.

It has also been observed that certain herbs like the company of some species of herbs and seek their company and the tend to shy away from other species avoiding contact with them, showing that there is even sympathy and antipathy between herbs themselves.

The Essences of the Herbs

In the descriptions that follow of the herbs, when the "essence" of the herb or substance is referred to, it means the type of energy that it radiates. The term "hot" means that the herb or substance has a stimulating, electric, or aggressive effect and the term "cold" refers to a relaxing, passive or magnetic effect.

Herbs According to Their Properties

The following lists of herbs are given as a reference to facilitate the search of herbs with certain properties or effects.

Aphrodisiac
Amber, Clove, Nutmeg, Patchouli, Peppermint, and Spikenard

Astral Projection
Benzoin, Hyssop, Lemon, Mugwort, Sage, Saint John's Wort and Sandalwood

Chapter X — Herbs and Spices

Attract Good Spirits
Catnip, Gardenia and Jasmine

Clairvoyance
Angelica, Anise, Bay, Bistort, Cinnamon, Eyebright, Frankincense, Gum Arabic, Honeysuckle, Mastic, Mugwort, Nutmeg, Patchouli, Rose and Wormwood

Clarity of Thought
Fenugreek

Divinations and Predictions
Anise, Bistort, Camphor, Iris, Lavender, Sage and Wormwood

Eliminate Bad Vibrations
Basil, Benzoin, Broom, Clove, Fenugreek, Flax, Garlic, Hyssop, Lemon, Marjoram, Nutmeg, Peppermint, Rose, Rosemary, Rue, Sage, Snapdragon, Solomon's Seal and Vervain

Eliminate Fears
Agrimony, Garlic, Rosemary, Snapdragon and Yarrow

Fortune and Money
Cinnamon, Fumitory, Honeysuckle, Garlic, Ginger, Nutmeg, Orange, Parsley, Sandalwood, Spikenard, Sweet Flag, and Vervain

Healing
Bay, Carnation, Cinnamon, Eucalyptus, Eyebright, Gardenia, Geranium, Pennyroyal, Peppermint, Rosemary, Sage and Sweet Flag

Invisibility
California Poppy

Love and Passion
Basil, Bay, Benzoin, California Poppy, Cassia, Catnip, Chamomile, Cinnamon, Clove, Cyclamen, Frankincense, Gardenia, Geranium, Hyacinth, Iris, Jasmine, Juniper, Lavender, Lemon, Lemon Balm, Marjoram, Mate, Meadowsweet, Mullein, Myrrh, Myrtle, Nutmeg, Orange, Patchouli, Rose, Rosemary, Saint John's Wort, Sandalwood, Snapdragon, Spikenard, Thyme, Vervain and Yarrow

Luck
Basil, Benzoin, California Poppy, Catnip, Chamomile, Cinnamon, Clove, Ginger, Hyssop, Jasmine, Lemon, Lemon Balm, Myrtle, Nutmeg, Orange, Parsley, Patchouli, Pennyroyal, Peppermint and Thyme

Meditation
Chamomile, Gum Arabic and Hyacinth

Prevent Nightmares
Anise, Betony, Bistort, Garlic, Hyacinth, Mullein, Rosemary, Thyme and Vervain

Prophetic Dreams
Bay, Benzoin, Calendula, Cassia, Honeysuckle, Iris, Jasmine, Lavender, Lemon, Peppermint, Mugwort, Myrrh, and Rose

Protection
Agrimony, Aloe Vera, Anise, Basil, Bay, Betony, Broom, Calendula, Camphor, Carnation, Cinnamon, Clove, Cyclamen, Eucalyptus, Flax, Frankincense, Fumitory, Garlic, Gardenia, Geranium, Ginger, Greater Burnet, Gum Arabic, Horehound, Hyacinth, Hyssop, Iris, Juniper, Lavender, Lemon Balm, Lotus, Marjoram, Mate, Mugwort, Mullein, Myrrh, Nutmeg, Parsley, Patchouli, Pennyroyal, Pokeweed, Rosemary, Rue, Sage, Saint John's Wort, Solomon's Seal, Sandalwood, Snapdragon, Sweet Flag, Thyme, Vervain and Wormwood

Psychic and Spiritual Development
Aloe Vera, Anise, Bay, Calendula, Carnation, Cassia, Cinnamon, Eyebright, Flax, Frankincense, Gum Arabic, Honeysuckle, Horehound, Hyssop, Iris, Juniper, Lemon, Lotus, Marjoram, Mastic, Meadowsweet, Mugwort, Patchouli, Peppermint, Rosemary, Sage, Sandalwood, Spikenard, Thyme, Wallflower, Wormwood and Yarrow

Purification
Angelica, Anise, Basil, Bay, Benzoin, Betony, Broom, Clove, Flax, Frankincense, Fumitory, Garlic, Ginger, Greater Burnet, Hyssop, Juniper, Lavender, Mugwort, Mullein, Myrrh, Orange, Parsley, Peppermint, Rose, Rosemary, Rue, Sandalwood, Solomon's Seal, Thyme, Vervain and Yarrow

Repel Evil Spirits
Agrimony, Betony, Bistort, Camphor, Juniper, Lotus, Mate, Mullein, Myrrh, Rue and Saint John's Wort

Spiritual Cleansing
   Basil, Gardenia, Garlic, Marjoram, Mate, Patchouli, Rue and Thyme

Success
   Amber, Benzoin, Calendula, California Poppy, Cinnamon, Clove, Frankincense, Ginger, Honeysuckle, Iris, Lemon Balm, Nutmeg, Sandalwood, Spikenard and Vervain

Visions
   Angelica, Cinnamon, Clove, Eyebright, Frankincense, Iris, Jasmine, Mugwort, Myrrh, Nutmeg and Spikenard

Herbs Related to the Planets

The following lists of herbs are given as a reference to facilitate the search of herbs with each planet.

Sun
   Aloe Vera, Amber, Angelica, Bay, Benzoin, Calendula, Camphor, Carnation, Cassia, Chamomile, Cinnamon, Clove, Eyebright, Frankincense, Gum Arabic, Iris, Juniper, Lemon Balm, Mastic, Mugwort, Myrrh, Orange, Parsley, Patchouli, Rose, Rosemary, Rue, Sandalwood and Saint John's Wort

Moon
   Aloe Vera, California Poppy, Bay, Cinnamon, Eucalyptus, Flax, Frankincense, Gardenia, Ginger, Honeysuckle, Hyacinth, Iris, Jasmine, Lavender, Lemon, Lotus, Myrrh, Myrtle, Orange, Rosemary, Sandalwood, Sweet Flag and Wormwood

Mercury
   Aloe Vera, Amber, Anise, Bay, Benzoin, Cassia, Chamomile, Cinnamon, Clove, Fenugreek, Greater Burnet, Gum Arabic, Honeysuckle, Horehound, Jasmine, Lavender, Lemon, Marjoram, Nutmeg, Parsley, Peppermint, Sage, Sandalwood and Vervain

Mars
   Basil, Benzoin, Betony, Broom, Garlic, Ginger, Geranium, Honeysuckle, Patchouli, Pennyroyal, Pokeweed, Rue
Snapdragon, Vervain and Wormwood

Jupiter
   Agrimony, Amber, Anise, Betony, Frankincense, Greater Burnet, Hyssop, Honeysuckle, Iris, Jasmine, Juniper, Lavender, Lemon Balm, Meadowsweet, Nutmeg, Sage and Vervain

Venus
 Aloe Vera, Amber, Angelica, Benzoin, Calendula, Carnation, Catnip, Cinnamon, Cyclamen, Geranium, Hyacinth, Iris, Juniper, Lavender, Mugwort, Myrtle, Nutmeg, Patchouli, Peppermint, Rose, Sandalwood, Snapdragon, Spikenard, Thyme, Vervain, Wallflower and Yarrow

Saturn
 Agrimony, Angelica, Bistort, Carnation, Eucalyptus, Flax, Frankincense, Fumitory, Horehound, Mullein, Myrrh, Patchouli, Parsley, Rue, Solomon's Seal, Sandalwood, Spikenard and Vervain
Yarrow

Neptune
 Amber, Carnation, Clove, Iris and Nutmeg

Uranus
 Benzoin, Cinnamon, Flax, Sage and Vervain

Pluto
 Basil and Rosemary

Herbs Related to the Elements
 The following lists of herbs are given as a reference to facilitate the search of herbs with each element.

Air
 Agrimony, Angelica, Anise, Benzoin, Broom, Cassia, Catnip, Cinnamon, Eyebright, Fenugreek, Greater Burnet, Gum Arabic, Horehound, Lavender, Marjoram, Mastic, Mugwort, Nutmeg, Parsley, Peppermint, Rose, Sage, Sandalwood, Thyme and Wallflower

Water
 Anise, Aloe Vera, California Poppy, Chamomile, Camphor, Catnip, Cyclamen, Eucalyptus, Gardenia, Geranium, Hyacinth, Iris, Jasmine, Lemon, Lotus, Lemon Balm, Meadowsweet, Myrrh, Myrtle, Orange, Rose, Solomon's Seal, Sandalwood, Sweet Flag, Thyme, Vervain and Yarrow

Fire
 Aloe Vera , Angelica, Basil, Bay, Betony, Broom, Calendula , Chamomile, Carnation, Cassia, Cinnamon, Clove, Flax, Frankincense, Garlic, Geranium, Ginger, Honeysuckle, Hyssop, Juniper, Lemon Balm, Meadowsweet, Mullein, Myrrh, Nutmeg, Pennyroyal,

Chapter X — Herbs and Spices

Pokeweed, Rosemary, Rue, Saint John's Wort, Snapdragon and Wormwood

Earth

Amber, Bistort, Eucalyptus, Fumitory, Jasmine, Honeysuckle, Horehound, Iris, Mugwort, Myrtle, Parsley, Patchouli, Rue, Sage, Solomon's Seal, Spikenard, Sweet Flag, Vervain and Yarrow

Agrimony

Agrimony
(Agrimonia eupatoria L.)
Rosaceae

Essence:	Hot
Planets:	Jupiter, Saturn
Element:	Air
Parts Used:	The Aerial Parts

Effects: Eliminates Fear, Protection, Repels Evil Spirits

Other Names: Church Steeples, Cocklebur, Philanthropos, Stickwort

Description: Native of Europe, this perennial herb is dark green, with a brown cylindrical stem covered with soft and silky hair. The whole herb is slightly aromatic and the flowers have a spicy odor.

Flowers:	Yellow, with five egg shaped petals, growing in a slightly curved form.
Leaves:	Hairy (divided alternately).
Fruit:	Red and sticky.
Height:	1 to 2 meters.

Care: Full sunlight or partial shade. It requires soil low in nutrients and moderate watering. pH: tolerates a wide range.

History:
Its name comes from the Greek "Argemón". They used it medicinally to cure illnesses of the eyes. A tradition from the Middle Ages says that if Agrimony is placed under the pillow, the sleep of who ever lies there will last until the herb is removed. It was also used to detect the presence of witches.

Uses:
It's most notorious property is that of eliminating fears. When there has been an event that has produced fear, burn a little bit of Agrimony to clear the environment of the vibrations caused by the fear. It is carried in little bags of herbs as protection, to repel evil spirits and dissipate negative energy. In the bath it is also used to eliminate fears.

Broom

Broom
(Cytisus ssp.)
Leguminosae

Essence: Hot
Planet: Mars
Elements: Air, Fire
Parts Used: The Aerial Parts

Effects: Eliminates Bad Vibrations, Protection, Purification

Other Names: Banal, Genista, Irish Broom, Scotch Broom

Description: Native of Europe and northern Africa, broom is a shrub with many thin rigid stems.

Flowers: Bright yellow or white, pea like in shape that bloom alone or in pairs along the branches.

Leaves: Found sparsely on the stems; growing alternately along the stem. The lower leaves are oval shaped and the upper leaves are lance shaped.

Fruit: Looks something like a bean, dark brown with seeds.

Height: 3 meters.

Care: Needs full sunlight and light soil with good drainage. It needs moderate but deep watering. pH: more acid than alkaline.

History:
In the Middle Ages this herb was used to sweep the houses to repel negative vibrations and evil spells. The procedure was very specific, if you swept when the herb was in flower you would sweep away the life of the master of the house and bring very bad luck. The Celts recommended burning the flowers to calm the winds.

Uses:
The herb (without flowers) is used to "sweep" the area where outdoor rituals are to take place to eliminate bad vibrations and astral detritus. It is used in purification incenses. One or two cups of tea made from Broom are used to wash the floors to eliminate astral detritus. In the bath it also works as an astral broom, eliminating inferior astral influences. Soaked in alcohol it is used to cleanse the aura.

Calendula

Calendula
(Calendula officinalis)
Compositae

Essence:	Hot
Planets:	Sun, Venus
Element:	Fire
Parts Used:	Flowers

Effects: Psychic and Spiritual Development, Success, Protection, Prophetic Dreams

Other Names: Gold, Holigold, Marigold, Pot Marigold

Description: This annual herb is cultivated as an ornamental garden flower. Originally from warm climates it is erect with many branches. The whole herb is covered with fine hairs and gives off a characteristic scent when the leaves or branches are squeezed.

Flowers: Varying from pale yellow to bright orange, they are found in solitary terminals of 10 cm in length.

Leaves: In general oblong shaped.

Fruit: Seeds.

Height: 30 to 60 cm.

Care: Calendulas should be planted in early spring. They accept almost any type of soil and need frequent watering and good drainage. pH: 6.6

History:
The Druids considered this herb sacred and used it by placing petals under their pillows for clairvoyant dreams and by placing petals on their eyelids to see fairies.

Uses:
In incense it is an excellent condenser of astral forces. It is used in herbal bags as an amulet for success and psychic and spiritual development. Magic mirrors can be made with an alcoholic extract of the flowers, covering the mirror with the solution. (The glass must be clean or the astral charge will constantly reveal itself through the glass). Flowers are sprinkled under the bed or their scent inhaled for prophetic dreams and protection. In the bath it helps to gain respect and admiration from others. In oil it has the same effect and also helps with self-confidence. Calendulas attract fairies.

California Poppy

California Poppy
(Eschscholzia californica)
Papaveraceae

Essence: Cold
Planet: Moon
Element: Water
Parts Used: Seeds, Flowers

Effects: Love, Success, Fertility, Invisibility, Luck

Other Names: Dormidera

Description: Native of California, this perennial herb has many separate stems.

Flowers: Very noticeable, from bright yellow to deep orange, they have 4 petals and many stamens.

Leaves: Green-grey in color they are usually much divided and grow in a rosette at the base of the stem.

Fruit: Seeds.

Height: 1 meter.

Care: In general they care for themselves; they are very resistant herbs that need fertile soil with good drainage and moderate watering. It needs full sunlight or partial shade.

History:
Native Californian Indians used this herb for love and fertility even before the days that the Spanish Jesuits planted them while they traveled (on horse or on foot) to find their way in later trips. The ships that traveled near the coast could see the bright yellow and orange flowers from a long distance and called California Tierra del Fuego (Land of Fire).

Uses:
The flowers and seeds are used in teas to induce sleep, for fertility and luck. The seeds are carried for luck and to attract love. Teas are also made from the seed for invisibility of persons and objects. In incense it is used for success. Smelling the flowers inspires and promotes intuition, contact with nature and helps to see the aura.

Camphor

Camphor
(Cinnamomum camphora)
Lauraceae

Essence: Cold
Planets: Moon, Sun
Element: Water
Parts Used: Essential Oil, Roots

Effects: Predictions, Protection, Repels Evil Spirits

Description: Camphor comes from the camphor tree which is native to southern Asia. Its wood repels insects and moths.

Flowers: Very fragrant
Height: 20 meters

Care: The roots of this tree are very competitive so it should not be planted near other trees. It needs soil with good drainage and plenty of water.

History:
It has been known in the Orient for over 2.000 years and was a favorite among the Alchemists in Europe. The Buddhists and Taoists planted this tree around their temples for protection.

Uses:
The oil is added to incense for predictions and for protection. Placed in the corners of rooms, it protects from nocturnal psychic intruders. A mixture of camphor oil and vinegar placed in the corners of a room on open plates protects from evil spirits and poltergeists. It is also used for anointment of candles in rituals to repel spells and illnesses. Sprayed, it cleans the environment and protects against negative forces. The root can also be used in fumigations for protection.

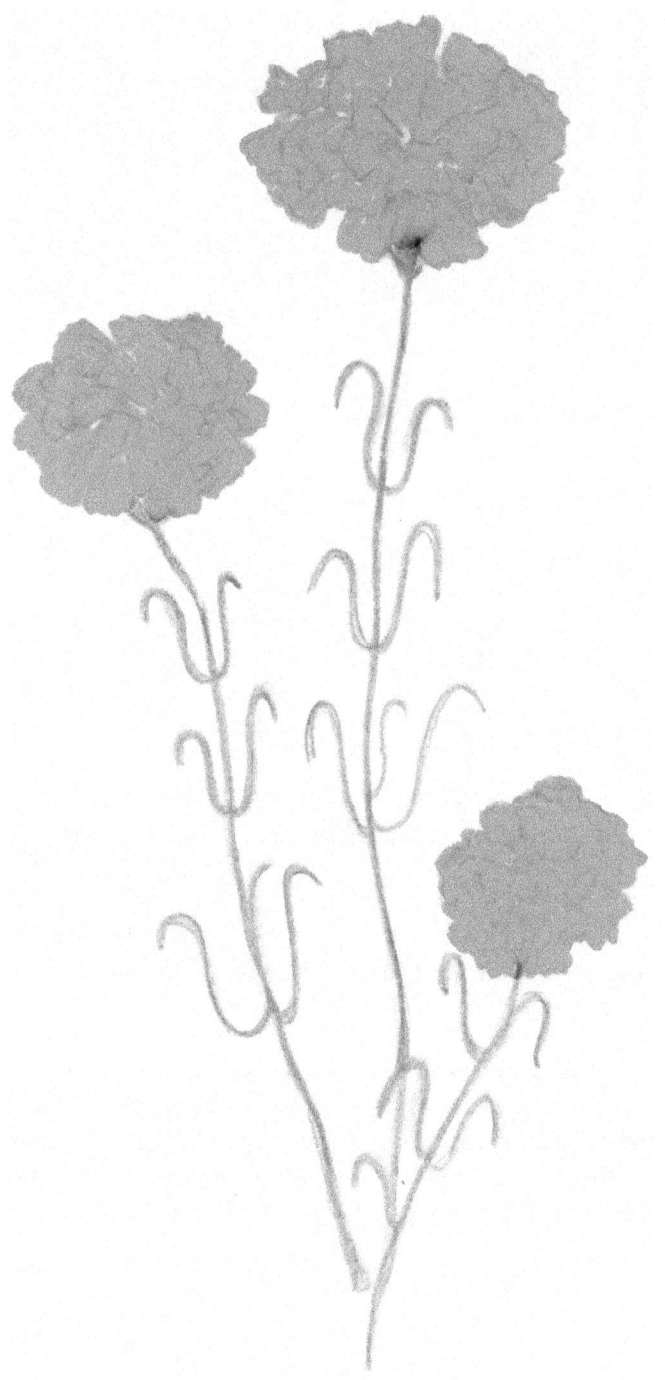

Carnation

Carnation
(Dianthus caryophyllus)
Caryophyllaceae

Essence: Hot
Planets: Sun, Venus, Saturn, Neptune
Element: Fire
Parts Used: Flowers

Effects: Healing, Psychic Development, Protection

Other Names: Jove's Flower, Nelka

Description: This perennial herb is native of Europe. It has a spicy scent, weak woody stems that are dark green with nodules.

Flowers: Solitary terminals with a cylindrical calyx originally white (it is cultivated in several colors), whose sepals end in serrated petals.
Leaves: Blue-green, long and narrow and lance shaped.
Fruit: Seeds.
Height: 30 to 40 cm.

Care: It needs full sunlight during the morning and shade in the afternoon. It needs fertile soil and moderate amounts of water.

History:
The Greeks called it the Flower of Zeus. Its name, Dianthus, means Flower of God. In the Middle Ages, witches supposedly carried it as a means of protection.

Uses:
It is a powerful herb which gives energy when used in incenses. It is said that it is most powerful when harvested when the Sun is under the sign of Leo. The presence of flowers helps eliminate emotional and mental alterations. In the bath it is used to cleanse the aura. In oil it is used for spiritual healing and to increase psychic powers.

Cassia

Cassia
(Cinnamomum cassia)
Lauraceae

Essence:	Hot
Planets:	Sun, Mercury
Elements:	Fire, Air
Parts Used:	Bark

Effects: Love, Psychic Development, Prophetic Dreams

Other Names: Chinese Cinnamon

Description: Cassia is obtained from the bark of the cassia tree. It has a peculiar scent, very much like cinnamon.

Flowers: Very little noticeable, yellow.

Leaves: Bright red when young that turn green as they mature; shiny, opposite, of oval shape of 3 to 4 cm in length.

Fruit: Seeds.

Height: 20 meters.

Care: The root of this tree is very competitive and it should not be planted near other trees. It needs soil with good drainage and plenty of water.

History:
Arabian doctors were the first to describe the medicinal uses of this herb. Since then it has been widely used.

Uses:
It is used in love potion incenses. In oil it induces prophetic dreams and increases psychic abilities.

Catnip

Catnip
(Nepeta cataria)
Labiatae

Essence: Cold
Planet: Venus
Elements: Water, Air
Parts Used: The Aerial Parts

Effects: Love, Attracts Good Spirits, Luck

Other Names: Catmint, Calamint, Cat's Wort, Field Balm

Description: This perennial herb from the mint family, grows with straight square stems, with soft white hairs on its stems and leaves.

Flowers: Small, tubular shaped, found in white, pale lavender or purple and grow from the principal and secondary stems.

Leaves: Opposite, heart shaped, toothed and light green.

Fruit: Very small nuts.

Height: 1 to 1 1/2 meters.

Care: It needs full sunlight, fertile soil with good drainage and moderate watering. pH: 6.6

History:
From Europe to China, Catnip has been used as medicine and as a cat herb for last 2.000 years. The Druids considered it a sacred herb and would chew it for strength before going to war.

Uses:
The leaves of this herb are used to strengthen the psychic ties with cats. Under certain conditions one can see through the eyes of the cat. It is also added to herbal sacks and incenses together with Rose petals for love. Its scent promotes peace. It is grown or placed on doors to attract good spirits and good luck. It is used in certain spells to increase physical beauty. Dried leaves are very good as bookmarks, especially for magical books.

Chamomile

Chamomile
(Matricaria chamomilla L.)
Compositae

Essence: Hot
Planets: Sun, Mercury
Elements: Water, Fire
Parts Used: Flowers

Effects: Love, Meditation, Luck

Other Names: Camomile, Chamaimelon, German Chamomile, Manzanilla, Maythen

Description: Native of Europe, this annual herb has a much ramified erect stem.

Flowers: White petals with a yellow center and a scent similar to that of an apple.
Leaves: Alternate, light green, featherlike, divided into segments.
Fruit: Seeds.
Height: 30 cm.

Care: It grows in almost any type of soil. It needs full sunlight or partial shade and moderate watering. pH: 7.0

History:
The Chamomile flowers reminded the ancient Egyptians of the sun and Egyptian women used this herb to highlight blond colors in their hair.

Uses:
It is used in spells for luck and to attract money. When burned it produces drowsiness and favors the serene spiritual attitude necessary for meditation and creating an interior equilibrium. In oil it refreshes and relaxes, calms the nerves and attracts love. It is carried to attract good luck and to induce sleep. In the bath it also helps to attract love.

Cinnamon

Cinnamon
(Cinnamomum zeylanicum)
Lauraceae

Essence: Hot
Planets: Sun, Mercury, Venus, Uranus, Moon
Elements: Fire, Air
Parts Used: Bark

Effects: Clairvoyance, Healing, Psychic Development, Success, Fortune, Passion, Protection, Luck, Visions

Other Names: Cassia, Sweet Wood

Description: Native of Sri Lanka, it is a small tree with a very characteristic scent, produced by a volatile essence in the bark that is obtained by distillation.

Flowers: Very little noticeable, yellow.
Leaves: Bright red when young that turn green as they mature; shiny, opposite of oval shape of 3 to 4 cm in length.
Fruit: Seeds.
Height: 15 meters.

Care: The roots of this tree are very competitive, it should not be planted near other trees. It needs soil with good drainage and plenty of water.

History:
It has been considered a sacred tree for millennia. The Chinese were already using this herb for medicinal purposes in the year 2.700 B.C. The Egyptians used it among other things to embalm their dead. Moses was said to have received direct instructions on how to use it. The Hebrews, Greeks and Romans used it as an aphrodisiac perfume.

Uses:
It can be burned to generate highly spiritual vibrations and to attract good fortune. It is recommended for potions of healing incenses and to favor clairvoyance, visions and concentration. It is also used to awaken and stimulate passion. One of its best uses is to protect from envy and jealousy of others. In the bath it helps to resolve problems at home and work and to increase income, especially when combined with Parsley. In oil it is used for luck and to stimulate vital and sexual energy. It is carried for success and psychic and spiritual development.

Clove

Clove
(Syzygium aromaticum)
Myrtaceae

Essence:	Hot
Planets:	Sun, Mercury, Neptune
Element:	Fire
Parts Used:	Flower Buds
Effects:	Aphrodisiac, Love, Eliminates Bad Vibrations, Success, Protection, Purification, Luck, Visions
Description:	Native of tropical Indonesia, the clove is an evergreen, pyramidal shaped, aromatic tree.
Flowers:	White, pink or red, with many stamens; they are found in bunches.
Leaves:	Oblong or lance shaped, bright green, with veins, fragrant and sometimes hairy.
Fruit:	The clove.
Height:	20 meters.
Care:	Since it comes from tropical areas it requires high temperatures and humidity all year long.

History:
In the Han dynasty (207 B.C. to 220 A.D.) all those that addressed the Emperor had to carry a Cove in their mouths so as not to offend him with their breath. Throughout history many nations have fought over this herb.

Uses:
It can be carried or consumed to expulse negative and hostile energies. It stimulates the memory capacity and is added to herbal sacks to seduce the opposite sex. Hung on the crib it protects the baby from all evil. In incense it attracts luck and success, rejects negative and hostile energies, generates positive spiritual vibrations, purifies the environment and favors visions. In oil it is used as an aphrodisiac and to promote love. It protects and cleans the aura.

Cyclamen

Cyclamen
(Cyclamen europaeum)
Primulaceae

Essence:	Cold
Planet:	Venus
Element:	Water
Parts Used:	The Aerial Parts

Effects: Love, Fertility, Protection

Other Names: Groundbread

Description: Native of Europe and Asia, cyclamen is an ornamental perennial herb. It is grown in gardens, greenhouses and as a house plant.

Flowers: Dark red dark, white, pink or purple, with a main petal that curves abruptly downwards.
Leaves: Bright green or silver white with patches of white along the nerve terminals.
Fruit: Tubers that curve downwards.

Care: It needs partial shade, porous soil with fertilizer. The soil should be kept humid.

History:
Cyclamen comes from the Greek kyklaminos meaning "circle". They believed that if you ate it or drank it you would fall in love.

Uses:
Placed in the bedroom it protects during the night. It is used to repel and break spells. Planted in the garden it protects the garden and the house. The flowers are carried to alleviate the pain of a broken relationship. It is also carried to favor fertility. In incense it is used for love. It is also used in charms for happiness.

Eucalyptus

Chapter X — Herbs and Spices

Eucalyptus
(Eucalyptus globulus)
Myrtaceae

Essence:	Cold
Planets:	Moon, Saturn
Elements:	Water, Earth
Parts Used:	Leaves, Berries

Effects: Physical and Spiritual Healing, Protection

Other Names: Blue Gum, Fever Tree

Description: Native of Australia, it is one of the tallest and fastest growing trees in the world. It grows in areas with high temperatures and its roots can literally drain marshes. Its trunk is straight, light grey in color and whose bark breaks off in strips.

Flowers: Small with conical cover that falls off when opened, found in groups of 3 or 4 without petals, the stamens are white, pink, yellow, orange or red.

Leaves: The young leaves are opposite, bluish green and heart shaped. Adult leaves are alternate, dark green and lance shaped.

Fruit: Capsules with seeds.

Height: 90 meters.

Care: Its roots are very shallow and it needs heavy and frequent watering with full sunlight. pH: tolerates a wide range.

History:
It has been used traditionally for physical health; for fever, colds and grippe.

Uses:
The leaves can be used to decorate blue candles for healing vibrations. Leaves can also be placed in the room of a sick person for same purpose. In incenses it affects are spiritually healing and protective. In oil it protects and assists in spiritual healing. To clean a house of negative psychic energy place a few drops of oil in the corners around the house. The leaves can also be carried for protection.

Eyebright

Eyebright
(Euphrasia officinalis L.)
Scrophulariaceae

Essence: Hot
Planet: Sun
Element: Air
Parts Used: The Aerial Parts

Effects: Clairvoyance, Healing, Psychic and Spiritual Development, Visions

Other Names: Euphrosyne, Meadow Eyebright, Pimpernel

Description: This is a small delicate annual herb with square stems and low branches.

Flowers: Very small, red or white with a superior double lobe and an inferior triple lobe.
Leaves: Vary in shape from round to thin and pointed, they grow in opposite pairs.
Fruit: Seeds.
Height: 1 to 4 cm.

Care: This is a parasitic herb that attaches its roots to the roots of other herbs that are close, making in difficult to transplant. To cultivate it must be planted next to other herbs that it can parasitize. pH: alkaline.

History:
  Its botanical name Euphrasia comes from the Greek "good cheer", it has been used since then for medicinal purposes related to the eyes. The Druids recommended boiling this herb and drinking the water to stimulate clairvoyance.

Uses:
 It is used in incenses for spiritual healing. It helps develop psychic-spiritual abilities and promotes visions and divination. It is carried for spiritual development. It is drunk in teas to clear the mind, improve the memory and stimulate clairvoyance

The Book of Herbs and Magic — Heather Eaton

Fenugreek

Fenugreek
(Trigonella foenum-graecum L.)
Leguminosae

Essence: Cold
Planet: Mercury
Element: Air
Parts Used: The Aerial Parts

Effects: Clarity of Thought, Eliminates Bad Vibrations

Other Names: Greek Hayseed, Trigonella

Description: This is an annual herb, native of central Europe and the Orient, which has very thin stems and leaves.

Flowers: Simple, double to triple, white, measuring about 1 cm and growing alone or in pairs.
Leaves: Alternate with three oval leaves of 2 to 3 cm.
Fruit: Cylindrical pod that contains the seeds (similar to beans), long and some times hairy, 2 to 4 cm with very aromatic seeds.
Height: 1 meter.

Care: It requires dry soil without fertilizer, full sunlight and very little water.

History:
Used in the Mediterranean and the Middle East as a medicinal herb and as food even before it became popular in Egypt. The Egyptians used it in incenses as an offering to their gods.

Uses:
Used in a few incenses, but mostly as a hair rinse to improve the clarity of thought. In the bath it destroys any negative vibrations or thoughts sent by others.

Flax

| Chapter X | Herbs and Spices |

Flax
(Linum usitatissimum L.)
Linaceae

Essence: Hot
Planets: Moon, Saturn, Uranus
Element: Fire
Parts Used: The Aerial Parts

Effects: Psychic Development, Eliminates Bad Vibrations, Protection, Purification

Other Names: Linseed, Lint Bells

Description: Flax is an annual herb with a straight thin stem and secondary stems emerging from the top of the stem.

Flowers: Completely symmetrical, delicate, sky blue with 5 sepals, 5 petals and 10 stamens.
Leaves: Small, pale green or light blue, they grow alternately on the stems.
Fruit: Seeds, brilliant dark brown or yellow.
Height: 1 meter.

Care: It needs full sunlight, light soil with good drainage and moderate watering.

History:
Archaeologists have identified fibers of flax 10.000 years old in prehistoric areas of Switzerland. It has been cultivated in Mesopotamia, Assyria and Egypt for more than 5.000 years. In Teutonic mythology, this herb was under the protection of the goddess Hulda. In the Middle Ages it was used as protection against black magic. Flax is was and is still used to elaborate the white tunics used in the religious practices of the Hebrews, the Egyptians and the Greeks.

Uses:
 In incense it is used as protection against black magic, and the Evil Eye. When it is carried it dissolves negative energy and forms a sort of protective shield. The flowers are carried for protection, to increase psychic abilities and to absorb and neutralize negative energy.

Incense

Frankincense
(Boswellia carteri)

Essence: Hot
Planets: Sun, Moon, Jupiter, Saturn
Element: Fire
Parts Used: Resin

Effects: Love, Clairvoyance, Psychic Development, Success, Meditation, Protection, Purification, Visions

Other Names: Incense, Olibanum

Description: A tree native of Arabia, India and parts of Africa. The resin is obtained from the sap of the tree.

History:
 Mentioned frequently in the Bible, Frankincense was one of the incenses that the three Kings of the Orient gave to the baby Jesus, because it represents saintliness. The Egyptians burned it every day at sunrise in honor of their god Ra.

Uses:
It is burned to generate purifying vibrations that consecrate and protect from the Evil Eye. It is a powerful protector and purifier, also used in incenses for love and success. It is carried as an amulet for protection, to stimulate visions and for meditation. It can replace any other type of resin or be used alone. In oil it protects and stimulates psychic development.

Fumitory

Fumitory
(Fumaria officinalis L.)
Fumariaceae

Essence: Cold
Planet: Saturn
Element: Earth
Parts Used: The Aerial Parts

Effects: Money, Protection, Purification

Other Names: Earth Smoke, Wax Dolls

Description: Annual herb with thin stems and thick roots.

Flowers: Small purple-pink with red tips, they appear in long bunches at the tips of the stems, they have 2 sepals 4 petals and 6 stamens.
Leaves: Green-grey subdivided into triangular leaflets.
Height: 20 cm.

Care: Needs full sunlight, moderately fertile soil and moderate watering.

History:
It has been cultivated for medicinal purposes since the Neolithic times in Europe, burned to repel evil spirits and dispel negative energy.

Uses:
This herb is used in incenses for protection, and purification, it has very positive vibrations. Very powerful on All Hallow's Eve (Halloween) to dispel negative energy. Sprayed around the house or rubbed on shoes it is used to attract money.

Gardenia

Gardenia
(Gardenia ssp.)
Rubiaceae

Essence:	Cold
Planet:	Moon
Element:	Water
Parts Used:	Flowers

Effects: Love, Attracts Good Spirits, Spiritual Healing, Psychic Development, Spiritual Cleansing, Passion, Protection

Other Names: Cape Jasmine

Description: A slow growing shrub, native of the tropics. Grows well in greenhouses.

Flowers: Beautiful and fragrant, snow white and extremely delicate; they bruise when touched and turn yellow with time. Funnel-shaped with a tubular calyx that opens at the top.

Leaves: Lance shaped dark green with a leather-like texture.

Fruit: Berries.

Height: 3 meters.

Care: Ideally grown in greenhouses, needs high temperatures and humidity, bright light (not direct sunlight), fertile soil, frequent watering with good drainage and fertilizing. It can handle frost, but it needs high temperatures to flower.

History:
It owes its name to Alexander Garden, American naturalist and doctor from the XVIII century.

Uses:
The flowers are carried to attract love and new friends, to seduce a lover and to stimulate spiritual healing. Incenses made from dried ground petals are used for protection and spiritual healing. It stimulates lunar energy and promotes harmony, especially between married couples. In oil it is used for protection for spiritual cleansing and psychic development. Fresh flowers in sickrooms stimulate spiritual healing. It is grown to attract good spirits.

Garlic

Garlic
(Allium sativum)
Amaryllidaceae

Essence:	Hot
Planet:	Mars
Element:	Fire
Parts Used:	Cloves, Clove Skins

Effects: Healing, Money, Eliminates Fear and Bad Vibrations, Spiritual Cleansing, Protection, Purification, Prevents Nightmares

Other Names: Garleac, Stinky Rose

Description: Native of central Asia, Garlic is a perennial herb with a bulb composed of small cloves with a very pungent scent.

Flowers: Very small, white or pink divided into 6 segments, found in umbels, globe shaped with 6 stamens.
Leaves: Grow from the base; with 4 to 6 long straight and very thin leaves.
Fruit: Bulb with cloves.
Height: 1 meter.

Care: Planted in spring, and harvested when the leaves fall off. pH: 4.5 to 8.3.

History:
It is one of the oldest herbs known. Remains of Garlic have been found in caves that were inhabited 10.000 years ago. The Egyptians supossed fed the workers who made the pyramids with Garlic and they also used it to swear by. Sailors carried it for protection. Many cultures believed that it had magical powers against evil and it was used widely in charms and spells for protection.

Uses:
To conserve money and eliminate bad thoughts, the skin from cloves is burned over the kitchen fire. Minced Garlic with brown sugar and Benzoin makes an incense used for spiritual purification. In the bath it is used for spiritual cleansing, and to eliminate negative vibrations in general. It is carried to repel the Evil Eye and attract money and hung on doors and windows to avoid evil, envy, thieves and vampires. It is eaten to avoid nightmares and eliminate fears and rubbed on objects to eliminate bad vibrations. Garlic cloves can be spread around the room at night and collected and eliminated in the morning to absorb negative vibrations.

Geranium

Geranium
(Pelargonium ssp.)
Geraniaceae

Essence: Cold
Planets: Mars, Venus
Elements: Water, Fire
Parts Used: Flowers

Effects: Love, Healing, Fertility, Protection

Other Names: Pelargonium, Stork's Bill

Description: Native of South Africa, it is a bushy shrub with soft woody, many branched, brittle stems.

Flowers: Varied in color, they grow in clusters on each stalk, with one or more layers of five spoon shaped petals.
Leaves: The most common are circular with slightly lobed edges that give off a particular s cent when touched.
Fruit: Seeds.
Height: 1 meter.

Care: In costal areas it needs full sunlight and in valleys, partial shade. It needs fertile soil with good drainage, and moderate watering.

History:
It was introduced to Europe at the beginning of the XVI century. It was rumored that witches planted this herb around their houses and when strangers came the flowers would point out the direction that they were coming from.

Uses:
Geranium flowers are carried for love, to calm the mind and stabilize emotions. White flowers favor fertility while red ones have healing and protective effects. Planted in the garden, (especially pink and red varieties) this herb provides protection from negative thought forms. In oil it helps create a calm environment and is used in rituals for protection, and to reject misfortune.

Ginger

Ginger
(Zingiber officinalis)
Zingiberaceae

Essence: Hot
Planets: Mars, Moon
Element: Fire
Parts Used: Roots

Effects: Money, Success, Protection, Purification, Luck

Other Names: Gingerroot

Description: Native of India, it is a tropical perennial herb that grows directly from its aromatic root or rhizome.

Flowers: Appear in dense tassels at the end of the stem and have yellow-green segments and a single purple and yellow petal.

Leaves: Thin, dark green and lace shaped.

Height: 1 to 2 meters.

Care: Since this herb is tropical, it needs a lot of heat and humidity and should be grown in partial shade. The soil must be rich in nutrients and be watered frequently.

History:
 This herb is one of the oldest medicinal herbs. It was a very important herb described in the first great herbal book of China, the *Pen Tsau Ching* (Classic Book of Herbs), published in 3.000 B.C. by the emperor Shen Nung. In the India it was known as *shringara* and the Greeks called it *zingiberis*.

Uses:
 In small quantities dry Ginger root can be added to almost any incense to improve its effects It must be used in less quantity than the other components or it will overwhelm the effects. In oil it generates energy, creates harmony and attracts luck. In the bath it is used for purification and it is carried for protection. It is grown for money and success. It is consumed to empower rituals.

Greater Burnet

Greater Burnet
(Sanguisorba officinalis L.)
Rosaceae

Essence:	Hot
Planets:	Mercury, Jupiter
Element:	Air
Parts Used:	The Aerial Parts
Effects:	Protection, Purification
Other Names:	Burnet, Great Burnet, Pimpernel, Salad Burnet
Description:	Perennial herb, forming a basal rosette about 50 cm wide with pinnate compound leaves.
Flowers:	Very small club shaped, deep red that appear on thin upright stalks from the center of the rosette.
Leaves:	Toothed leaflets of 7 to 8 cms. in length, they are green on top and whitish underneath.
Height:	2 meters.
Care:	Needs full sunlight or partial shade, soil low in nutrients and abundant water with good drainage. pH: 6.8

History:
This herb has been used for last 2.000 years for medicinal purposes, very popular in Europe and America.

Uses:
It is used in incenses for purification and protection. It is carried for protection and to avoid being duped. When it is grown in the garden it helps avoid accidents and prevents illnesses.

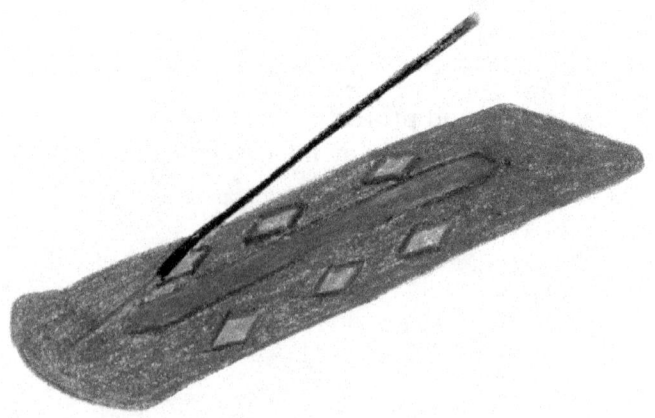

Incense

Gum Arabic
(Acacia senegal)
Leguminosae

Essence:	Hot
Planets:	Sun, Mercury
Element:	Air
Parts Used:	Branches, Wood, Resin, Flowers

Effects: Clairvoyance, Psychic Development, Meditation, Protection

Other Names: Acacia, Cape Gum, Egyptian Thorn

Description: It's a tree found in India and Africa. It's sap is used for magical and medicinal purposes.

Flowers:	White or yellow, spongy, bases with 5 sepals and 5 petals and 10 stamens.
Leaves:	Fern like with thorns.
Fruit:	Seeds.
Height:	2 or 3 meters.

Care: It needs fertile soil and moderate but deep watering.

History:
The Egyptians discovered it more than 3.700 years ago and have used its resin for centuries, among other things as a glue for gems and a as base for painting. In India it is still used religiously in sacred fires and in building temples.

Uses:
Burned with Sandalwood it is used as meditation incense, for mental clarity and to develop psychic abilities. When it is burned alone, the smoke is used to see things that are happening in other places It stimulates psychic powers, especially intuition. The wood is carried or placed under the bed for protection against evil. In oil it is a powerful psychic developer. A branch placed in the doors or windows will protect the room during the night.

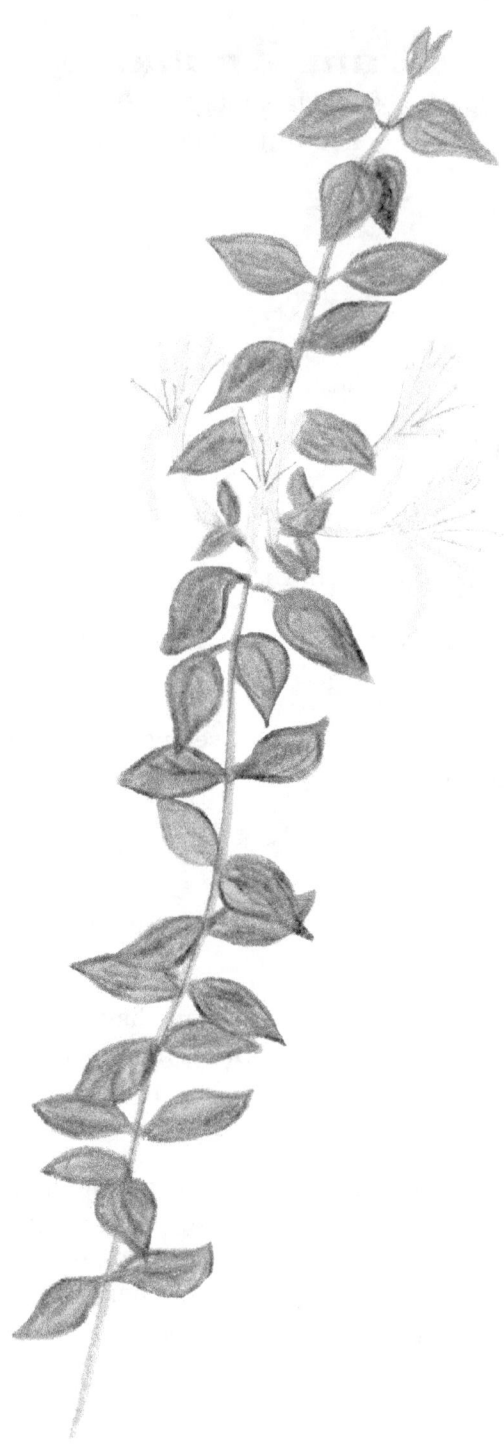

Honeysuckle

Honeysuckle
(Lonicera caprifolium)
Caprifoliaceae

Essence:	Hot
Planets:	Jupiter, Moon, Mercury, Mars
Elements:	Earth, Fire
Parts Used:	Flowers, Leaves

Effects: Clairvoyance, Psychic Development, Success, Fortune, Prophetic Dreams

Other Names: Woodbine

Description: It is a climbing shrub with hairy young stems and woody older stems, native of the Andes.

Flowers: White, yellow, pink or red, found in terminals with long flower heads. The calyx and the corolla are welded on top of the ovary, with 5 stamens inside the tubular corolla.

Leaves: Opposite, dark green and heart shaped.

Fruit: Berries, generally red.

Care: It grows in full sunlight or partial shade. In general it accepts any soil and requires moderate watering.

Uses:
Flowers are placed around green candles to attract money. For clairvoyance and prophetic dreams, the leaves are rubbed on the forehead (over the third eye). The fragrant flowers are used in incenses for success in businesses. It is said that people who understand things quickly are attracted to the scent of the flower, and it is also used to boost self confidence. In oil it is used to create environments adequate for clearing up fishy situations and to increase psychic abilities. In incense it is used for success. Grown in the garden it attracts good luck.

Horehound

Horehound
(Marrubium vulgare)
Labiatae

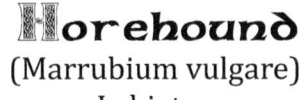

Essence:	Hot
Planets:	Mercury, Saturn
Elements:	Air, Earth
Parts Used:	Leaves, Flowers
Effects:	Psychic Development, Protection
Other Names:	Hoarhound, Eye of the Star, Marrubium, Marvel, White Horehound
Description:	Native of Eurasia, Horehound is a perennial herb with square hairy stems.
Flowers:	Small, white, found in verticillated inflorescences, with a tubular calyx, asymmetrical corolla, 4 stamens and 1 pistil.
Leaves:	White-grey opposite, dented, oval or round. On the surface of the leaves there are small glands with aromatic oil.
Fruit:	Nut.
Height:	50 cm.
Care:	It grows in poor soil or sand in full sunlight and requires moderate watering. pH: 6.9

History:
This herb got its name from Horus, the Greek god of heaven and light. Legend said that it could break spells of black magic. In ancient Rome it was used for medicinal purposes.

Uses:
It is used in herbal sacks for protection against negative energy. In incense it eliminates bad vibrations. It is consumed to clear the mind and stimulate mental powers.

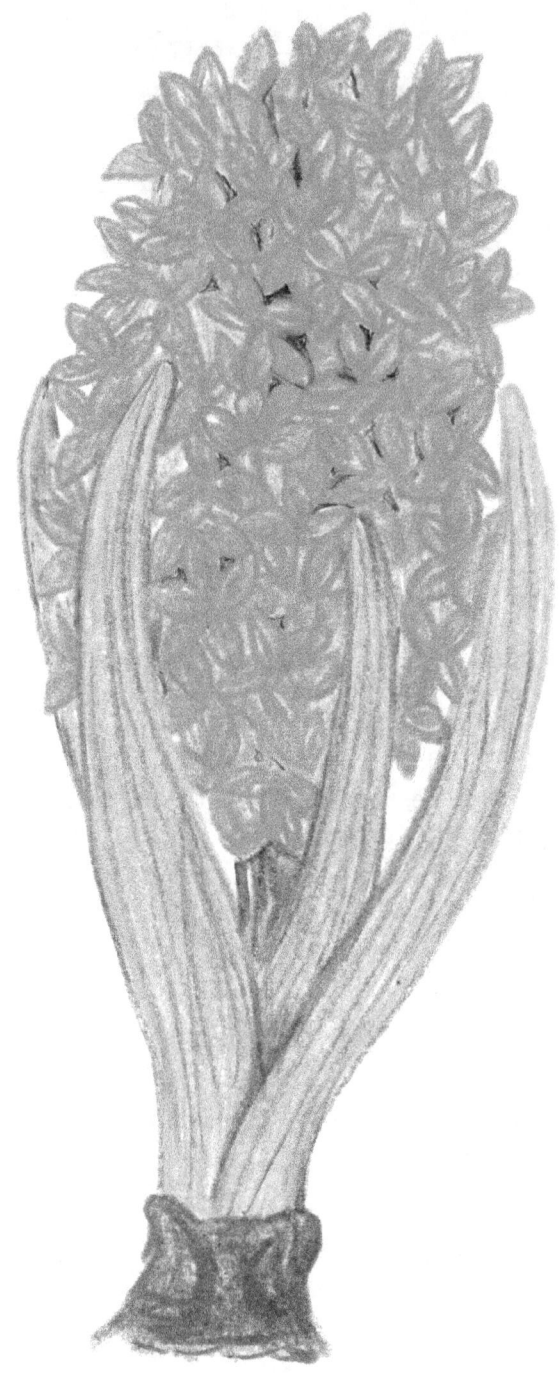

Hyacinth

Hyacinth
(Hyacinthus orientalis)
Liliaceae

Essence:	Cold
Planets:	Venus, Moon
Element:	Water
Parts Used:	Flowers, Leaves

Effects: Love, Meditation, Protection, Prevents Nightmares

Other Names: Jacinth

Description: It is a bulb herb from Mediterranean climates, native of Greece and Asia. Hybrid hyacinths are aromatic and flower in spring.

Flowers: Found in white, sky blue, purple, pink and red, they have 3 petals, 3 sepals and 6 stamens. The flowers are 17 to 19 cm. long.

Leaves: Dark green, long and lance shaped.

Fruit: Capsule.

Height: 40 cm.

Care: Hyacinths should be planted early in the spring in soil or water. They need plenty of sun and water.

Uses:
The flowers are used in herbal sacks as protection and to avoid nightmares. Incense (made from the leaves) is good for calming people who are always in a hurry, and is also used to avoid nightmares. The scent of fresh flowers alleviates spiritual pain and depression. The oil is used for tranquility, peace and meditation.

Hyssop

Hyssop
(Hyssopus officinalis L.)
Labiatae

Essence: Hot
Planet: Jupiter
Element: Fire
Parts Used: The Aerial Parts

Effects: Spiritual Development, Eliminates Bad Vibrations, Protection, Astral Projection, Purification, Luck

Other Names: Ysopo

Description: It is a perennial shrub native to Eurasia. It is a member of the mint family and is very aromatic; it has square woody, erect stems, with many branches.

Flowers: Blue-purple, blue or white, in a tubular form, that appear in bunches on the superi or part of the stems.
Leaves: Green, thin, opposite and aromatic.
Fruit: Very small nuts.
Height: 60 cm.

Care: Needs full sunlight with light soil and moderate watering. pH: 6.7.

History:
Rabbis used Hyssop 2.500 years ago to purify and consecrate the temple of Jerusalem and other places of adoration. The Greeks and Romans recommended it as a sedative.

Uses:
It is carried in herbal sacks for protection. In incense it eliminates negative feelings, protects and purifies the soul. In the bath it protects and purifies and is used for spiritual illumination. In oil it increases finances, attracts luck and assists in astral projection. It can be sprayed to eliminate heavy vibrations. Hung around the house it cleans it of negative energy.

Iris

Iris
(Iris florentina)
Iridaceae

Essence:	Cold
Planets:	Venus, Sun, Moon, Jupiter, Neptune
Elements:	Water, Earth
Parts Used:	Roots
Effects:	Love, Psychic Development, Success, Predictions, Protection, Prophetic Dreams, Visions
Other Names:	Florentine Iris, Liver Lily, Orris, Poison Flag
Description:	This kind of iris is native to Europe, it has thick erect stems. Its root is used in perfumes.
Flowers:	White, sky blue or blue with three petals and six petaloid segments.
Leaves:	Green, long and lance shaped with parallel veins.
Fruit:	Capsules with seeds.
Height:	15 cm.
Care:	Needs full sunlight with neutral or slightly acid soil and abundant water during the flowering period. pH: 7.0

History:
The ancient Egyptians and Greeks discovered that the root of this herb has a notable fragrance and used it for perfumes. Its name comes from the Greek word for rainbow. In Japan it is used even today as protection against evil spirits.

Uses:
In powder and oil it is used to attract love and for protection against evil spirits. It can be added to the talcum powder. The root is carried to attract the loved one. It is a useful ingredient for any ritual destined to improve communications. Sprayed around a room before a meeting, it stimulates people to speak sincerely. In incense it is used where astral manifestations are expected, to favor visions, for prophetic dreams and for success. In the bath it stabilizes or improves communications with loved ones and also protects. In oil it attracts the opposite sex and is also used as anointment for charms. The root makes an excellent pendulum.

Jasmine

Jasmine
(Jasminum officinalis)
Oleaceae

Essence:	Cold
Planets:	Jupiter, Moon, Mercury
Elements:	Earth, Water
Parts Used:	Flowers
Effects:	Love, Attracts Good Spirits, Prophetic Dreams, Luck, Visions
Other Names:	Jessamine, Jazmin
Description:	This herb, originally from India and Persia (Iran), is a climbing plant with stems that are almost square.
Flowers:	White or pink, very aromatic, with a calyx and corolla of 5 to 8 lobes, 2 stamens and one pistil. The flowers appear in summer.
Leaves:	Five to 7 leaves with no stem.
Fruit:	Berries.
Height:	3 meters.
Care:	Jasmine grows in almost any kind of soil and requires full sunlight or partial shade and moderate watering. Frequent pruning is recommended to control its shape.

History:
This herb was sacred in ancient Persia.

Uses:
The flowers attract spiritual love and it is very useful in herbal sacks for love. In incense, its scent is ideal to fight off depression, stimulate optimism, energy and a sense of well being. It eliminates anguish and gives a feeling of self confidence, and can awaken sensuality. Its fragrance stimulates fantasy and attracts good luck. In oil it has inspiring effects, attracting good spirits, neutralizing envy, clearing negative environments and stimulating clairvoyance. It is used in rituals to increase personal charm. The flowers are boiled and added to love baths. The scent of the flowers can help induce prophetic dreams.

Juniper

Juniper
(Juniperus communis)
Cupressaceae

Essence:	Hot
Planets:	Sun, Venus, Jupiter
Element:	Fire
Parts Used:	Leaves, Berries
Effects:	Love, Psychic and Spiritual Development, Protection, Purification, Repels Evil Spirits
Other Names:	Hackmatack, Horse Savin
Description:	It is found growing in dry fields, valleys and hills. It is an evergreen shrub, native of the northern hemisphere.
Flowers:	The female flowers are green and the male flowers are yellow.
Leaves:	Needle shaped. Lighter green when young and darken when older.
Fruit:	Seeds, berry-like red or purple
Height:	15 meters.
Care:	Plant at least a meter or two from each other, with a pile of compost earth. Item will protect from weeds and they will grow faster. The roots will rot if waterlogged therefore good drainage is necessary. It needs full sunlight or in very hot climates, partial shade.

History:
During the Middle Ages it was believed that Juniper planted next to the front door would scare away evil doers (unless they could guess the correct number of leaves). People would burn Juniper when a baby was born so it wouldn't be stolen by hobgoblins. It was also used to repel evil spirits and spells. The Druids burned the incense to promote psychic visions.

Uses:
A stem protects the carrier against accidents, thefts and evil spells. A necklace made from the berries will help attract the loved one and stimulate psychic powers. Burned as incense it purifies the environment and the people, it scares away evil entities and ghosts it can help cure the possessed and stimulate psychic and spiritual development. Planted in front of the house it protects from thieves and physical injuries. It is also used in herbal sacks for love.

Lavender

Lavender
(Lavandula officinalis)
Labiatae

Essence: Hot
Planets: Mercury, Jupiter, Moon, Venus
Element: Air
Parts Used: Flowers

Effects: Divination, Love, Protection, Purification, Prophetic Dreams

Other Names: Elf Leaf, Lavandula

Description: Native of the Mediterranean, it is perennial shrub with many branches.

Flowers: Small, blue-purple or lilac, in long bunches or tassels, with four stamens, one pistil, tubular corolla. It has between six and ten flowers in the end of the stems.
Leaves: Small and narrow, soft opposite borders, that are green-gray, about 5 cm. in length.
Fruit: Small nuts.
Height: 3 meters.

Care: Needs full sunlight, in loose soil with good drainage and moderate watering. pH: 7.1

History:
Greeks and Romans used Lavender for their soaps and baths. In fact the name of the herb derives from the Latin *lavare* (to wash). It was said that on certain summer nights Wiccans would throw it into fires as offering to ancient Gods. In the Middle Ages it was considered as an herb of love and was the favorite flower of Queen Elizabeth I of England.

Uses:
Used in love incenses; for purification, protection and prophetic dreams. It is used to seduce men. Carrying this herb helps to see spirits and ghosts and reduces the psychic tension. In oil it helps to obtain mental peace from obsessions, it inspires love and is used for divination. In herbal sacks in the bath it is used for purification, to counter insomnia and stress and for spiritual power. The Lavender flowers are sprinkled around the house to create harmony and peace, it helps in the fulfillment of dreams and wishes.

Lemon

Lemon
(Citrus limon)
Rutaceae

Essence:	Cold
Planets:	Mercury, Moon
Element:	Water
Parts Used:	Flowers, Leaves

Effects: Love, Spiritual Development, Eliminates Bad Vibrations, Astral Projection, Prophetic Dreams, Luck

Description: Citric tree that produces fruit all year.

Flowers: White on top and pink underneath, small and very aromatic, with five sepals, five petals and only one pistil.

Leaves: Green and lance shaped.

Fruit: Sour yellow fruit called lemon.

Height: 3 to 6 meters.

Care: It grows ideally in warm climates producing fruit all year round. In hot climates it produces fruit in winter, spring and fall. It needs full sunlight or partial shade, very fertile soil with good drainage and moderate water.

Uses:
Incenses (made from flowers) stimulate prophetic dreams. Sprayed in the environment it refreshes and stimulates, it is also used to repress people who talk too much. In incense potions, together with Frankincense and Myrrh it stimulates astral projection. In oil it is used in rituals for lucidness or to improve states of mind and for prophetic dreams. The oil used in the bath increases personal magnetism. A mixture of water and lemon juice is used to clean second hand jewels to eliminate the vibrations of the previous owner. A bath with Lemon flowers taken with a full moon is recommended for its healing powers.

Lemon Balm

Lemon Balm
(Melissa officinalis L.)
Labiatae

Essence:	Cold
Planets:	Sun, Jupiter
Elements:	Water, Fire
Parts Used:	The Aerial Parts

Effects: Love, Success, Protection, Luck

Other Names: Balm, Melissa

Description: Originally from Europe this fragrant lively perennial herb has straight, hairy and square stems, with a scent like lemon.

Flowers:	Small, white or yellow, growing in the junctures of the stems.
Leaves:	Light green, oval, they grow in pairs opposite each nodule.
Fruit:	Seeds.
Height:	1 meter.

Care: It needs very fertile and humid soil in full sunlight or partial shade with frequent watering. pH: 7.0.

History:
For more than 2.000 years (in different cultures) Lemon Balm has been recommended to lighten the mind and heart; also used as an antidote for melancholy.

Uses:
Used in incenses for luck, protection and success. Consumed for positive energy, to awakening inspiration and carried for love. In oil it is used to stimulate fantasy and inspiration and for its sedative effects.

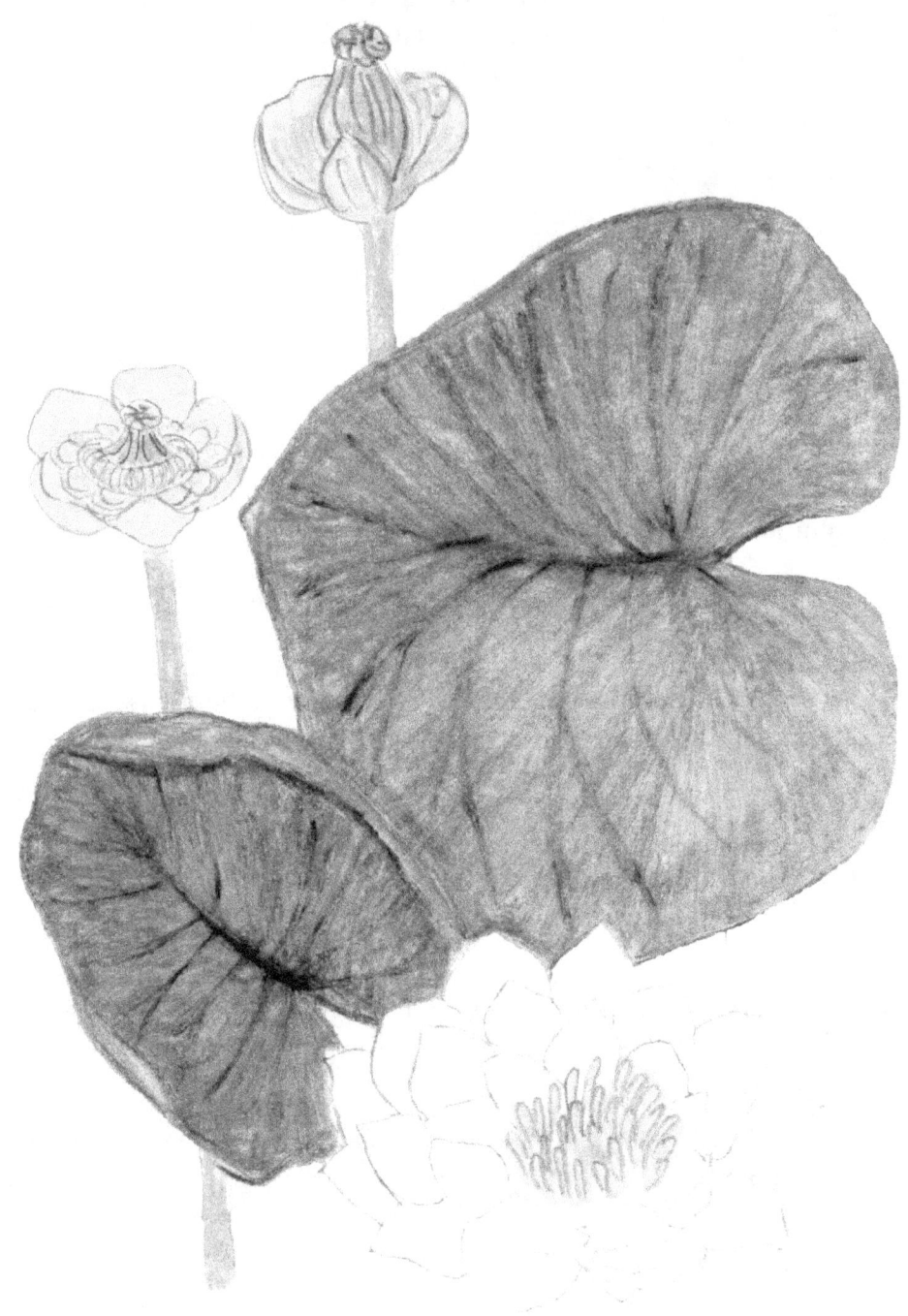

Lotus

Lotus
(Nymphaea lotus)
Nymphaeaceae

Essence: Cold
Planet: Moon
Element: Water
Parts Used: Flowers, Roots

Effects: Spiritual Development, Protection, Repels Evil Spirits

Description: Native of Eurasia it grows in swampy zones and lakes, it is an aquatic perennial herb.

Flowers: White, round with a leather-like texture.
Leaves: Shaped like cups, white or yellow, the leaves grow on the surface of the water.
Height: From the surface; 10 to 15 cm.

Care: Being an aquatic herb, it needs a body of water of at least 10 cm deep with soil on the bottom. In very cold climates these herbs die in winter, and in warmer climates they will lose their foliage but survive.

History:
Both Egyptians and Hindi considered the Lotus as the mystical symbol of life and the center of the Universe. It is still used today in temples in Tibet and Nepal. The Egyptians considered it worthy of offering to their Gods and used both blue and white Lotus flowers in their art. In Greek mythology, who ever ate Lotus would lose the desire to see their native homeland. The botanist, R. A. Salisbury (1761-1829) gave it is current name Nymphaeceae, alluding to the nymphs in Greek mythology.

Uses:
The person who inhales the aroma of Lotus incense receives protection against evil spirits and it is commonly used in incenses for protection. In oil it is used for spiritual development. It is considered as a mystical symbol of the universe, of life and of spirituality. It is said that if you carry a piece of Lotus root under your tongue you can open any door.

Majoram

Marjoram
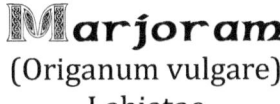
(Origanum vulgare)
Labiatae

Essence:	Hot
Planet:	Mercury
Element:	Air
Parts Used:	The Aerial Parts
Effects:	Love, Psychic-Spiritual Development, Eliminates Bad Vibrations, Spiritual Cleansing, Protection
Other Names:	Joy of the Mountains, Mountain Mint, Oregano, Wintersweet
Description:	A perennial herb with central erect, purple square stem, whose flower stems are hairy. Its roots are shallow but dense.
Flowers:	They look like knots before they open, they are very small, white, pink or purple of about 2 cm. at the top of hairy stems.
Leaves:	Small, oval, hairy with a peculiar odor; opposite, whitish or grey, lance shaped.
Fruit:	Very small nuts that look like a tear.
Height:	1 meter.
Care:	Full sunlight, regular soil with good drainage and moderate watering. pH: 6.9

History:
The Greeks called this herb "joy of the mountains" and believed that it was cultivated by Aphrodite, Goddess of love. Greek couples carried garlands of Marjoram at their weddings.

Uses:
Used in incenses to eliminate negative thought forms and other forms of negativity. In oil it has both calming and stimulating effects; depending on the emotional state at the time. It helps to organize the interior forces. Carried it is useful for spiritual cleansing and psychic and spiritual development. Used in the ritual preparation of food for positive energy and to strengthen love. It is grown in the garden to protect against evil. A tea prepared with Marjoram is given to persons who are depressed to raise their spirits since it generates positive energy.

The Book of Herbs and Magic — Heather Eaton

Incense

Mastic
(Pistacia lenticus)
Anacardiaceae

Essence: Hot
Planet: Sun
Element: Air
Parts Used: Resin

Effects: Clairvoyance, Psychic Development, Invocations

Other Names: Lentisk

Description: Mastic is the resin from mastic tree; native of the Mediterranean, almost exclusively confined to the Island of Chios in Greece. The resin is obtained by "bleeding" the tree and drying the resin in the air.

Flowers: The female flowers have one pistil and the male flowers have five stamens.
Leaves: Compound, appearing in pairs.
Fruit: Small globe shaped, red when ripe and then black.
Height: 7 meters.

History:
In the Orient, Mastic was traditionally used by the magus as an aphrodisiac.

Uses:
Used in incenses to empower psychic development and clairvoyance. Also used in incense potions to invoke spirits. Mastic can be added to any incense recipes destined to intensify personal power.

Mate

Mate
(Ilex paraguariensis)
Aquifoliaceae

Essence: Hot
Parts Used: Leaves

Effects: Love, Spiritual Cleansing, Protection, Repels Evil Spirits

Other Names: Paraguay Tea, Yerba Mate

Description: A shrub native of South America.

Flowers: Very tiny, (hermaphrodites), usually white.
Leaves: Alternate, lance shaped, persistent, oval, opaque green.
Fruit: Bright red drupe.
Height: 6 meters.

Care: Slightly acid soil rich in nutrients. It tolerates full sunlight or partial shade, full sun light being preferable. It needs plenty water and good drainage.

History:
More than 300 years ago Jesuit missionaries watched the South American Indians drinking mate tea for medicinal and ceremonial purposes.

Uses:
This herb is used in cleansing baths because it eliminates astral detritus. In powder it is used to free a person, object or place from the influence of spirits of the dead. Mate in the pillows reduces the nocturnal activities of spirits in the bedrooms. In incense potions it is also used for spiritual cleansing and for love charms. It is carried to attract the opposite sex.

Meadowsweet

Meadowsweet
(Filipendula ulmaria)
Rosaceae

Essence:	Hot
Planet:	Jupiter
Elements:	Water, Fire
Parts Used:	The Aerial Parts

Effects: Love, Psychic Development

Other Names: Bridewort, Meadowwort, Queen of the Meadow, Steeplebush

Description: It grows in marshes or very humid soil. It is a strong perennial herb with nodules in its roots.

Flowers: Very small, fragrant, creamy white with five petals that grow in bunches.
Leaves: Bright green, oval shaped, with grayish-white hair and a predominant vein underneath.
Fruit: Seeds.
Height: 2 meters.

Care: Needs partial shade and warm moist soil rich in nutrients; frequent watering with good drainage.

History:
One of the three most sacred herbs of the Druids. They used it to decorate their altars for love charms. During the Middle Ages, the delicate scent of this herb turned it into a popular herb spray. In the 1800's, salicylic acid was obtained from this herb. Meadowsweet flowers were said to be one of the favorites of Queen Elisabeth I.

Uses:
Popularly used in love incenses. It has particularly positive vibrations. Meadowsweet flowers sprinkled around or in the house preserve the peace; its scent cheers the heart. It is drunk in infusions to increase psychic powers.

Mugwort

Mugwort
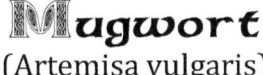
(Artemisa vulgaris)
Compositae

Essence:	Cold
Planets:	Venus, Sun
Elements:	Air, Earth
Parts Used:	The Aerial Parts

Effects: Clairvoyance, Psychic Development, Protection, Astral Projection, Purification, Prophetic Dreams, Visions

Other Names: Artemisia, Cingulum, Sailor's Tobacco, Saint John's Plant, Witch Herb

Description: Perennial shrub with many branches. It has angular red or brown hairy stems.

Flowers: Many small flowers in loose bunches, in yellow, red and brown.
Leaves: Dark green dark on top and white underneath that smell like sage and contain essential oils.

Fruit: Seeds.

Height: 1 to 3 meters.

Care: Needs full sunlight. It is resistant to droughts and requires very little water.
Since it is an herb of rapid growth it is convenient to prune it frequently.

History:
This particular herb has been surrounded by legends and superstitions for centuries. In the Middle Ages crown of Mugwort were worn on the night of Saint John to protect the bearer from demonic possession. In Europe pillows were stuffed with this herb to generate prophetic dreams. According to the Druids the effects are more powerful if Mugwort is harvested in the full moon. The Chinese use it in the Dragon Festival (the 5th day of the 5th month) to reject evil spirits.

Uses:
Worn inside shoes it prevents fatigue. It is carried for psychic-spiritual development consumed for clairvoyance. Rubbing freshly cut leaves over magical mirrors or crystal balls empowers their effects. Used in incense for clairvoyance, divinations and visions. It is also used in incense for purification. In oil it is used for protection. The energies generated by this herb are more powerful when it is harvested in the full moon. Placed under the bed it helps in astral projection.

Mullein

Mullein
(Verbascum thapsus L.)
Scrophulariaceae

Essence: Cold
Planet: Saturn
Element: Fire
Parts Used: The Aerial Parts

Effects: Love, Protection, Purification, Repels Evil Spirits, Prevents Nightmares

Other Names: Bunny's Ears, Candlewick Plant, Feltwort, Flanel Leaf, Jupiter's Staff, Mullen, Shepherd's Herb, Torches, Velvet Plant

Description: Bi-annual herb with velvety stems and leaves.

Flowers: A long tassel with yellow flowers appears the second year.
Leaves: Appear in rosette form.
Fruit: Seeds.
Height: 4 meters.

Care: Needs sunlight and moderate watering.

History:
Many ancient cultures considered Mullein as a magical, protector against evil spirits. It was planted around the house for protection and used as torches for same purpose.

Uses:
Used to repel evil spirits. Added to incenses for protection and purification. It is carried for protection against savage animals, the Evil Eye and to attract love. It is considered a powerful guardian against evil spirits and is commonly hung on doors and windows for protection. Under the pillows it protects from nightmares.

Myrrh

Myrrh
(Commiphora myrrha)
Burseraceae

Essence:	Cold
Planets:	Sun, Saturn, Moon
Elements:	Water, Fire
Parts Used:	Resin

Effects: Love, Protection, Purification, Repels Evil Spirits, Prophetic Dreams, Visions

Other Names: Karan, Mirra

Description: A small tree (shrub) with a grey-white stem native of Africa. The resin is a mixture of resin and essential mirrol oil. Its bark is a chestnut red.

History:
The aromatic resin of this herb was greatly appreciated even 4.000 years ago The Bible makes more than a dozen references to this herb. The Egyptians used it to prepare balsams and it appears in Greek and Roman mythology.

Uses:
Myrrh is used in incenses for protection against the Evil Eye, for purification and to induce visions and prophetic dreams. Its smoke is used to consecrate, purify and bless objects such as rings, amulets, and talismans. It can be carried together Frankincense as a protecting amulet. In oil it rejects the Evil Eye and evil spirits. Used as an offering to dissipate evil.

Myrtle

Myrtle
(Myrtus communis)
Myrtaceae

Essence:	Cold
Planets:	Venus, Moon
Elements:	Water, Earth
Parts Used:	Leaves
Effects :	Love, Luck
Other Names:	Candleberry, Myrtlewood, Myrtus, Wax Myrtle

Description: A shrub with many branches and aromatic leaves, typical of the west Mediterranean coast.

Flowers:	White or pink, solitary and aromatic. It flowers in summer.
Leaves:	Dark green, lustrous and very fragrant, they are pointy oval shape.
Fruit:	Black-blue berries.
Height:	5 meters.

Care: It will grow in partial shade but full sunlight is recommended. It grows in almost any soil with good drainage and requires moderate watering. It can not stand frost.

History:
In Greek mythology this herb was considered an herb of love and consecrated to their Goddess Venus.

Uses:
Used to attract positive spiritual influences. It should be used in small quantities for incense potions. It is considered as an herb of love and sexual attraction bringing spiritually positive influences. Carrying Myrtle wood conserves youth and attracts love. When grown on both sides of the house it will help maintain love and harmony. In oil it attracts money and good luck. Added to herbal sacks for love.

Nutmeg

Nutmeg
(Mysristica fragans)
Myristicaeae

Essence:	Hot
Planets:	Jupiter, Mercury, Venus, Neptune
Elements:	Air, Fire
Parts Used:	Nuts
Effects:	Aphrodisiac, Love, Clairvoyance, Money, Eliminates Bad Vibrations, Success, Protection, Luck, Visions
Other Names:	Calabach
Description:	Native of the Mollusk Islands in Indonesia, Nutmeg is a perennial tree.
Flowers:	Inconspicuous.
Fruit:	Yellow drupe which divides itself in two leaving the seed visible.
Height:	15 meters.

History:
It has been used for eons as an amulet for good luck.

Uses:
It is eaten or carried to empower clairvoyance and for protection. In a ritual bath it makes people more willing to listen and eliminates negative thoughts; good for job interviews. In oil it promotes personal equilibrium, helps in meditation and is also considered as an aphrodisiac. In incense potions it empowers love, clairvoyance, visions and increases friendliness. It is also used in incense to attract luck and success and eliminate negative thoughts and bad vibrations. Sprinkling powdered Nutmeg on green candles attracts money and prosperity. Rubbing oil on the forehead (over the third eye) helps receive prophetic messages.

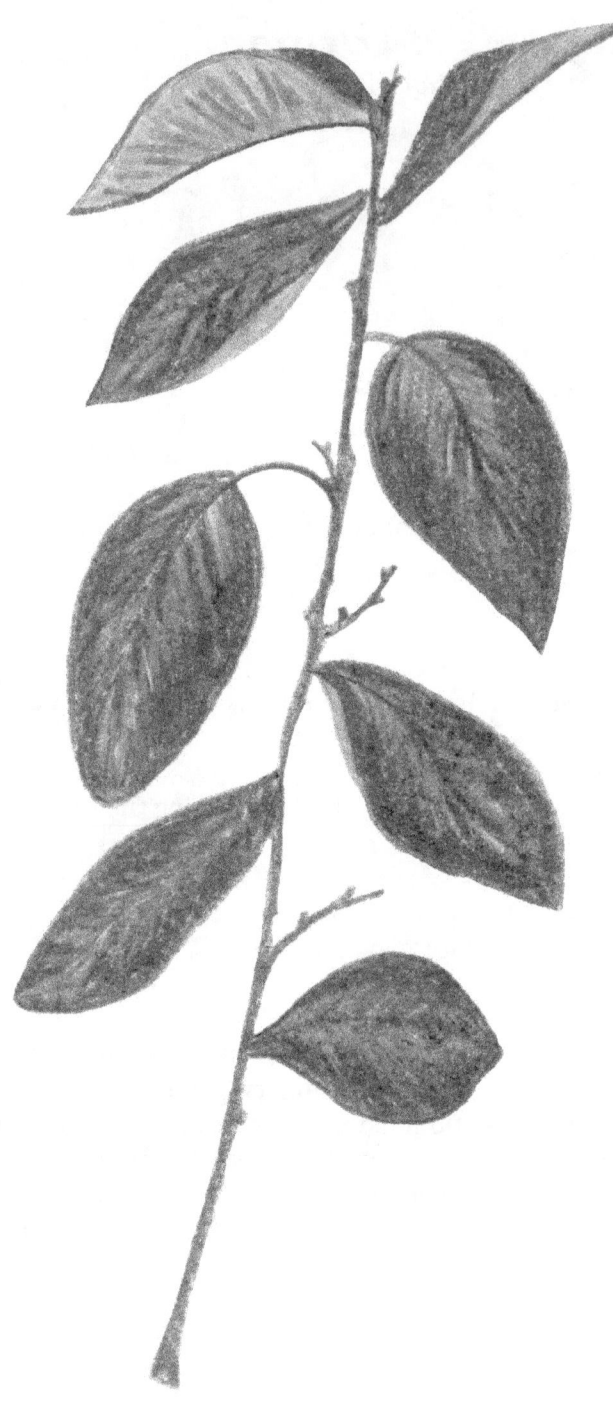

Orange

Orange
(Citrus sinensis)
Rutaceae

Essence:	Hot
Planets:	Sun, Moon
Element:	Water
Parts Used:	Flowers, Fruit
Effects:	Love, Fortune, Purification, Luck
Other Names:	Love Fruit
Description:	Native of Southeast Asia, orange is a perennial, tree.
Flowers:	White, small and fragrant.
Leaves:	Green, oval and shiny.
Fruit:	Orange. Peel contains essential oils.
Height:	10 meters.
Care:	It grows ideally in warm climates where it produces fruit all year round. In hot climates it produces fruit in winter, spring and fall. It needs full sunlight or partial shade, soil with good drainage and moderate watering.

History:
The Chinese have considered for millennia the orange as a symbol of luck and good fortune.

Uses:
Dry Orange peel is used in herbal sacks for love and for purification. In a spray it acts stimulating the mind and promoting the exhibition of emotions, good for parties or meetings. To attract people of the opposite sex a ritual bath with fresh or dry flowers will help. In incense potions it is used to heal. Its oil is famous for attracting good luck and fortune. Teas are made of Orange flowers to protect from drunkenness.

Parsley

Parsley
(Apium petroselinum)
Umbelliferae

Essence:	Hot
Planets:	Sun, Saturn, Mercury
Elements:	Air, Earth
Parts Used:	The Aerial Parts

Effects: Psychic Development, Luck, Money, Fertility, Protection, Purification,

Other Names: Cilantro

Description: Common kitchen herb grown in gardens with long and thin stems.

Flowers:	White, very small, found in bunches at the top of the stem.
Leaves:	With serrated edges.
Fruit:	Seeds.
Height:	20 cm.

Care: Requires soil with medium quantity of nutrients, full sun and abundant water with good drainage.

History:
It has been used for centuries in the Seder, the Jewish ritual meal at Passover, as a symbol of new beginnings. The Greeks used it in funeral ceremonies. The Romans carried it for protection. In the Middle Ages it was considered bad luck.

Uses:
This is an herb especially beneficial for women. Spraying it around the house calms and protects. Used in purifying baths and baths to end bad fortune, and improve finances (for money it is more effective when combined with Cinnamon). It is carried to promote the development of psychic powers and for protection. In oil it calms and attracts good luck. Placed on a plate of food as decoration it eliminates poison and corruption. It is consumed for fertility, love and spiritual purification.

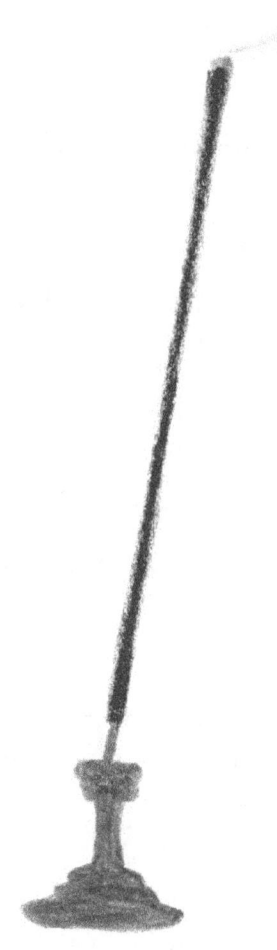

Patchouli Incense

Patchouli
(Pogostemon cablin)

Essence: Cold
Planets: Sun, Mars, Saturn, Venus
Element: Earth
Parts Used: The Aerial Parts

Effects: Aphrodisiac, Love, Clairvoyance, Psychic Development, Spiritual Cleansing, Passion, Predictions, Protection, Luck

Description: There are around 30 varieties of this herb, which grows in India, Southeast Asiatic and Indonesia. The essence of Patchouli is obtained by the distillation of the leaves.

Flowers: Small.
Leaves: Opposite and dented.

Uses:
Because of its intense spicy scent, this herb is related to passion and lust. Its essence is used in love potions. Carried it attracts love and passion, both in men as well as women. It is burned in incense potions to favor love and to stimulate clairvoyance, divination and psychic development. In the morning Patchouli generates creative energy and in the evening it becomes the reputed aphrodisiac. In oil it protects and inspires mental peace and harmony. Also used for spiritual cleansing. It awakens the desire to broaden boundaries and stimulates spiritual power. It is used on occasions to bless objects for magical purposes. In baths it is used for love and passion.

Pennyroyal

Pennyroyal
(Mentha pulegium L.)
Labiatae

Essence: Hot
Planets: Mars
Element: Fire
Parts Used: The Aerial Parts

Effects: Healing, Protection, Luck

Other Names: Mosquito Plant, Piliolerian, Squaw Mint

Description: A perennial herb of the mint family.

Flowers: Tubular, pink or lilac with two petals. They grow in bunches on the top of the stems between the branches.
Leaves: Hairy and oval shaped with a strong peppermint like smell.
Fruit: Small nuts.
Height: 1 meter.

Care: It grows in almost any soil but ideally prefers light soil, medium in nutrients and humid. It needs partial shade and abundant watering. pH: acid.

History:
The Chaldeans called this herb blieth and the Greeks called it ketus. It was popular both in Europe and Americas as a repellent of fleas and mosquitoes. This herb is still used for medicinal purposes and the herb in itself is not toxic, although only two teaspoons of the oil extract would be enough to kill a person.

Uses:
Placed in shoes it prevents fatigue and stimulates vital forces. Added to summer healing incenses and other potions to energize the body and calm the mind. When carried it protects against the Evil Eye by creating a protective shield. It is also used to promote good business.

Peppermint

Peppermint
(Mentha piperita L.)
Labiatae

Essence:	Hot
Planets:	Venus, Mercury
Elements:	Fire, Air
Parts Used:	The Aerial Parts

Effects: Aphrodisiac, Healing, Psychic Development, Eliminates Bad Vibrations, Purification, Prophetic Dreams, Luck

Other Names: Brandy Mint, Mint

Description: A native of Europe, this perennial herb is also from the mint family.

Flowers:	Small, lilac or pink growing in thin bunches.
Leaves:	Opposite, simple, oval, serrated edges and very aromatic.
Fruit:	Very small nuts.
Height:	1 meter.

Care: It grows in almost any soil but the ideal is light and humid soil, medium in nutrients. It needs partial shade and abundant watering. pH: 6.5

History:
Peppermint is mentioned as a stomach soother in the Papiro Ebers, one the oldest known Egyptian medical books. In Greek mythology Persephone, jealous because her husband Pluto had fallen in love with Minthe, turned her into the herb. Mint is considered a symbol of hospitality by the Gods Zeus and Hermes. The Druids used it for protecting their homes and altars.

Uses:
This herb is used in healing incenses and to purify. Used in fumigations to clean up negative energy generated during a prolonged illness. Since it has aphrodisiac properties it is used in a love potions and incenses. In oil it is used to increase physical powers and to attract luck. It is sprayed to stimulate the mind and the emotions, improving positive vibrations and eliminating bad ones. Under the pillow it induces prophetic dreams. As a hair rinse it eliminates the Evil Eye. It is carried for psychic and spiritual development. Teas of Peppermint are consumed to calm the mind and alleviate psychic tensions.

Pokewood

Pokeweed
(Phytolaca americana L.)
Phytolacaceae

Essence:	Hot
Planet:	Mars
Element:	Fire
Parts Used:	Roots

Effects: Protection

Other Names: Dove Blood, Garget, Poke Root, Scoke

Description: A perennial herb with a reddish stem that is very poisonous.

Flowers:	White in tassels.
Leaves:	Green pointed at the tip.
Fruit:	Purple or black berries.
Height:	6 meters.

Care: It grows in almost any type of humid soil with good drainage. It needs full sun or partial shade and moderate watering.

History:
Historically Pokeweed has had a bad reputation because of its toxic effects on humans. The American Indians have used it for centuries as a fabric dye.

Uses:
The berries are used to make a dye, known as "Dove Blood dye". It is especially effective after of the New Moon. The root has a valuable astral influence. In the bath it eliminates bad vibrations

Rose

Rose
(Rosa spp.)
Rosaceae

Essence: Cold
Planets: Venus, Sun
Elements: Water, Air
Parts Used: Flowers, Leaves

Effects: Love, Clairvoyance, Eliminates Bad Vibrations, Purification, Prophetic Dreams

Other Names: China Rose

Description: Perennial green erect herb with thorny stems.

Flowers: Solitary or in bunches at the end of the stems; with an oval or round calyx and corolla with five petals.
Leaves: Dark green, alternate, rough and an odd number of elliptical follicles.
Fruit: Called rose-hip; it is a fleshy berry with many hairy seeds.
Height: Varies according to the variety.

Care: Full sunlight, good drainage and frequent watering. While flowering, fertilize and prune frequently. pH: 6.5 - 6.8.

History:
Roses have been grown since ancient times in China, and were the favorite flowers of the Egyptians, who used the fragrance to freshen the environment and rose water as perfume. When Cleopatra invited Marc Anthony to the palace, she ordered the floors to be covered knee high in Rose petals. This herb has been considered for centuries as the most notorious symbol of love and beauty.

Uses:
The rose scent is the queen of the perfumes. In oil it produces a sensation of peace and calm, it actives female energies, increases spiritual power and heals broken hearts. It is used in rituals for artistic inspiration and for protecting secrets. To prepare love incenses it is recommendable to wash your hands in rose water first. To induce clairvoyance and prophetic dreams a rose tea is ingested or leaves from the bush are burned. Rose petals are burned for a refreshing sleep. The flowers absorb bad vibrations, especially white ones. Spraying purifies and eliminates heavy vibrations. Rose bushes planted in the garden attract fairies. In ritual baths it is used for love and sensuality.

Rosemary

Rosemary
(Rosmarinus officinalis)
Labiatae

Essence:	Hot
Planets:	Sun, Moon, Pluto
Element:	Fire
Parts Used:	Leaves, Flowers
Effects:	Love, Healing, Purification, Psychic Development, Eliminates Bad Vibrations, Protects, Prevents Nightmares
Other Names:	Incensier, Rosmarine, Rosmarinus, Sea Dew
Description:	Native to the Mediterranean, perennial with a woody grey or brown stem.
Flowers:	Small, sky blue or blue, two petals; divided into 2 upper and 3 lower lobes, with 4 stamens, in clusters along the stem.
Leaves:	Dark green on top, silvery and hairy underneath, needle shaped 3 cm long with a peculiar scent and volatile oil.
Fruit:	Very small nuts.
Height:	2 to 3 meters.
Care:	Survives in soil with few nutrients, needs full sunlight and good drainage. Can stand droughts, infrequent but deep watering. pH: 6.5 - 7.0.

History:
The Greeks used it to symbolize memory. It was used in matrimonial ceremonies as a symbol of fidelity and in funerals so that the living would remember the dead. In the Middle Ages it was used as an amulet for love and for protection.

Uses:
It is used to wash or rinse hair to improve the memory, for healing in fumigations mixed with Juniper. It releases very powerful purification vibrations when used to cleanse. Furniture may be washed with a tea to eliminate bad vibrations. In the corners of rooms or under the bed, it calms and protects from nightmares and harm. Hung in doors and windows it avoids thieves. In oil it protects, purifies, and promotes courage. It also predisposes the mind towards realism, creativity and a sense of stability. In ritual baths it is used to preserve youth and for spiritual purification. It is carried to stimulate psychic powers.

Rue

Rue
(Ruta graveolens)
Rutaceae

Essence: Hot
Planets: Sun, Saturn, Mars
Elements: Fire, Earth
Parts Used: The Aerial Parts

Effects: Eliminates Bad Vibrations, Spiritual Cleansing, Protection, Purification, Repels Evil Spirits

Other Names: Bashoush, Herb of Grace, Herbygrass, Mother of Herbs, Ruta

Description: Originally from Europe, it's a perennial shrub. Its base is woody and the whole herb has a very characteristic smell.

Flowers: Yellow with a green center, slipper shaped, in loose clusters at the end of the stems. It has five petals, with uneven borders.
Leaves: Blue-green, divided into fleshy segments, alternate, oval that contain aromatic glands.
Fruit: Round capsule with lobes and seeds shaped like a half moon.
Height: 2 meters.

Care: Needs very fertile soil, full sunlight and frequent watering. pH: 7.0.

History:
The Greeks named it "rueo" which means "liberate", they believed that it liberated the magic of others. In the Middle Ages it was used as defense against witches and charms. The Romans consumed Rue to eliminate the Evil Eye. The Druids and the Christians consider it the "herb of grace".

Uses:
A freshly cut branch of Rue submerged in spring water is used for consecrations and blessings. It is carried to mend broken hearts and for protection. In incense potions it adds virtue, protects and repels evil spirits. In ritual baths it is used for spiritual cleansing, to assist spiritual illumination and the path to follow. It is also commonly used in baths to eliminate bad vibrations and to protect against them. It is hung on the doors for protection. It is sprayed to eliminate negativity.

Sage

Sage
(Salvia officinalis)
Labiatae

Essence:	Hot
Planets:	Jupiter, Mercury, Uranus
Elements:	Air, Earth
Parts Used:	The Aerial Parts

Effects: Divination, Healing, Psychic Development, Eliminates Bad Vibrations, Protects, Astral Projection

Other Names: Carlove, Meadow Sage

Description: Native of the Mediterranean, it is a perennial shrub type herb, with square stems, that is woody at the base.

Flowers: Tubular, pink, purple, blue or white with two petals, with hair at the tip of the stems.

Leaves: Green-grey, dentated, whitish with wrinkled borders, oblong, hairy in opposite pairs along the stem. The leaves contain oil.

Fruit: Seeds.

Height: 1 meter.

Care: It needs soil low in nutrients but with a good drainage, ideally in full sunlight, it supports droughts moderately well. It needs moderate watering and pruning after it flowers. pH: 6.4.

History:
The Greeks called it "Carlove" and as the Romans, they used it to conserve the memory. In Arabia it was associated with longevity and the improvement of the mental capacities. One of its most common medical uses was for insomnia. Native American Indians considered it sacred.

Uses:
It is added to herbal sacks, incenses and amulets for healing purposes. It is carried to assure a long life. Sprayed around the house it creates a protective barrier against negativity and eliminates what is already there, it also and tends to increase the mental clarity of those present. It awakens curiosity for new and unknown. In ritual baths it helps gain authentic wisdom and mental clarity. In oil it also awakens curiosity for the unknown and opens new horizons. It is also used for divination and astral projection. It is consumed for wisdom and patience. When it is burned, the smoke cleanses the aura of negative energy.

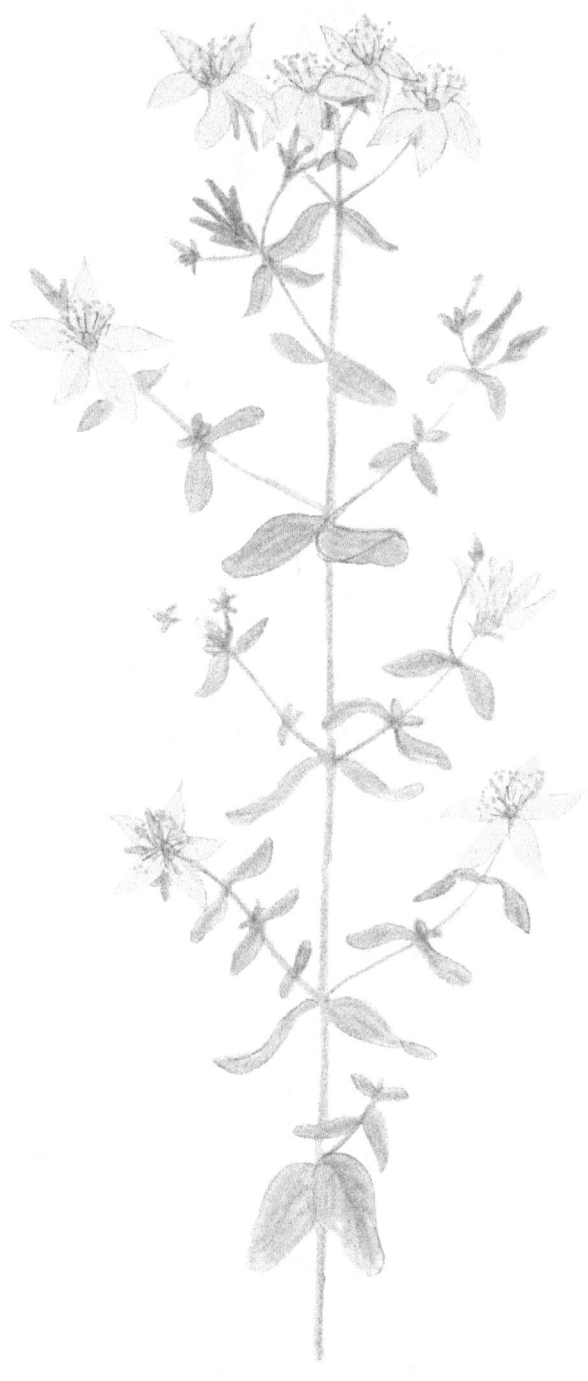

Saint John's Wort

Saint John's Wort
(Hypericum perforatum L.)
Hypericaceae

Essence:	Hot
Planet:	Sun
Element:	Fire
Parts Used:	Leaves, Flowers

Effects: Love, Protection, Repels Evil Spirits, Astral Projection

Other Names: Amber, Rosin Rose

Description: Native of Europe, this perennial herb has a slightly woody base and yellow brown roots that branch out. The leaves and flowers contain essential oils.

Flowers: Brilliant golden yellow with little black spots on the tips, they have five petals and numerous stamens.
Leaves: Light green, small, oval in opposite pairs.
Fruit: Seeds.
Height: 60 cm.

Care: Ideally grown in coastal areas with high humidity, it grows in almost any soil and can stand droughts but does better with moderate watering. In coastal areas it needs full sunlight and in warmer valleys partial shade. pH: acid or alkaline.

History:
The Druids burned it on the summer solstice to be invincible in battle. The Greeks and Romans believed that the fragrance of Saint John's Wort caused evil spirits to leave and that it protected against evil spells. For centuries this herb has been considered to have power to repel devils. In the Middle Ages Catholic priests used it in exorcisms.

Uses:
Placed on the doors or windows to block the passage of negative forces. It protects against feelings of anguish. In incense potions it is one of the most powerful herbs, protecting, and scaring away evil spirits. A tea prepared with the flowers is used to cover crystal balls creating a "doorway" for astral projection. It is carried to attract love, to block negative forces and to detect evil. It is consumed in teas for spiritual tranquility. Inhaling the scent of the flowers stimulates lucid dreams and psychic energy.

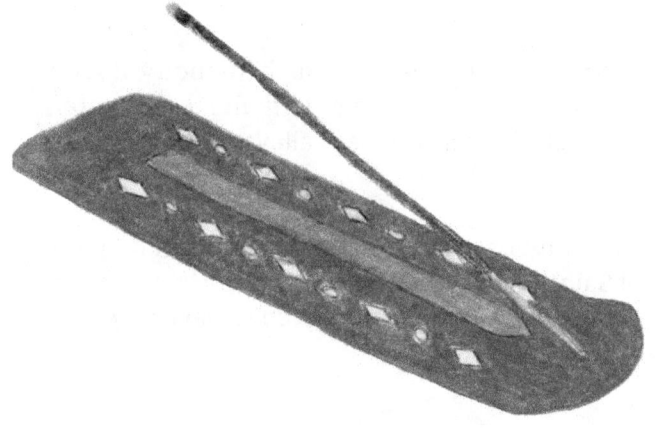

Sandalwood Incense

Sandalwood
(Santalum album)
Santalaceae

Essence:	Cold
Planets:	Moon, Sun, Mercury, Venus
Elements:	Water, Air
Parts Used:	Bark

Effects: Love, Psychic Development, Success, Fortune, Invocations, Protection, Astral Projection, Purification

Other Names: Sandal, Santal, White Saunders

Description: It is a tree from subtropical climates, native of Indonesia, that parasites the roots of other trees. Sandalwood is one of the main components in many incense potions and perfumes.

History:
Sandalwood has been used by many cultures and religions since the 5th century. Even today it is used in India and China in Buddhist rituals and ceremonies.

Uses:
The perfume relaxes the body and calms the mind; it is used for meditation because it facilitates concentration. In incense, combined with Lavender, it is used to invoke spirits and for success. In ritual fumigations, mixed with Frankincense it is used for lunar rituals due to its elevated vibrations. It is burned by itself for protection, to stimulate fantasy, for creativity and to awaken spiritual powers. In oil it protects, stimulates fantasy and creativity, awakens spiritual forces, and attracts luck and fortune. It is also used in rituals to invoke spirits of ancestors . It is carried to empower spirituality. Sprinkling powered Sandalwood eliminates negative energy. It is mixed and burned with Benzoin and Mugwort for astral projection.

Snapdragon

Snapdragon
(Antirrhinum majus)
Scrophulariaceae

Essence: Hot
Planets: Venus, Mars
Element: Fire
Parts Used: Flowers

Effects: Love, Eliminates Fear and Bad Vibrations, Protection

Other Names: Dragon Flower

Description: An annual and lively herb from warm regions, Native of the Mediterranean.

Flowers: Pocket shaped in bunches with a five piece calyx. When the flowers are pinched at their base, it opens to looks like the mouth of dog or dragon.
Leaves: Green, lance shaped.
Fruit: Seeds.
Height: 20 cm.

Care: It germinated in a greenhouse in the fall it will produce flowers in the spring, planted in a garden only after the frost. It requires frequent watering.

Uses:
Snapdragon flowers placed in a vase are a powerful protecting amulet. When carried, the flowers serve as a protecting amulet and help guess evil intentions of others. Used in incense potions to break charms. In oil and in baths this herb is used to break charms and eliminate fear. To eliminate bad vibrations or negative energy, flowers are placed on an altar in front of a mirror.

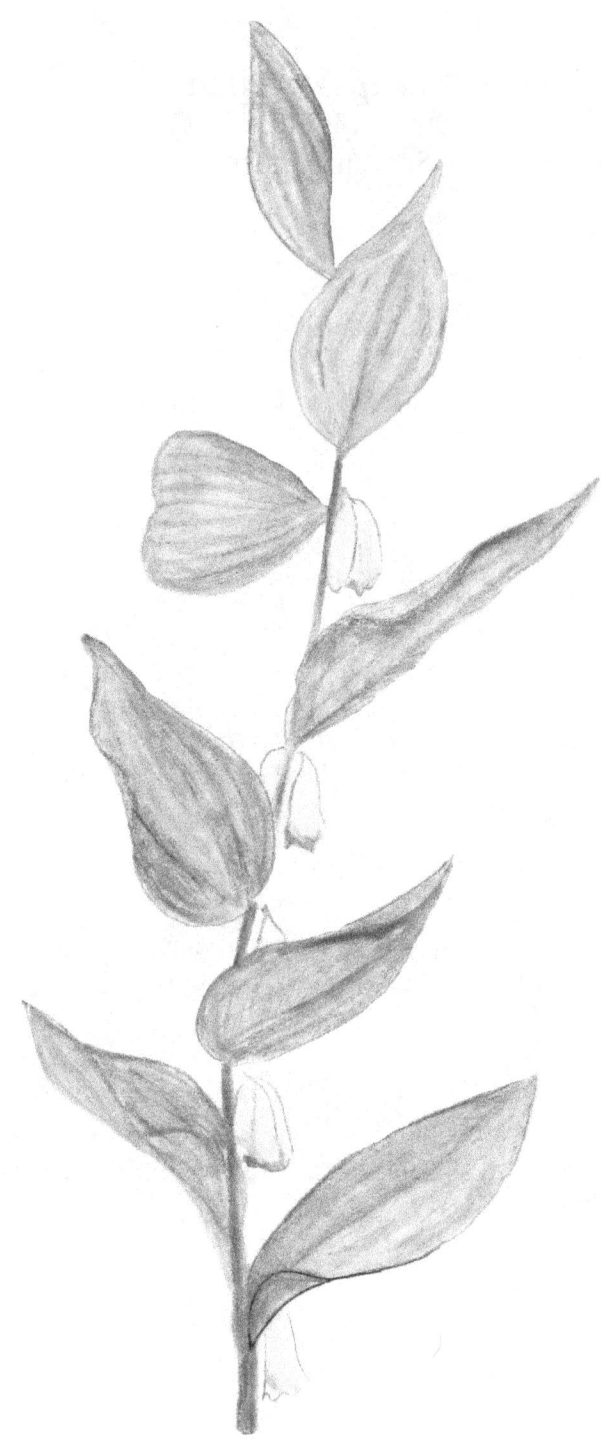

Solomon's Seal

Solomon's Seal
(Polygonatum multiflorum)
Liliaceae

Essence:	Cold
Planet:	Saturn
Elements:	Water, Earth
Parts Used:	Leaves, Roots

Effects: Eliminates Bad Vibrations, Invocations, Protection, Purification

Other Names: Sealroot, Sealwort

Description: Perennial herb with a fleshy root and an angular erect stem.

Flowers:	Cylindrical, white or yellow-green.
Leaves:	Big and curved alternating on the blue-green stem.
Fruit:	Black berries.
Height:	2 meters.

Care: It needs plenty of shade, relatively fertile soil and frequent watering.

History:
The Druids burned it as an offering to the Elemental Spirits. Since the Middle Ages it has also been used for medicinal purposes.

Uses:
Carried in herbal sacks for protection. In incense it is used to purify and protect. The powdered root is burned in incenses for rituals destined to invoke spirits. It is sprayed to clean bad vibrations and repel evil. It is placed in the corners of the house for protection against evil.

Spikenard

Spikenard
(Aralia racemosa L.)
Araliaceae

Essence:	Cold
Planets:	Saturn, Venus
Element:	Earth
Parts Used:	Roots

Effects: Aphrodisiac, Love, Psychic Visions, Development, Money, Success,

Other Names: Indian Root, Sarsaparilla

Description: Perennial herb, originally from the Americas. It is reproduced by bulbs.

Flowers: White, with a waxy texture, they are found in pairs in tassels, they have three sepals, many petals, six stamens and one pistil.

Leaves: Divided in many oval green leaflets.

Fruit: Purple berry.

Height: 1 meter.

Care: It needs humid climates and plenty of shade.

History:
Traditionally used by several North American Indian tribes for medicinal purposes.

Uses:
It attracts blessings, money and economic stability. In incense, mixed with Sandalwood it is excellent for businesses. In other incense potions it is used to stimulate visions. In oil potions it empowers spiritual qualities, psychic powers and is considered an aphrodisiac. Carried it attracts love and good business.

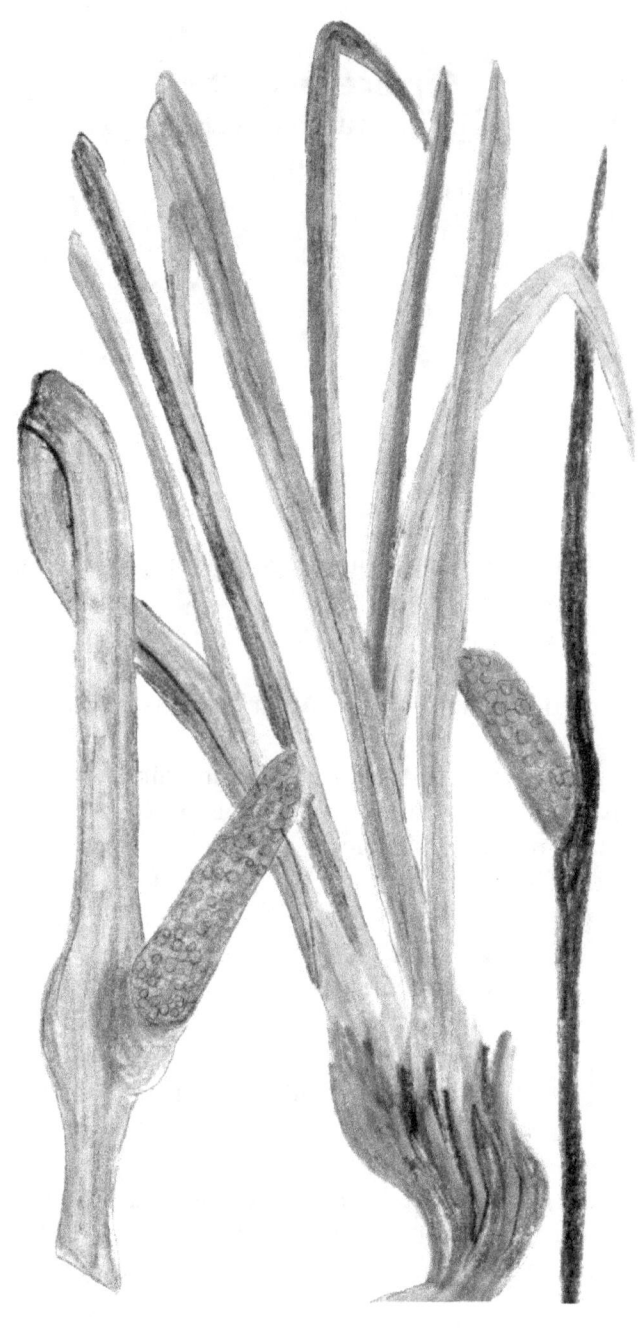

Sweet Flag

Sweet Flag
(Acorus calamus)
Araceae

Essence:	Cold
Planets:	Moon
Elements:	Water, Earth
Parts Used:	Roots

Effects: Healing, Fortune, Protection

Other Names: Calamus, Sweet Calamus, Sweetroot

Description: Originally from Asia aquatic herb grows in the shores of swamps. It is perennial with flat subterranean stems.

Flowers: Small brownish yellow, cylindrical of 4 to 8 cm, they grow out of the main stem.
Leaves: Straight, thin and sword shaped.
Height: 2 meters.

Care: Being a marsh herb, it needs to be planted in water.

History:
It has been used for centuries as a medicinal herb. The Arabs used it as an aphrodisiac.

Uses:
The powder root is used in incense potions to heal, to attract money and fortune. It should not be taken internally because it is very toxic. Small pieces of the root are kept in the corners of the kitchen to protect from hunger and poverty. It is very good luck whoever grows it.

Thyme

Thyme
(Thymus vulgaris)
Labiatae

Essence:	Cold
Planet:	Venus
Elements:	Water, Air
Parts Used:	The Aerial Parts

Effects: Love, Psychic Development, Spiritual Cleansing, Purification, Protection, Luck, Prevents Nightmares

Description: Native of Europe, it is a very aromatic perennial herb, with stiff woody stems and many stems.

Flowers: Pink, lavender or white, they flower in small bunches.
Leaves: Small, green almost linear and highly aromatic, very thin of about 2 cm that grow in opposite pairs.
Height: 15 a 25 cm.

Care: Needs full sunlight, soil with good drainage and moderate watering. pH: 6.3.

History:
The name "thymus" comes from Greek and means "courage". In the Middle Ages it was also associated with courage. Thyme was believed to have a psychological effect that was an antidote for nightmares and nervous disorders. It was also believed that drinking teas made from this herb would allow one to see nymphs and fairies. The Druids used it under their pillows to avoid nightmares and wore it in their hair when assisting funerals so as not to be affected by the negativity of the environment.

Uses:
In incense potions it is burned to purify places for rituals for luck, against depression and for love. It increases self-confidence and courage. Ritual baths are taken in spring for spiritual cleansing, protection and purification and to expand psychic abilities. A twig of Thyme placed under the pillow avoids nightmares. It is eaten or carried to activate psychic abilities and to purify. Women who wear a branch of this herb in their hair become irresistible. It is grown for prosperity.

Vervain

Vervain
(Verbena officinalis)
Verbenceae

Essence:	Cold
Planets:	Mars, Mercury, Saturn, Jupiter, Venus, Uranus
Elements:	Earth, Water
Parts Used:	The Aerial Parts
Effects:	Love, Money, Eliminates Bad Vibrations, Success, Protection, Purification, Prevents Nightmares
Other Names:	Enchanter's Plant, Herb of Grace, Herb of the Cross, Juno's Tears, Verbena
Description:	Native of the Mediterranean its perennial with straight, long and thin stems.
Flowers:	Lilac or purple with five petals in bunches.
Leaves:	Opposite, lower leaves are oblong and with sharp edges; top leaves are thin lanced-shaped with indentations.
Fruit:	Very small nuts.
Height:	1 to 2 meters.
Care:	Full sunlight and high temperatures to flower, it needs soil with good drainage and moderate watering, although it can stand droughts.

History:
In Egypt, Vervain was born from the tears of Isis. The Druids considered it one of the most sacred herbs; they burned it against psychic attacks and placed it on their altars for magical rituals. The Romans consecrated it for purification of their temples. In Christianity it was the herb that was placed over the wounds of Christ. It was said to be an ingredient in love potions made by medieval witches.

Uses:
In ritual baths, incenses and amulets, it favors personal security and purification. It should be harvested at noon during summer. On the bed it avoids nightmares and transmits the sensation of security and comfort. Sprayed it eliminates heavy vibrations and malicious thought forms. In oil it is used to eliminate the Evil Eye and to avoid negative influences. It is used in ritual baths for protection and purification. When it is grown in the house or garden it attracts money and prosperity. It is carried for love and success.

Wallflower

Wallflower
(Cheiranthus cheiri L.)
Cruciferae

Essence: Hot
Planet: Venus
Element: Air
Parts Used: Flowers

Effects: Psychic Development

Description: A perennial herb with many stems and notorious flowers.

Flowers: Yellow, very fragrant, forming tassels with four round petals.
Leaves: Oblong, lance shaped two cm. in length growing alternately on the stem.
Fruit: Seeds.
Height: 1 meter.

Care: Needs full sunlight or very little shade and soil good drainage. Flowers appear the second year.

History:
Since 130-200 B.C. Greek doctors have recommended this herb for medicinal purposes. In the XIV century, in Scotland it was considered adverse to love.

Uses:
The big and aromatic flowers are used in incenses to reveal the intentions of others. It is said that people who like the scent of the flowers are very sensitive, and live more in the past than in the present. In incense potions it is used for psychic development.

Wormwood

Wormwood
(Artemisia absinthium)
Compositae

Essence:	Hot
Planets:	Mars, Moon
Element:	Fire
Parts Used:	The Aerial Parts

Effects: Clairvoyance, Psychic Development, Invocations, Predictions, Protection

Other Names: Absinthium, Green Ginger, Madderwort

Description: Native of the mountains in southern Europe, it is a very resistant perennial herb with grey stems.

Flowers:	Small, white or yellow, they grow from one central stem.
Leaves:	Light grey or white, very divided and feather like.
Fruit:	Seeds.
Height:	2 meters.

Care: Needs full sunlight. It resists droughts and needs very little water. Frequent pruning is recommended. pH: 6.6.

History:
The Egyptians have known about this herb since 1.600 B.C., when they used it for intestinal parasites. The Druids considered it sacred and consecrated it to their Moon Gods. They used it rituals for clairvoyance, evocations and prophecies. Its name comes from the Greeks who dedicated it to their Goddess Artemisa.

Uses:
Used in incense potions to increase psychic powers, stimulate clairvoyance and predictions (especially when combined with Mugwort). Also used in incense potions for protection. On the night of All Saints this herb is thrown into ritual fires for protection against evil spirits. To invoke good spirits, it is powdered and burned as incense on charcoal. It is carried to increase psychic powers, protect from the Evil Eye, spells and accidents. It is also used in incenses for protection.

Yarrow

Yarrow
(Achillea millefolium)
Compositae

Essence:	Cold
Planets:	Venus, Saturn
Elements:	Water, Earth
Parts Used:	Leaves, Stems, Flowers

Effects: Love, Psychic Development, Eliminates Fear, Purification

Other Names: Achillea, Bloodwort, Ladies Mantle, Milfoil, Millefolium, Sanguinary, Thousand Seals

Description: Perennial herb with fern type foliage, straight stem covered with silky hair.

Flowers:	White, pink or cream on flower heads with five petal-like flowers.
Leaves:	Fern like, very thin and growing alternately on the stems.
Fruit:	Nuts.
Height:	1 meter.

Care: Needs full sunlight, fertile soil with good drainage and moderate water. Prune after flowering. pH: 6.1.

History:
This herb has been associated with the human race for over 60.000 years. Known above all for it's use in the I Ching. It played a role in the Trojan War 3.000 years ago when Achilles used it to heal the wounds of his solders. The Druids used it in incenses and love spells, and believed that it had the power of maintaining happy and united marriages. In the Americas it was used for love charms.

Uses:
When the fresh leaves are harvested immediately after the new Moon of Taurus, they become a powerful element for love and to increase self-esteem. It is an ideal herb for love amulets. It is very effective in love baths as well; telling the universe that we are ready for love. Drinking it increases psychic powers and spraying it increases love. When carried it protects from fears, fantasies or visions, gives courage, and attracts friends and loved ones. A powder from the dried flowers inhaled inhibits the sensation of fear for a period of hours.

Table of Herbs

Table of Herbs

Herb	Incense	Oil	Bath	Other
Anise	* Induces clairvoyance and visions * Protects	* Stimulates psychic powers	* The seeds in the bath produce a sensitive psychological state ideal for spiritual development	* Consumed for protection * Carried for psychic and spiritual development * Leaves placed in the corners of rooms protect from evil spirits
Basil	* Eliminates bad vibrations * Purifies, protects love * Ends discussions between lovers	* Creates a harmonious environment * Stimulates the mind and alleviates sorrow	* Protects from and cleanses the negativity and accumulations of negative influences provoked by other people	* Sprayed to clean / lighten the place * Carried to stimulate passion, increase luck and for protection
Bay	* The leaves are burned to stimulate psychic abilities and to generate visions * Used for love, protection and purification	* Attracts luck when placed with green candles * Generates energy and creates harmony	* The leaves are added to herbal sacks in baths for psychic and spiritual purification	* Placed under the pillow for prophetic dreams, clairvoyance and to awaken inspiration * Carried to attract love, for protection against the Evil Eye and negative energy * Consumed in teas to generate visions and stimulate the psyche
Benzoin	* Purifies the soul and is used for success and love * Attracts good spiritual vibrations, clears the mind and eliminates bad vibrations * Combined with *Sandalwood* and *Mugwort* for astral projection	* Used to bless objects * Breaks spells and curses * Produce charm in women * Attracts clients and friendships		* Mixed with *Cinnamon* it attracts success * With *Myrrh* and Musk it scares away evil spirits

The Book of Herbs and Magic — Heather Eaton

Herb	Incense	Oil	Bath	Other
Anise	* Induces clairvoyance and visions * Protects	* Stimulates psychic powers	* The seeds in the bath produce a sensitive psychological state ideal for spiritual development	* Consumed for protection * Carried for psychic and spiritual development * Leaves placed in the corners of rooms protect from evil spirits
Basil	* Eliminates bad vibrations * Purifies, protects love * Ends discussions between lovers	* Creates a harmonious environment * Stimulates the mind and alleviates sorrow	* Protects from and cleanses the negativity and accumulations of negative influences provoked by other people	* Sprayed to clean / lighten the place * Carried to stimulate passion, increase luck and for protection
Bay	* The leaves are burned to stimulate psychic abilities and to generate visions * Used for love, protection and purification	* Attracts luck when placed with green candles * Generates energy and creates harmony	* The leaves are added to herbal sacks in baths for psychic and spiritual purification	* Placed under the pillow for prophetic dreams, clairvoyance and to awaken inspiration * Carried to attract love, for protection against the Evil Eye and negative energy * Consumed in teas to generate visions and stimulate the psyche
Benzoin	* Purifies the soul and is used for success and love * Attracts good spiritual vibrations, clears the mind and eliminates bad vibrations * Combined with *Sandalwood* and *Mugwort* for astral projection	* Used to bless objects * Breaks spells and curses * Produce charm in women * Attracts clients and friendships		* Mixed with *Cinnamon* it attracts success * With *Myrrh* and Musk it scares away evil spirits

Table of Herbs

Herb	Incense	Oil	Bath	Other
Betony	* Used in incense potions for protection and purification			* Under the pillow it protects from nightmares * Grown to repel evil spirits and to protect the house * Carried to protect against intoxication
Bistort	* Used in predications and divinations, especially when mixed with *Frankincense*			* Carried by women who desire to become pregnant * Sprayed to scare away evil spirits * Placed under pillows to avoid nightmares
Broom	* Added to purification incenses		* Used in baths as an astral broom * Eliminates influences of the inferior spheres	* Using the stems (without flowers) to sweep or wash eliminates astral detritus and bad vibrations * In alcohol, it cleanses the aura
Calendula	* An incense made with the flowers is an excellent condenser of astral force	* Helps win respect and admiration	* Helps win respect and admiration by boosting self-confidence	* Magical mirrors are made with an extract of the flowers * Carried to develop the psyche and the spirit * Flowers are sprinkled under the bed for prophetic dreams and for protection

The Book of Herbs and Magic — Heather Eaton

Herb	Incense	Oil	Bath	Other
California Poppy	* Used in incenses for luck and fertility			* Seeds are carried as a protecting amulet * Used in infusions for invisibility of persons and objects * The flowers are smelled for intuition and to see auras
Camphor	* Added to incenses for divination * Protects health	* Placed in the corners of bedrooms, it repels psychic intruders * Used to anoint candles to break spells * Empowers psychic abilities		* Sprayed it cleanses and adds a vibration for protection against negative forces
Carnation	* When burned it liberates a lot of energy. It is very powerful, providing enormous amounts of astral energy * Favors visions and luck	* Spiritual healing * Increases psychic powers	* Completely cleanses the aura * It is one of the best spiritual cleansing baths	* The presence of carnations eliminates emotional and mental alterations
Cassia	* Used in love incenses	* Induces prophetic dreams * Increases psychic powers		

Table of Herbs

Herb	Incense	Oil	Bath	Other
Catnip	* Together with *Rose* petals makes an excellent love incense			* Added to *Rose* petals in herbal love sacks or sprayed for the same effect * Grown to attract luck and good spirits * Used to strengthen psychic ties with cats * Used in spells for beauty
Chamomile	* Favors a calm spiritual attitude for meditation and relaxation; produces drowsiness	* Creates interior equilibrium and calms nerves * Used as a sedative to induce sleep * Attracts love	* In the bath it helps attract love	* Carried for luck * Sprayed to repel spells * Used in herbal sacks to induce sleep * Used in spells for luck and money
Cinnamon	* Attracts high spiritual vibrations and good fortune * Stimulates concentration, clairvoyance and favors visions * Attracts love and success * Protects from envy and jealousy	* Attracts good fortune * Stimulates courage and vital and sexual energies * Also used to bless places	* Helps resolve problems at work and home * Increases income and stimulates vital energies	* Carried for success and for psychic and spiritual development
Clove	* Expulses negative energy * Purifies the environment, generates spiritual energy * Brings luck and favors visions	* Aphrodisiac * Cleans and protects the aura		* Carried or consumed to expulse negative energy * Also good to attract the opposite sex * Consumed to stimulate the memory * Hung on cribs to protect babies

The Book of Herbs and Magic — Heather Eaton

Herb	Incense	Oil	Bath	Other
Cyclamen	* Added to love incenses			* In the bedrooms protects the sleep and rejects spells * Grown around the house it protects * Carried for fertility
Eucalyptus	* Blue candles decorated with *Eucalyptus* leaves are lit to liberate healing vibrations * Stimulates spirituality	* Protects sleep * Stimulates spiritual healing * Is an excellent cleanser of negative energy		* Branches hung in the rooms of sick people help the healing process * Carried for protection
Eyebright	* In incenses helps in the development of the spirit and the psyche * Favors visions * Spiritual healer			* Carried to develop psychic abilities and uplift the spirit * A drink clears the mind and stimulates clairvoyance
Fenugreek	* Used as offering to the Gods * Stimulates clarity of thought		* Washing or rinsing the hair produces mental clarity * Destroys strange or negative thoughts sent by others	

Table of Herbs

Herb	Incense	Oil	Bath	Other
Flax	* Used in incenses for purification and protection, against the Evil Eye			* When carried it forms a protective shield that dissolves negative energy * Also carried to increase psychic powers
Frankincense	* Protects from the Evil Eye * It is a purifier and protector, a very powerful consecrator * Attracts love, success and spirituality	* Heals the effects negative energy * Purification and psychic development		* It is a vigorous protector * Carried to favor meditation and visions
Fumitory	* Used in incenses for purification and protection			* Sprayed around the house it attracts money
Gardenia	* Channels lunar energy and attracts the opposite sex * Added to incense potions for healing and protection	* Protects and prevents others from provoking unrest in ours lives * Attracts love and courage		* The flowers are carried to attract love and new friends and to stimulate spiritual healing * Grown it attracts good spirits

The Book of Herbs and Magic — Heather Eaton

Herb	Incense	Oil	Bath	Other
Garlic	* Keeps the money at home * Eliminates bad thoughts from the environment		* A bath rinse eliminates the Evil Eye (boil 20 cloves in a big pot of water for an hour and cool before using)	* Consumed to avoid nightmares * Carried it protects from the Evil Eye and attracts money * Hung on doors or windows it avoids envy, thieves and vampires
Geranium	* Red flowers are used in incenses for protection and healing and pink flowers are used in love incenses	* Protects and breaks spells * Stimulates physically and psychically * Attracts love * Reject misfortune and protects from it		* Flowers (especially the red and pink) are grown for protection * Carried in herbal sacks for love, to calm the mind and to stabilize emotions
Ginger	* It acts improving the effects most incenses	* Attracts friendship * Boosts energy and creates harmony * Induces passion		* Consumed for success * Carried for protection * Grown to attract money and success
Greater Burnet	* Used in incenses for purification and protection			* Carried for protection against deceits of others * Grown in the garden to prevent accidents and illnesses

Table of Herbs

Herb	Incense	Oil	Bath	Other
Gum Arabic	* Purifies a ceremonial room for rituals * Produces clairvoyance and stimulates psychic powers * Reverses curses	* Increases intuitive powers * Powerful psychic developer * Used for meditation		* Used as an amulet for protection * A branch under the bed or on the windows repels evil and protects during the night
Honeysuckle	* Dry flowers may be used in any almost incense destined to the success of businesses	* The oil helps create a favorable environment to clear up sticky situations * Increases psychic powers		* Green candles are decorated with the flowers and burned for money * The leaves are rubbed on the forehead for clairvoyance * Grown for luck
Horehound	* Used in incense potions to break charms and spells			* Used in herbal sacks to protect against negativity * Consumed to clear the mind and increase the mental powers
Hyacinth	* The incense is good to calm hyperactive people * Protects against nightmares	* Peace, harmony and tranquility * Meditation		* The scent of fresh flowers mitigates spiritual pain * Carried in herbal sacks for protection and to avoid nightmares

The Book of Herbs and Magic — Heather Eaton

Herb	Incense	Oil	Bath	Other
Hyssop	* Eliminates negative feelings, protects and purifies the soul	* Increases finances and attracts luck * Used for astral projections * Used for spiritual assistance	* Cleanses and purifies the soul assists in spiritual illumination * Protects and purifies	* Sprayed it purifies and cleans the environment from heavy vibrations * Carried for protection * Hung around the house to eliminate negative energy
Iris	* Used for love, burned when expecting visitors * Favors visions and prophetic dreams	* Attracts people of the opposite sex * Empowers crystals or tools for charms	* Improves and stabilizes communications and protects * Very powerful in love baths	* Sprayed to stimulate sincerity * The root is carried to attract love and protect from evil spirits
Jasmine	* Combats depression and stimulates optimism * Eliminates anguish and boosts self-confidence * Attracts good luck and good spirits	* Attracts good spirits, brings good luck, inspiration and neutralizes envy * Clears negative environments and stimulates clairvoyance * Stimulates fantasy		* The flowers are carried for luck and for love * Carried it attract spiritual love and inspire prophetic dreams * The scent of the flowers induces prophetic dreams * Used in rituals to increase personal charm
Juniper	* Used to scares away evil entities and avoid nightmares * Helps in psychic and spiritual development and purifies * Purifies people and places	* Used for love and protection * A cleanser of negative psychic energy		* Grown it protects against theft * The berries are carried to stimulate passion, protect from accidents and stimulate psychic powers * Carried to attract love

Table of Herbs

Herb	Incense	Oil	Bath	Other
Agrimony	* Eliminates fear		* Eliminates vibrations of fear	* Carried in herbal sacks for protection, to eliminate negative energy, to repel evil spirits and to break curses
Aloe Vera	* Spiritually healing		* Used to develop patience and to stimulate spiritual development	* Carried to stimulate passion and protect from accidents and malignant influences * Grown to repel evil and attract good luck
Amber	* It is a remedy for nervous maladies and is also used as an aphrodisiac	* Social success, good spiritual environment; favors luxury and comfort		* Its scent attracts those who wish to do big things
Angelica	* Protects and purifies * Burning the seeds produces clairvoyance and visions	* Stimulates energies necessary to contact angels and favors visions	* Eliminates curses and spells * Protects from the accumulation of negative influences	* Carried in necklaces or planted in the garden as protection * Smoking the leaves produces visions

The Book of Herbs and Magic — Heather Eaton

Herb	Incense	Oil	Bath	Other
Marjoram	* Eliminates negative thought forms and clears the environment of bad vibrations	* Helps restore the interior forces * Tranquilizes and stimulates		* Consumed for positive energy and to attract love * Carried to attract money and for psychic and spiritual development * Grown in the garden it protects from evil * Given in tea to depressed persons to cheer them up
Mastic	* Used in fumigations to empower extra-sensorial energies * Used in rituals to invoke spirits * Increases personal power			
Mate	* Astral cleanser		* Spiritual cleanser * Eliminates astral detritus and the Evil Eye	* In the pillows it reduces nocturnal psychic activity and reduces the influences of evil spirits * Carried to attract the opposite sex
Meadowsweet	* For love and peace, it generates very positive vibrations			* Flowers sprinkled around the house conserves the peace * Consumed in teas to increase psychic powers

Table of Herbs

Herb	Incense	Oil	Bath	Other
Mugwort	* Produces lucid dreams, protects and purifies * Used in incenses for clairvoyance and divinations	* Protects		* Carried or consumed for psychic and spiritual development * Under the bed it helps in astral projection * Placed in the shoes it prevents fatigue
Mullein	* Added to incenses for purification and protection			* Carried or hung in the windows for protection against the Evil Eye * Also carried to attract love * Under the pillow it avoids nightmares
Myrrh	* It favors visions and prophetic dreams, eliminates the Evil Eye and curses * Turns dreams into reality, attracts love and success * The smoke is used to consecrate rings, amulets and others.	* Rejects evil spirits and the Evil Eye * Protects friends * Used as an offering to dissipate evil * Induces prophetic dreams		* Together with *Frankincense* in herbal sacks it is carried as amulet for protection
Myrtle	* Increases sexual attraction and attracts spiritually positive influences	* Attracts money and good luck		* Carried or consumed it conserves youth * Added to herbal sacks for love * Grown to conserve youth and peace and love at home

The Book of Herbs and Magic — Heather Eaton

Herb	Incense	Oil	Bath	Other
Nutmeg	* Increases congeniality * Favors clairvoyance * Attracts love and luck	* Attracts good luck * Helps in meditation and personal spiritual equilibrium * Attracts the opposite sex	* Makes people listen, useful in interviews * Attracts luck and eliminates bad thoughts	* Rubbed on the forehead to receive messages * Consumed for protection and clairvoyance * Carried for protection
Orange	* The flowers are used in healing incenses	* For reaching objectives quickly * Favors concentration and creates a calm and quiet atmosphere * For luck and love	* The flowers are used in the bath to attract the opposite sex or to seduce a lover	* Sprayed it stimulates the mind and the emotions * The peel used in herbal sacks for love * An infusion of the flowers is consumed against the drunkenness
Parsley		* Calms the nerves * Attracts good luck	* Used for money problems (more effective when combined with *Cinnamon*) * Also used to end streaks of bad luck and to purify	* Sprayed it calms and protects * Consumed for spiritual purification, fertility and love * Carried to develop psychic powers and for protection * Used to decorate plates of food to eliminate poison
Patchouli	* Used for clairvoyance, divination and love * In the morning it generates energy and in the evening it stimulates sensuality and love	* Creates mental peace, harmony and protects * Used to bless objects * Awakens the desire to surpass limits and stimulates spiritual power	* Used to attract love	* Carried to attract love and passion, both in men and women

Table of Herbs

Herb	Incense	Oil	Bath	Other
Pennyroyal	* Used in healing incenses and summer incenses * Used to energize the body and calm the mind			* It is good for business * Placed in the shoes it prevents fatigue and repels the Evil Eye * When carried it forms a protective shield against the Evil Eye
Peppermint	* Aphrodisiac * Helps sleep and purifies the place * Burned to clean negative energy generated by illnesses	* Increases physical force * Attracts luck	* As a hair rinse it eliminates the Evil Eye	* Sprayed to stimulate the mind * Carried to develop psychic and spiritual powers * Under the pillow it induces prophetic dreams * Consumed to calm the mind and alleviate psychic tensions
Pokeweed				* Its root has a valuable astral influence
Rose	* *Rose* leaves are burned for clairvoyant dreams * Its scent inspires love, spiritual peace and calms the mind	* Used in rituals for artistic inspiration * Inspires love, peace, harmony and spiritual power * Sedative	* Love and sensuality	* Sprayed to purify and eliminate heavy vibrations * *Rose* buds are carried to attract love * Consumed for clairvoyance and to induce prophetic dreams

The Book of Herbs and Magic — Heather Eaton

Herb	Incense	Oil	Bath	Other
Rosemary	* Protects and purifies, rejecting bad vibrations * Awakens and increases the mental capacities * Used for protection, love and purification	* Vanquishes fear and gives courage * Protects and purifies * Predisposes realism, creativity, stability and love	* Conserves youth, good for concentration and eliminating bad vibrations * A hair rinse improves the memory and mental capacities * Protects against all harm	* Carried for love, protection and psychic development * Under the bed it induces happy dreams and alleviates stress
Rue	* Protects in general * Repels evil spirits * Stimulates virtue * Alerts to danger	* Breaks spells and protects from them * Forms a protective shield against bad vibrations	* In the bath it eliminates religious confusion * It illuminates the spiritual path to follow	* Sprayed or hung in the doors it eliminates negativity and produces calming spiritual vibrations * Carried for comfort and protection * Used to bless
Sage	* Used for healing and to finish projects with success	* It awakens curiosity for the new and unknown * Opens up horizons, used in divinations and astral projection	* Stimulates mental clarity * Helps gain authentic wisdom	* Sprayed for mental clarity and to form a protective shield * Consumed for wisdom and patience * Used in herbal sacks to assure a long life
Saint John's Wort	* One of the most powerful protection incenses * Neutralizes evil spirits			* Carried as protection against the Evil Eye and to attract love * Consumed for spiritual tranquility * Harvested on Saint John's Day it rejects evil * On crystal balls it helps in astral projection * The scent of the flowers stimulates psychic energy and lucid dreams

Table of Herbs

Herb	Incense	Oil	Bath	Other
Sandalwood	* Stimulates fantasy and awakens spiritual forces * Attracts love, success and good psychic vibrations * Relaxes the body and mind * Used with *Frankincense* for Lunar rituals * Used with *Benzoin* and *Mugwort* for astral projection	* Protects, calms and purifies the soul and empowers psychic equilibrium * Attracts luck and fortune * Stimulates fantasy * Invokes spirits of ancestors		* Mixed with *Lavender* it is excellent for invoking spirits * Sprinkled to cleanse of negative energy * Carried to develop spirituality
Snapdragon	* Used to break charms	* Breaks charms and frees personal fears	* Used to break charms and eliminate fears	* Carried as a protective amulet and to divine the intentions of others
Solomon's Seal	* Used for protection and purification * Burned to invoke spirits * Attracts love and success			* Carried in herbal sacks for protection * Sprayed around the house to repel evil and bad vibrations * Placed in the corners of the rooms protects from evil
Spikenard	* Mixed with *Sandalwood* it is excellent for business * Burned alone it attracts high spiritual vibrations	* Attracts spiritual qualities and blessings * Aphrodisiac * Stimulates psychic powers		* Carried to attract love and for good bussiness

The Book of Herbs and Magic

Herb	Incense	Oil	Bath	Other
Sweet Flag	* The powdered root is used in incenses for healing and to attract fortune and money			* In the kitchen protects from hunger and poverty * When grown it brings good luck to the gardener
Thyme	* Burned in small quantities for luck, purification and love		* Ritual baths are taken in spring to expand the psychic abilities * Eliminates negativity	* Consumed or carried to purify and activate psychic and spiritual abilities * Under the pillow it protects from nightmares * Grown for prosperity
Vervain	* Eliminates malicious or heavy thought forms * Used to purify and in love incenses	* Removes effects of Evil Eye * Predisposes creativity and has a leveling effect	* Used in ritual purifying and protection baths (very powerful)	* Sprayed it eliminates heavy vibrations and malicious thought forms * Carried to attract love and success * Under the bed it avoids nightmares * Grown for prosperity and to attract money
Wallflower	* Used to reveal the intentions of others * Stimulates psychic powers			

Table of Herbs

Herb	Incense	Oil	Bath	Other
Wormwood	* Eliminates the Evil Eye * Invokes good spirits * Increases psychic power, clairvoyance and predictions	*Do Not Use in Oils*		* Carried to increase psychic powers, for protection against the Evil Eye, spells and accidents
Yarrow	* Ideal for love and purification incenses	* Used as perfume to find a lover	* Used in the bath to find a lover	* Used in amulets for love, protection and to eliminate fear * Spraying stimulates love * Consumed to increase psychic powers

Bibliography

Agee, Doris, Edgar Cayce on ESP, Avenel, New Jersey, USA, Assoc. For Research and Enlightenment, Random House, 1969.
Agrippa, Henry Cornelius, The Philosophy of Natural Magic, Secaucus, New Jersey, USA, University Books, 1974.
Ashcroft-Nowicki, Dolores, Highways of the Mind, The Aquarian Press, 1987.

Baker, Douglas, Dr., The Opening of the Third Eye, Wellingborough, Northhamptonshire, England, Aquarian Press, 1986.
Blavatsky, H.P., Isis Unveiled, Pasadena, California, USA, Theosophical University Press, 1988.
Budge E.A., Wallis, The Egyptian Book of the Dead, (Papyrus of Ani) Egyptian Text Transliteration and Translation, New York, NY, USA, Dover Pub.
Buchland, Raymond, Practical Candle Burning Rituals, Saint Paul, MN, USA, Llewellyn Publications, 2004.
Butler, W.E., The Magician: His Training and Work, Melvin Powers Wilshire Book Co., North Hollywood, CA, USA, 1969.
Butler, W.E., How to Read the Aura, Practice Psychometry, Telepathy & Clairvoyance, Rochester, Vermont, USA, Destiny Books, 1987.

Calbot, Laurie, Power of the Witch, New York, NY, USA, Bantam Doubleday Dell Publishing Group, Inc. 1990.
Calais, Roger, Las Plantas y el Ocultismo, Barcelona, Spain, Ediciones Dalmau Socias.
Caland, Marianne and Patrick, El Uso Mágico y Espiritual de Las Velas, Madrid, Spain, Editorial EDAF, 1995.
Caland, Marianne and Patrick, El Uso Mágico y Espiritual de Inciensos y Sahumerios (Original Title: Weirook, Over Het Gebruik Invloed in Samenstelling), Madrid, Spain, Editorial EDAF, 1995.
Campbell, Eileen and Brennan, JH, Dictionary of Mind, Body & Spirit, Hammersmith, London, England, Aquarian Press, 1990.
Caradeau, J. L., El Gran Libro de las Velas y Candelas, Ediciones Robinbook SL.,1997.
Castleman, Michael, Hierbas Curativas (Original Title: The Healing Herbs), Rodale Press, USA, 1994.

Cayce, Hugh Lynn, The Edgar Cayce Collection, Avenel, NJ, USA, Wings Books, 1969.
Conway, D.J., Celtic Magic, St. Paul MN, USA, Llewellyn Publications, 1993.
Conway, D.J., Magic of Gods and Goddesses, St. Paul MN, USA, Llewellyn Publications, 1996.
Cunningham, Donna, An Astrological Guide to Self-Awareness, Vancouver, WA, USA, CRCS Publications, 1978.
Cunnigham, Scott, Cunnigham's Encyclopedia of Crystal, Gem & Metal Magic, St. Paul, MN, USA, Llewellyn Publications, 1994.
Cunnigham, Scott, Cunnigham's The Complete Book of Incense, Oils & Brews, St. Paul, MN, USA, Llewellyn Publications, 2000.
Cunnigham, Scott, Earth, Air, Fire and Water, St. Paul, MN, USA, Llewellyn Publications, 1997.
Cunnigham, Scott, Enciclopedia de las Hierbas Mágicas (Original Title: Cunningham's Encyclopedia of Magical Herbs), St. Paul, MN, USA, Llewellyn Publications, 1995.
Cunnigham, Scott, Magical Aromatherapy, St. Paul, MN, USA Llewellyn's New World of Mind and Spirit, ,1989.
Cunnigham, Scott and Harrinton, David Spell Crafts, Creating Magical Objects, St. Paul, MN, USA, Llewellyn Publications, 1997.
Currot, Phyllis, Book of Shadows, New York, NY, USA, Broadway Books, 1999.

Dalichow, Irene and Booth, Mike, Aura-Soma, Aribau, Barcelona, Spain, Ediciones Uranus S.A., 1997.
Davidson, Gustav, A Dictionary of Angels, New York, NY, USA, The Free Press, 1967.
De Tervagne, Simone, Los Poderes Mágicos de las Joyas (Original Title: Le Collier Magnifique), Barcelona, Spain, Ediciones Martínez Roca, 1994.
Denning and Phillips, The Development of Psychic Powers, St. Paul, MN, USA, Llewellyn Publications, 1997.
Dobelis, Inge N., et.al, Magic and Medicine of Plants, USA, The Reader's Digest Association, Inc., 1986.
Doring Kindersley Ltd, Success with House Plants, USA, The Reader's Digest Association, Inc., 1987.
Doyle, Arthur Conan, The History of Spiritualism, New York, NY, USA, Arno Press, 1975.
Du Bois, Fils, Los Inciensos y Su Magia, Grupo Editorial Tomo S.A., Mexico, 1998.

E
Eaton, Heather, The Encyclopedia of the Divine, Spiritual and Occult, Portland, OR, USA, One Spirit Press, 2012.
Encyclopaedia Britannica, printed by Encyclopaedia Britannica, Inc., USA, 1972.
Enciclopedia Planeta, Santa Perpétua de Mogoda, Spain, Editorial Planeta, Cayfo, S.A. 1984.
Encarta 99, USA, Enciclopedia Multimedia, Microsoft Windows, Microsoft Corporation, 1998.

Bibliography

Fortune, Dion, Aspects of Occultism, London, England, The Aquarian Press, 1962.
Fortune, Dion, Esoteric Orders and Their Work, York Beach, ME, USA, Samuel Weiser, Inc. 2000.
Fortune, Dion, Psychic Self Defense, York Beach, ME, USA, Samuel Weiser, Inc. 1993.
Fortune, Dion, The Esoteric Philosophy of Love and Marriage, London, England, The Aquarian Press, 1974.
Fortune, Dion, The Training and Work of an Initiate, Wellingborough, Northhamptonshire, England, Aquarian Press, 1982.
Fortune, Dion, The Cosmic Doctrine, London, England, The Aquarian Press, 1988.
Fortune, Dion, What is Occultism, York Beach, ME, USA, Samuel Weiser, Inc., 2001.
Frédérick, Robert, Sensibilidad y Psiquismo, (Original Title: L'Intelligence des Plantes), Barcelona, Spain, Ediciones Marzo 80, 1985.

Garret, Eileen J., Many Voices: The Autobiography of a Medium, New York, NY, USA, Del Publishing Co., 1969.
Garret, Robert, La Magia de Los Cristales, Madrid, Spain, M.E. Editoriales S.L.
Gaynor, Frank, Dictionary of Mysticism, New York, NY, USA, Philosophical Library, 1953.
Green, Marian, Magic for the Aquarian Age, Wellingborough, Northhamptonshire, England, The Aquarian Press, 1986.
Greer, John Michael, The New Encyclopedia of the Occult, St. Paul, MN, USA, Llewellyn Publications, 2004.

Hawken, Paul, The Magic of Findhorn: An Eyewitness Account, New York, NY, USA, Bantam Books, 1976.
Hodali H. Salim, et.al, Maestros Espirituales, Santiago de Chile, Chile, Editorial Grijalbo, S.A., 2000.
Howard, Michael, Finding Your Guardian Angel, Through Incense & Candle Burning, San Francisco, California, USA, Thorsons, 1996.
Hoffman, A. et. al, Plantas Medicinales de Uso Común en Chile, Santiago de Chile, Chile, Ediciones Fundación Claudio Gay, 1989.

Kingston, Karen, Creating Sacred Space With Feng Shui, New York, NY, USA, Broadway Books, 1996.
Kowalchik, Claire and William H. Hylton, Rodale's Illustrated Encyclopedia of Herbs, USA, Rodale Press, 1998.

L

Leadbeater, C.W., How Theosophy Came to Me, Wheaton, IL, USA, The Theosophical Publishing House, 1930.

Leadbeater, C.W., Man Visible and Invisible, Wheaton, IL, USA, The Theosophical Publishing House, 1969.

Leadbeater, C.W., The Chakras, Wheaton, IL, USA, The Theosophical Publishing House, 1987.

Leadbeater, C.W., The Masters and The Path, Chicago, IL, USA, The American Theosophical Society, 1925.

Leek, Sybil, Diary of a Witch: The Private Life of One of the World's Most Famous and Colorful Psychics, New York, NY, USA, Signet Classics, 1969.

Levi, Eliphas, The History of Magic: Including a Clear & Precise Exposition of Its Procedure, Its Rites and... Los Angeles, CA, USA, Borden Pub. Co.

Linn, Denise, Quest: A Guide for Creating Your Own Vision Quest, New York, NY, USA, The Ballentine Publishing Group, 1997.

M

Malbrough, Ray T., Conjuros, Hechizos y Formulas, (Original Title: Charms, Spells & Formulas), Madrid, Spain, Tecnología Gráfica S.A., 1988.

Manning, Al. G., Ayúdese con la Magia Blanca, (Original Title: Helping Yourself with White Witchcraft), Spain, Editorial Diana, 1976.

Masters, Robert, The Goddess Sekhmet: Psycho-Spiritual Exercises of the Fifth Way, St. Paul, MN, USA, Llewellyn Pub., 1991.

Matthews, Catilín, The Celtic Tradition, Rockport, MA, USA, Elements Books Inc. 1992.

Matthews, Catilín, The Elements of the Goddess, Dorset, England, Elements Books Inc. Longmead, Shaftesbury, 1989.

Matthews, Catilín and John, The Encyclopaedia of Celtic Wisdom, Rockport, MA, USA, Elements Books, Inc. 1996.

Matthews, John, The Grail Tradition, Longmead, Shaftesbury, Dorset, England, Elements Books Inc., 1990.

Mickaharic, Draja, Proteccion Espiritual, (Original Title: Spiritual Cleansing), Madrid, Spain, Editorial EDAF, 1990.

Mickaharic, Draja, Manual de Modernos Hechizos, (Original Title: A Century of Spells), Madrid, Spain, Editorial EDAF, 1989.

Monroe, Robert, Journeys Out of the Body, New York, NY, USA, Doubleday, 1971.

Monroe, Robert, Ultimate Journey, New York, NY, USA, Doubleday, 1994.

Moine, Michele and Degaudenzi, Jean-Louise, Manual de Experimentos Geobiológicos (Original Title: Guide of Géobiologie), Constitution, Barcelona, Spain, Libergraf, 1991.

Morrison, Sarah Lyddon, Recetario de la Bruja Moderna, (Original Title; The Modern Witch's Spellbook), Madrid, Spain, Editorial EDAF, 1992.

Bibliography

O'Hara, Gwydion, The Magick of Aromatherapy, St. Paul, MN, USA, Llewellyn Publications, 1998.

Oxford, The New Oxford Annotated Bible: With the Apocrypha, New York, NY, USA, Oxford University Press Inc., 1973.

Peale, Norman Vincent, Power of the Plus Factor, New York, NY, USA, Ballentine Books, 1987.

Peterson, Robert, Out of Body Experiences: How to Have Them & What to Expect, Charlottesville, VA, USA, Hampton Roads Publishing Co. Inc., 1997.

Picknett, Lynn and Prince, Clive, The Templar Revelation: Secret Guardians of the True Identity of Christ, New York, NY, USA, Touchstone, 1998.

Piper, Don, 90 Minutes in Heaven – A True Story of Death and Life, Grand Rapids, MI, USA, Touchstone, 2004.

RavenWolf, Silver, To Stir a Magick Cauldron: A Witch's Guide to Casting & Conjuring, St. Paul, MN, USA, Llewellyn Publications, 2000.

RavenWolf, Silver, To Ride a Silver Broomstick: New Generation Witchcraft, St. Paul, MN, USA, Llewellyn Pub., 2000.

Reader's Digest, Family Guide to Natural Medicine – How to Stay Healthy the Natural Way, Pleasantville, NY, USA, The Reader's Digest Association, Inc., 1993.

Reader's Digest, Magic and Medicine of Plants, Pleasantville, NY, USA, The Reader's Digest Association, Inc., 1996.

Reid, Lori, The Dream Catcher, Singapore, Barnes & Noble, 1997.

Regardie, Israel The Complete Golden Dawn System of Magic, Phoenix, Arizona, USA, Falcon Press, 1984.

Regardie, Israel The Tree of Life, St. Paul, MN, USA, Llewellyn Publications, 2002.

Riviere, Jean, Amuletos, Talismanes y Pantáculos, (Original Title: Amulettes, Talismans et Pantacles), Barcelona, Spain, Ediciones Martínez Roca S.A., 1974.

Scheffer, Mechthild, Manual Práctico de la Terapia Floral de Bach, (Original Title: Selbstilfe durch Bach-Blütentherapie), Barcelona, Spain, Ediciones Uranus, S.A., 1997.

Sechrist, Elsie, Edgar Cayce, Dreams: Your Magic Mirror, New York, NY, USA, Warner Books, 1988.

Stone, Robert B., La Magia del Poder Psicotrónico, (Original Title: The Magic of Psychotronic), Madrid, Spain, Editorial EDAF, S.A., 1997.

Telesco, Patricia, Your Book of Shadows, Secaucus, NJ, USA, Carol Publishing Group, 1999.
The Holy Bible, King James Version, Light of the World Edition, Co., USA, The World Publishing, 1954.
Thies, Barbara and Peter, Plantas Medicinales en Casa (Original Title; Gesünder leben mit Heilkräutern), Barcelona, Spain, Cayfosa Sta. Perpetua de Mogoda, 1991.
Thompson, Janet, Magia Blanca en el Hogar, (Original Title: Magical Herat: Home for Modern Pagan), Spain, Artes Gráficas COFÄS, S.A., 1995.
Tomkins, Peter, The Secret Life of Plants, New York, NY, USA, Avon Books, 1973.

Underhill, Evelyn, Practical Mysticism: A Little Book for Normal People and Abba: Meditations Based.., New York, NY, USA, Vintage Books, 2003.

Van Gelder Kuntz, Dora, El Aura, (Original Title: The Aura), Barcelona, Spain, Ediciones Martínez Roca, S.A., 1992.
Vinci, Leo, Magia de las Velas, (Original Title: The Book of Practical Candle Magic), Madrid, Spain, Ediciones EDAF, 1983.

Webster's Encyclopedic Unabridged Dictionary of the English Language, New York, NY, USA, Random House Value Publishing Inc, 1996.
Whitmont, Edward C., Return of The Goddess, New York, NY, USA, The Crossroad Publishing Co., 1984.

Webliography

A

acourseinlight.com — A Course in Light – A Spiritual Path for Enlightenment
ahistoryofgreece.com — History of Greece
alchemylab.com — Alchemy Laboratory
alchemyofabundance.wordpress.com — Alchemy of Abundance
altavista.com — Altavista – Search Engine
americanmeditation.org — American Meditation Institute for Yoga, Science and Philosophy
amorc.org — Ancient Mystical Order Rosae Crusis - Rosicrucian
ancientegypt.co.uk — Ancient Egypt – The British Museum
ancientlibrary.com — Ancient Library
angelsghosts.com — Angels and Ghosts
annmourasgarden.com — Ann Moura's Garden – Wicca Dictionary
answers.com — Answers – Search Engine
aoda.com — Ancient Order of Druids in America
aol.com — America on Line – Search Engine
a-rainbow-of-spirituality.org — A Rainbow of Spirituality – Spiritual and Healing Information from all Pagan Paths
archaeonia.com — Religion and History
archangels-and-angels.com — Archangels and Angels
aromatherapy.com — Aromatherapy
aromaticplantproject.com — Aromatic Plant Project – Jeanne Rose
aromaweb.com — Aromatherapy and Essential Oils
asdreams.org — International Association for the Study of Dreams
asiya.org — Asiya's Shadow – Magick Informational Resources - Wicca
ask.com — Ask – Search Engine
aspr.com — American Society for Psychic Research
ascension-research.org — Ascension Research – Guy Ballard
astraldynamics.com — Astral Dynamics – A Little Light from Down Under – Astral Projection
astralvoyage.com — Astral Projection and Spirituality
astro.com — Astrology and Horoscope
astrocenter.com — Astro Center – Horoscope and Astrology
astrologers.com — American Federation of Astrologers
astrologicalgem.com — Astrological Gems - Jyotish Gemstones and Their Associated Planets
astrology.com — Astrology
astrology-numerology.com — Astrology and Numerology
astronautix.com — Encyclopedia Astronautica
astrorelocation.com — Astrocartography and Relocation Astrology

astro-software.com — Astrological Birth Charts
avalontraditions.com — Avalon Traditions – Wicca and Pagan
awakeningspirit.com — Awakening Spirit – Aromatherapy and Herbal Products
ayahuasca.com — Amazonian Great Medicine

beliefnet.com — Belief Net – Inspiration, Spirituality, Faith, Religion
beloit.edu — Beloit College
berkeley.edu — University of California Berkeley
berkshirehistory.com — Royal County of Berkshire History
bibliotecapleyades.net — Biblioteca Pleyades (site in Spanish) - Library
bing.com — Bing – Search Engine
bluffton.edu — Bluffton University
brown.edu — Brown University
bulfinch.englishatheist.org — Bulfinch's Mythology – Stories of Gods and Goddesses, Heroes and ..

cayce.com — Edgar Cayce – Health and Research Information
celticspirit.org — Chalice Center for Celtic and Western Magical Traditions – Mara Freeman
celtic-twilight.com — Celtic Twilight – Compendium of Celtic and King Arthur Legends and Resources
centerforsacredsciences.org — Center for Sacred Sciences – Exploring Mystical Traditions and Religions
chakraenergy.com — Chakra Energy - Chakras
columbia.edu — Columbia University
consciousness.arizona.edu — Center for Consciousness Studies
controverscial.com — Controversial – Wicca - Carl Llewellyn Weschcke
crcsite.org — The Rosicrucian Archive - Library
crystalinks.com — Crystal Links – Metaphysical and Science Website

daly-health.com — Daly Health – Therapy for Geopathic, Electromagnetic, Stress, Personal, ..
dimensionconnection.com — Dimension Connection – Psychic, Readings, Healing, Reiki, …
distancehealing.net — Quantum Distance Healing
divine-light-healing.com — Divine Light Healing
dowsers.com — Spiritual Dowsing and the Blessing Process
dowsers.org — American Society of Dowsers
dreamcatcher.com — Dream Catcher
dreamviews.com — Dream Views – Lucid Dreaming
druidnetwork.org — The Druid Network

Webliography

druidry.org   The Order of Bards, Ovates and Druids

E

edgarcayce.org   Edgar Cayce – Association of Research and Enlightenment
egyptianculture.net   Ancient Egyptian Mythology
egyptianmuseum.gov.eg   Egyptian Museum
egyptianmyths.net   Ancient Egypt: The Mythology
egyptpyramidhistory.com   Egypt – Pyramids - History
eldritchmaven.co.uk   The Healing Temple
elevatedtherapy.org.uk   Elevated Therapy – Akashic Records
emory.edu   Emory University
enchantedspirit.org   Enchanted Spirit - Metaphysical Resource Center
energyresearch.bizland.com   Energy Research – James Oschman
enlightened-spirituality.org   Enlightened Spirituality – Spiritual Awakening
enlightenment.com   Enlightenment
entheology.org   Entheology – Preserving Ancient Sacred Knowledge
eomega.org   Omega Institute – Personal Growth in Mind, Body, Spirit
espresearch.com   Remote Viewing and Spiritual Healing – Russell Targ
esotericgoldendawn.com   Esoteric Order of The Golden Dawn
esotericscience.org   Esoteric Science – Integrating Science and Spirituality
explorations-in-consciousness.com   Explorations in Consciousness – Out of Body Experiences, Lucid Dreams and Altered States
extrasensory-perceptions-guide.com   Extrasensory Perceptions Guide

F

flowerreadings.com   Design and Color as a Healing Art – Suzy Chiazzari
fmbr.org   Foundation for Mind Being Research

G

gems4friends.com   Gems for Friends - Alternative Medicine, Health and Healing
geomantica.com   Geomantica – Geomancy and Dowsing
geometrycode.com   The Geometry Code – Symbolic Wisdom of Natural Laws Within Us
georgiasouthern.edu   Georgia Southern University
georgetown.edu   Georgetown University
ghosthuntingsecrets.com   Ghost Hunting Secrets
ghostresearch.org   Ghost Research
globalspirit.org   World Commission on Global Consciousness and Spirituality
gnosis.org   The Gnosis Archive – Resources of Gnosticism and Gnostic Tradition w/ Library
gods-heros-myth.com   Gods, Heroes and Myth
golden-dawn.org   Hermetic Order of the Golden Dawn
google.com   Google - Search Engine

H

harvardsquarelibrary.org   Harvard Square Library
healingdeva.com   Alternative Therapies – Healing the Mind, Body and Spirit
hermetic.com   The Hermetic Library
hermeticgoldendawn.com   Hermetic Golden Dawn
holisticonline.com   Alternative Holistic Medicine
holybible.com   The Holy Bible
horoscope.com   Horoscope
how-to-meditate.org   How to Meditate - Guided Meditation Techniques - Buddhist Meditations
huna.com   Ancient Hawaiian Magical Shamanism and Healing
hyperdictionary.com   Hyperdictionary – Online Dictionary

 ## I

innerself.com   Inner Self – New Attitudes New Possibilities
insearchofspirit.com   In Search of Spirit – Philosophy of Spiritualism and Spirit Healing
insightjourneys.com   Insight Journeys – Mysteries and Science – Explore the Connection
institutespiritualsciences.org   The Institute of Spiritual Sciences – Expansion of Consciousness
invisibletemple.com   Invisible Temple – Sacred Sites, Sacred Places – Freddy Silva
ishk.com   Institute for the Study of Human Knowledge
issseem.org   The International Society for the Study of Subtle Energies and Energy Medicine
itp.edu   Institute of Transpersonal Psychology
iups.edu   International University of Professional Studies

 ## K

kineticchromotherapy.com   Kinetic Chromotherapy
kirlian.com   Kirlian – Energy - Aura Photography
kirlian.org   Kirlian Photography – Energy Works
knowledgefiles.com   Esoteric Orders
kundalininet.org   Kundalini Research Network

 ## L

laskow.net   Healing with Love – Leonard Laskow
law-of-attraction-info.com   Law of Attraction
learningmeditation.com   Learning Meditation
lib.byu.edu   Harold B. Lee Library
lightplanet.com   Light Planet – World Religion
lightworkers.org   Lightworker's Spiritual Social Network
llewellynencyclopedia.com   Llewellyn Encyclopedia

Webliography

M

manataka.org — American Indian Council
medicinewheel.com — Medicine Wheel – Native American Spirituality
metaphysics.com — University of Metaphysics
meta-religion.com — Multidisciplinary View of the Religious, Spiritual and Esoteric Phenomena
mother-god.com — A Chapel of Our Mother God – Goddess Mythology
mysteriousbritain.co.uk — Mysterious Britain and Ireland – Mysteries, Legends & the Paranormal
mysteriouspeople.com — Mysterious People – Strange Powers, Poltergeist Girls, Psychics, Occultists, Feral Children
mystic.wikia.com — Mystic Wikia – Wikia Philosophy - Encyclopedia
mysticvoodoo.com — Mystic Voodoo
mythencyclopedia.com — Myth Encyclopedia
mythinglinks.org — Myth*ing Links – Mythology, Fairy Tales and Folklore

N

nag-hammadi.com — Nag Hammadi Library
nativeremedies.com — Native Remedies
naturalcures.com — Natural Cures
natures-blessings.org — Natures Blessings – Healing – Distant Healing - Energy
natures-energies.com — Natures Energies – Discover the Secrets of Feng Shui, Flower Essences, Gem Essences, Protection
new-age-spirituality.com — New Age Spirituality - Spiritualism, Psychic Powers, Paranormal
newenergymovement.org — The New Energy Movement – Brian O'Leary
noetic.org — The Institute for Noetic Sciences – Edgar Mitchell
numii.net — Numii – Serving the Spiritual Search - Living Knowledge Base for Spirituality

O

occultopedia.com — Occultopedia - The Occult and Unexplained Encyclopedia
odinsvolk.ca — Odin's Volk Asatru – Spiritual and Cultural Organization – Nordic and Germanic
ofspirit.com — Of Spirit – Healing the Body, Mind and Spirit
ofspiritandsoul.com — Of Spirit and Soul
omsakthi.org — Om Sakthi – Spiritual Movement – World Religions
onegreatspirit.com — One Great Spirit – Universal Transformative Spirituality
ourdreamingmind.net — Our Dreaming Mind - Dreams
outofthedark.com — Out of the Dark - Wicca - Paganism

P

pagannews.com — Pagan News and Information
paleothea.com — Women in Greek Myths - Mythology

pantheon.org   Encyclopedia Mythica - Mythology
paranormalawarenesssociety.org   Paranormal Awareness Society
paranormal-encyclopedia.com   Paranormal Encyclopedia
paranormalhelp.com   Life Foundation – Paranormal Help
paranormalplus.com   Paranormal Plus
paranormality.com   Paranormality – A to Z of the Paranormal
parapsych.org   Parapsychological Association
parapsychologylab.com   American Institute of Parapsychology
personaltransformation.com   Personal Transformation – Inner Peace and Spiritual Awakening
philosophyprofessor.com   Philosophy Professor – A Dictionary of Philosophy and Philosophers
planetlightworker.com   Planet Lightworker Magazine
powerlawofattraction.com   Power Law of Attraction
power-of-imagination.com   Power of Imagination – Law of Attraction, Visualization, Meditation
probertencyclopaedia.com   Probert Encyclopaedia
psychic-experiences.com   Psychic Experiences
psychicinvestigators.net   Psychic Investigators into the Paranormal
psychics.co.uk   Psychics and Mediums Network
psychicscience.org   Psychic Science – Glossary of Terms in Parapsychology
psychicvista.com   Intuitive and Psychic Consultants
psychotherapy.net   Online Psychotherapy Magazine

religionfacts.com   Religious Facts – Just the Facts of Religion
religioustolerance.com   Religious Tolerance
renaissanceastrology.com   Renaissance Astrology
rhine.org   The Rhine Research Center – Parapsychology – Joseph Banks Rhine
rolfgordon.co.uk   Geopathic Stress

S

sapphyr.net   Pearls of Wisdom – Awakening Personal and Global Consciousness
selfgrowth.com   Self Growth – Online Self Improvement Encyclopedia – Carlos Warter
self-healing.org   School for Self-Healing – Meir Schneider
selftransform.net   Center for Self Transformation – Universal Ascension
servantsofthelight.org   Servants of the Light School of Occult Sciences
shamaniccenter.org   The Shamanic Center
shee-eire.com   Shee Eire – Irish Pagan Culture and Mythology
shiftinaction.com   Shift in Action – Institute of Noetic Sciences
sil.si.edu   Smithsonian Institution Libraries
sisterhoodofavalon.org   The Sisterhood of Avalon – Celtic Women's Mysteries Org. –

Webliography

Welsh Goddesses
soulfulliving.com   Soulful Living – Personal Growth, Spiritual Growth, Self Help and Self Improvement - Magazine
spaceclearing.com   Space Clearing – Feng Shui – Karen Kingston
spep.org   Society for Phenomenology and Existential Philosophy
spirit-medium.com   Spirit – Medium - Spiritual Dictionary
spiritofmaat.com   Spirit of Maat - Spirituality, Human Potential, and New Science
spiritsite.com   Spirit Site – Spirituality and Psychology Resource Site
spiritual-endeavors.org   Spiritual Endeavors - Spiritual, Holistic and Environmental Awareness
spiritual-experiences.com   Spiritual Experiences and Spirituality
spiritualists.org   Psychic and Mediums Network – Ghosts and Spirits of Spiritualism
spiritualityandpractice.com   Spirituality and Practice – Resources for Spiritual Journeys
spirituality-health.com   Spirituality and Health Magazine
spiritualnow.com   Spiritual Now – Your Guide to Spiritual Enlightenment
spiritualresearchfoundation.org   Spiritual Science Research Foundation
spr.ac.uk   Society for Psychical Research
stanford.edu   Stanford University
stregheria.com   Stregheria – The Home of the Authentic Italian Witchcraft
stillpointca.org   Stillpoint – The Center for Christian Spirituality
strangemag.com   Strange Magazine – Investigating Strange Phenomena - Magazine
successconsciousness.com   Success Consciousness – Awakening the Wisdom and Power in You
surnateum.org   Museum of Supernatural History
syr.edu   Syracuse University

T

templarhistory.com   Templar History - A History and Mythos of the Knights Templar
temple.edu/cfs   Center for Frontier Sciences at Temple University
theartofastralprojection.com   The Art of Astral Projection
theassc.org   Association for Scientific Study of Consciousness
theenigmagroup.com   The Enigma Group – Paranormal Investigations - Zachary Miller
thefreedictionary.com   The Free Dictionary
thegeomancer.netfirms.com   The Geomancer – Feng Shui, Geomancy and Chinese Numerology
thegoddessnetwork.net   The Goddess Network – Charlene Proctor
thehealingmind.org   The Healing Mind – The Power of Self Healing - Martin Rossman
thehermitsgrove.org   The Hermit's Grove – Paul Beyerl
themastersofattraction.com   The Masters of Attraction – Law of Attraction
themetaarts.com   The Meta Arts – The Magazine for the Metaphysical, Spiritual & Healing Communities
themystica.com   The Mystica - Encyclopedia
theoi.com   Theoi Greek Mythology

theologywebsite.com   Theology Website
theologyonline.com   Theology Online
theosophical.org   The Theosophical Society
theosophy.org   Theosophy Library Online
thepsychictimes.com   The Psychic Times – News Magazine
therapeutictouch.org   Therapeutic Touch – Dolores Krieger and Dora Kunz
thereconnection.com   The Reconnection – Heal Others, Heal Yourself - Eric Pearl
thespiritseekers.org   Spirit Seekers Paranormal Investigation Research and Intervention Team (SPIRIT)
thevisionandthevoice.com   The Vision and the Voice - Assisting in the Birth of the New Earth
timelessmyths.com   Timeless Myths – Greek, Roman, Norse, Celtic and Arthurian Legends
tm.org   Transcendental Meditation
truthseekingsouls.com   Truth Seeking Souls – New Thought, Spirituality, Metaphysics
tylwytheg.com   Witchcraft and Wicca with Welsh Paganism

unexplained-mysteries.com   Unexplained Mysteries – Paranormal Phenomena
unexplainedstuff.com   Encyclopedia of the Unusual and Unexplained
utexas.edu   University of Texas
uwm.edu   University of Wisconsin

wakeuplaughing.com   Wake Up Laughing - Steve Bhaerman
weare1.us   Esoteric Anatomy, Energy Healing, Energy Healer
weavings.co.uk   Weavings – Pagan Online Community
wholenesstherapy.com   Wholeness Therapy Website – Healing the Mind, Body and Spirit Together
wholistichealingresearch.com   Wholistic Healing Research – Daniel Benor
wicca.com   Wicca – The Celtic Connection
wicca.org   Wicca – Church and School of Wicca
wicca.dianic-wicca.com   Dianic University Online – Zsuzsanna Budapest
wikipedia.org   Wikipedia - Encyclopedia
wisn.org   Worldwide Indigenous Science Network
wisdomhunter.com   Wisdom Hunter - Books on Personal Development, Spirituality and Consciousness
wisdomuniversity.org   Wisdom University – Graduate Studies with World Renowned Leaders
witchcraftandwitches.com   Witchcraft and Witches
worldcat.org   WorldCat – The World's Largest Library Catalog
worldhistory.com   World History
world-mysteries.com   World Mysteries – Lost Civilizations, Ancient Ruins, Sacred Writings, Unexplained Artifacts, and Science Mysteries

worldwisdom.com   World Wisdom – Perennial Philosophy and the Worlds Great Spiritual Traditions

yahoo.com   Yahoo - Search Engine
yraceburu.org   Earth Wisdom – Maria Yraceburu

zodiac-signs-astrology.com   Zodiac Signs Astrology

0-9

0800-horoscope.com   Horoscope
4qf.org Four Quarters – An Inter Faith Sanctuary of Earth Religion

Glossary

Affirmation– is described as a statement frequently repeated to produce positive changes in oneself and one's environment.

Alchemy– originates from the Arabic phrase Al-kimia, meaning the "'Art of Egypt", although its roots are much older. The Chinese were practicing alchemy as early as 3,500 B.C.E and it is said that the people of Atlantis where the first to learn the art. The concepts of alchemy from the Aristotelian doctrine are consistent with the Theosophical, Esoteric, Qabbalistic and Occultist beliefs in spiritual evolution; that all things are on a path of evolution towards perfection. Practical alchemy refers to transforming a base material into a higher and more purified substance, such as lead into gold or the extraction of a purer medicinal substance from a plant to create a healing elixir. The Esoteric and Theosophical side refers to a system of spiritual development, a process of transformation, discipline and purification of turning something of low spiritual value into something with a high spiritual value, as "evolution" or "transmutation" of human beings; to the hastening of man's spiritual evolution towards God.

Altar– in most religions, Occultism, Wicca and other Pagan traditions the altar is the center of magical practices and can be described as a simple flat surface where magical tools and symbols are placed during rituals. In religion, an altar is described as a raised structure or place that is used for prayer, sacrifice or worship. The Greeks built altars at the entrances and in the courtyards of their houses, in public buildings and marketplaces, and in sacred groves outside the cities. When Christianity began to build Churches and altars, the remains of martyrs were customarily buried beneath them. Today the Roman Catholic Church uses the altar to hold a copy of the Bible and consecrated bread and wine.

Amen– is an expression of confirmation or agreement used in religious worship by Muslims, Christians and Jews, Amen is usually translated to mean "so be it". An orator who closes his speech with Amen is summing up and confirming what was said and is offering a prayer of thanksgiving. According to Occultists, Amen is a mystical word meaning "concealed".

Amulet– as passive magical empowered objects, amulets are used to deflect negative energy and carried to ward off evil, illness or misfortune, and to bring good fortune and health. Amulets are used as defense against black magic, the evil eye, and curses. Gems and semi-precious stones are commonly used as amulets but herbs as well as rabbit tails, animal teeth and bones are also used. The Egyptians used ritual formulas recited to empower their amulets, such as the Ankh and the Eye of Horus. Christians use amulets in the form of Saints or crucifixes that are blessed by priests or religious authorities. Traditionally Muslims carry verses of the Qur'an as protective amulets.

Angel– comes from Sanskrit Anigiras meaning a "divine spirit"; Persian Angaros, meaning "a courier" and Greek Angelos, meaning "a messenger." Angels are described in Judaism, Islam, Zoroastrianism, and Christianity as benevolent spiritual beings. Referred to in the Old Testament as the Company of Divine Beings and the Hosts of Heaven, the Bible describes Angels as messengers, whose function is to mediate between the divine and the human. According to Occult philosophy, an Angel is a superior being or entity within the divine hierarchy who has never incarnated in human form but who rather chose to assist humankind in their spiritual evolution from their own plane of existence. Each Angel has specific ruties and jurisdictions, ranging from simply delivering messages to being guardians over persons, places and even nations, and other heavenly duties. They are also called Sons of Twilight. In Occultism and Christian literature there are nine choirs of Angels:

> Archangels, described in Judaism, Christianity, Islam and Occultism as powerful Angels in the divine hierarchy who govern Choirs or Groups of Angels. They are said to be on a different evolutionary tract than humans but intrinsically related to us and our spiritual evolution. Archangels are one of the nine choirs of Angels in Heaven. They are also called Fire Spirits. The main Archangels are: Michael, Gabriel, Raphael and Uriel.
>
> Cherubim are described as God's highest angelic potencies, second only to the Seraphim, and the first Angels mentioned in the Old Testament. In Occultism, Cherubim are described as the charioteers of God, the Bearers of His Throne and personifications of the wind. Cherubim are also described in the Talmud as the order Ophanim (wheels or chariots), or the order Hayyoth (Holy beasts) who reside in the 6th or 7th Heaven.
>
> The singular form of Cherubim is Cherub. Jewish traditions describe Cherubim as handsome men but in modern Christianity they are described as beautiful infants with wings. Other spellings include Kerubim.
>
> Dominations– also called Dominions, they are also called Lords, Lordships, Principalities and Powers. The Dominations are described as having the duty of "Regulating the Angels". They are also called Spirits of Wisdom.
>
> Powers– have as their principle task is to see that there is order on the celestial pathways between Heaven and Earth. The Powers are also called Potentates, Dynamis and Authorities. They are also called Spirits in Form.
>
> Principalities– are the protectors of religion and watch over the leaders of nations and people, inspiring them to make the right choices and decisions. The Principalities are also called   Princedoms.
>
> Seraphim– from Hebrew meaning "The Flaming Ones", "The Fiery Ones", or "The Burning Ones". They are described as the Angelic host of Geburah and the highest order of Angels in the hierarchic scheme. In Judaism, Christianity and Islam, Seraphim are described as the celestial beings who serve as throne guardians of God. Seraphim are said to unceasingly chant "Holy, Holy, Holy…" and exist off the love emanated from God. They are also described in the Old Testament as six-winged, four-faced celestial creatures who praise God. The singular of Seraphim is Seraph. Seraphim are the first and foremost of the Angels.

Glossary

Thrones– also known as Ophnim. They are Angels who deliver and dispense God's justice to humans and who act as God's chariot. They are also called Many-Eyed-Ones and the Chariots.

Virtues– are described in Christianity as seven Angels, the Virtues relate to fundamental Christian ethics. There are seven Virtues, the first four relating to "Natural" virtues which are: Prudence, Temperance, Fortitude, and Justice, and the three "Theological" virtues which are: Faith, Hope and Love (or Charity). Within the same context Virtues are defined as the conformity of behavior in life with the principles of morality.

Archangels

Michael– known as the Prince of Splendor and Wisdom. His planet is Mercury, He rules the Elements of Fire and his color is red. He is the angel of truthfulness, knowledge, divination and philosophy.

Gabriel– known as the Prince of Change, the Archangel of the Annunciation. His planet is the Moon, He rules Elements of Water and his color is blue. He is the angel of magic, astral travel and herbal medicine.

Raphael– known as the Prince of Brightness, Beauty and Life. His planet is the Sun; He rules the Elements of Air and his color yellow. He is the angel of healing, balance, honor and contacting your guardian angel.

Uriel– known as the Prince Knowledge and Truth. He rules the Elements of Earth and his color is green. He is the angel of teaching, insight, endurance and stability, the bringer of knowledge from God.

Aromatherapy– is a therapeutic system for physical and spiritual healing based on the effects of pleasant aromas of distilled oils of flowers, herbs, perfumes and other aromas have on our bodies and minds. Aromatherapy uses fragrances to alter a person's mood, health or level of awareness. The principle is that the action of the scent reacts on the physical as well as on spiritual and mental levels producing the desired change.

Astral– from the Greek word astrum meaning "star", astral describes a substance, also called etheric, which belongs to the incorporeal level of being beyond the material or physical level.

Astral Body– is the spiritual double or mirror image of the physical body of every living being and the vehicle for the soul on the Astral Planes. It is composed of astral or etheric substance. The Astral Body accompanies the physical body during its lifetime and is able to leave the body at will; this occurs every night during sleep when the body is unconscious and can happen consciously in accidents, near death experiences, altered states of consciousness and other circumstances. The Astral Body is held together to the physical body by an etheric silver cord, at death this cord is broken and the Astral Body is freed from the physical world and becomes the Astral Shell which in turn becomes the Astral Corpse at the time of the Second Death. The Astral Body is also called Astral Double, Dream Body, Etheric Body, Second Body, Spiritual Body and Subtle Body.

Astral Detritus– can be defined as the accumulation of negative vibrations, thought forms, unresolved negative feelings or sticky psychic leftovers. Astral detritus can be received from other persons, places where negative psychic energies have accumulated and especially by one's own actions and thoughts.

Astral Link– is described as astral or etheric substance that forms links between beings on the astral level. The longer and closer a relationship with another human being, animal or plant, the closer the astral link that forms. The stronger the love (or hate) and the longer the relationship, the stronger the astral link. An astral link is also called a karmic tie.

Astral Plane– See Planes of Existence.

Astral Projection– also known as Out of Body Experience (or OBE), astral projection is used to describe the astral body leaving the physical body and moving around at will, with or without full consciousness. Occultists and theologians profess that everyone spontaneously projects from the physical body to recharge the astral body with spiritual or cosmic energy and to participate in astral activities.

Atlantis– also known as the Lost Continent, Atlantis was most famously described by Plato in the Timaeus and the Critias. Hundreds of books have been written on Atlantis and the descriptions vary widely. Occultists such as Madame Blavatsky and Dion Fortune, Theosophists such as Charles Leadbeater and Rudolf Steiner, and mediums such as Edgar Cayce have given similar versions. Plato's description of Atlantis as "just beyond the Pillars of Hercules" (Straits of Gibraltar) would refer to the last portion (Poseidonis) of the continent to disappear. Edgar Cayce placed Atlantis "between the Gulf of Mexico and the Mediterranean". He also said that the high technological advances of their civilization were based on an understanding and use of crystals and nuclear energy. Cayce and Blavatsky said that the destruction of Atlantis happened in three separate events, the 1st around 50,000 B.C.E., the 2nd around 28,000 B.C.E. and the last around 10,000 B.C.E. The survivors of these disasters are said to have relocated to North, Central and South America, the British Islands and Egypt. Other spellings include Atlantica and Atalantis. Cayce said that the remainder of Atlantis is today what are Bermuda, the Canary Islands and Azores.

Aura– as the electromagnetic field, astral energy or etheric substance that surrounds the body, the aura is also called; the Sphere of Sensation. It is described as a subtle energy that surrounds humans, animals, plants, gems and even the earth itself, visible by clairvoyance or by a process called Kirlian photography. The aura reflects the general state of mind at the time, including feelings, emotions and health issues by means of color vibrations. Edgar Cayce described through the colors that he saw in people's auras, not only the state of mind and health but surgical scars, fear of animals, bad digestion, worries, interest in music and much more. He describes the aura as being two-fold indicating the physical emanations and the spiritual development. Dion Fortune describes the aura as having three bands or levels: Etheric level or first band is the magnetic or heath aura is the innermost band in the auric field and indicates the health of the physical body; its colors vary from faint grey to shining silver light; Astro-mental level or second band is the astral aura where the colors denote the temperament, personality and mood; and Spiritual level or third band represents the Individuality, composed of many colors; it holds contact with the essential self and other cosmic potencies.

Glossary

Autosuggestion–A form of self-hypnosis, autosuggestion is the process by which one induces one's own acceptance of a belief or plan of action.

Ayurveda–from Sanskrit, ayur means "life" and veda means "knowledge", Ayurveda is a holistic system of medicine developed in ancient India that uses fasting, baths, enemas, diet, drugs and herbs.

Baptism– from the Greek baptein, meaning "to dip" a baptism is a ceremonial immersion or application of water as an initiatory rite of sacrament of most religions. Baptism is described as an initiation, dedication or purifying experience performed as a ceremony. It was particularly significant in the rituals of the Essenes. Baptism is a sign of dedication to the religious life chosen. Religious scholars, especially Christians disagree over whether it should be regarded as essential to new birth and membership in the Kingdom of God or whether it should be regarded only as an external symbol of inner regeneration.

Birth Chart– astrologers believe that the position of celestial bodies relative to a position on Earth at the exact moment of a person's birth reflect that person's character and destiny. This is called a Birth Chart or a Natal Chart.

Blessing– can be defined as the act, words or intention of a person who blesses; sometimes involving the formal invocation of God, Angel or spirit to favor or love someone or something. Frequently mentioned in the Old Testament, a Blessing is also described as a gift or favor bestowed upon by God and is also called a benediction.

Buddha– from Buddhism, Buddha is a Hindu and Tibetan term to describe an enlightened one, divine teacher, spiritual master or prophet, believed to incarnate at intervals to help human spiritual evolution. Buddha means, "One Who Has Attained Bodhi" (enlightenment). The last title of Buddha was conferred to Prince Siddhartha Gautama, founder of Buddhism and considered to be an Enlightened One, due to his supreme knowledge, self-realization, spiritual enlightenment, wisdom, healing and compassion. He has also known as Shakyamuni, Butsi and Gautama Buddha. He rules over the planet Mercury and is one of the nine Navagrahas.

Buddhism– religious philosophy developed in Tibet around 570 B.C.E. by Indian Prince Siddhartha Gautama, called Buddha or Enlightened One. Buddhism is based on Four Noble Truths: life is suffering; all suffering is caused by ignorance; suffering can be ended by overcoming ignorance and attachment. The path to The Middle Way which is comprised of the Noble Eightfold paths; right views, right intent, right speech, right action, right livelihood, right effort, right mindfulness and right concentration. It professes the doctrines of karma and reincarnation, and preaches that through enlightenment every person obtains Nirvana, which is a state of being where reincarnation is no longer necessary for further spiritual evolution. Buddhists have many Holy days that vary from place to place, following the lunar calendar, the most important ones are: Avalokitesvara's Birthday. This is a festival which celebrates the Bodhisattva ideal represented by Avalokitesvara; Buddhist New Year. This festival is usually celebrated for three days from the first full moon day in April; The Ploughing Festival. This festival is to celebrate the Buddha's first moment of enlightenment, said to have happened when the Buddha was seven years old and had gone with his father to watch the ploughing;

Ulambana (Ancestor Day). Throughout the Mahayana tradition this festival is celebrated from the first to the fifteenth days of the eighth lunar month. It is believed that the gates of hell are opened on the first day and the ghosts may visit the world for fifteen days. On the fifteenth day, Ulambana, people visit cemeteries to make offerings to their departed ancestors; and Vesak (Buddha Day). Buddha's Birthday, also known as Visakah Puja is the major Buddhist festival and it celebrates the birth, enlightenment and death of the Buddha on the first full moon in May, except in a leap year when the festival is held in June.

Celestial– related to the Heavens or the Divine.

Ceremonial Magic– also known as ritual magic, ceremonial magic is magic practiced through rituals aiming for command over elementals and invocations of power. Methods of ceremonial magic can be found in the Egyptian Mysteries, the Qabbalah and the Hermetic writings, among many others. In Western magical traditions ceremonial magic is one of two types of magic, the other being natural magic. The most well known modern systems of ceremonial magic are found in the Golden Dawn.

Ceremony– is defined as a formal religious or magical sacred rite or ritual.

Chakras– from Sanskrit, chakra means "wheel" or "lotus flower". From Eastern mysticism the chakras are described as vortices or psychic energy centers located along the spine and in the head that absorb life energy from the cosmos for the ethereal body the way that we eat to feed the physical body. Clairvoyants describe them as wheel-like vortices of energy within the aura. Other spellings include cakra. There are seven main Chakras:

> Sahasrara Thousand Petaled Lotus / Crown Chakra. – this chakra corresponds to the pineal gland. It governs spiritual illumination and cosmic consciousness and controls all aspects of the mind, body and soul. It is associated with the link between the human and the divine, its color is violet and its element is space. This Chakra has also been called the center of cosmic consciousness.
>
> Ajna Order or Brow Chakra (Third Eye)– this chakra corresponds to the pituitary gland, which governs psychic abilities and the spirit-to-spirit communication. It is associated with imagination, inspiration, perception and intuition, its color is indigo and its element is time. This chakra also known as the third eye has also been called the center of consciousness awareness.
>
> Vishuddha Purity / Throat Chakra.– this chakra corresponds to the thyroid gland. It governs will, intuition, potential, creativity and instinct. It is associated with the search for truth self-expression and creativity, its color is blue and its element is ether.
>
> Anahata Unstruck Sound / Heart Chakra.– this chakra corresponds to the thymus gland. It governs compassion, understanding, meditation and prayer. It is associated with love and self-acceptance, its color is emerald green and its element is air. This chakra has also been called the center of living love.

Glossary

    Manipura Diamond / Solar Plexus. – this chakra corresponds to the pancreas. It governs emotions and the emotional and mental bodies. It is associated with the seat of energy and identity and the perceptions of freedom, control and power, its color is yellow and its element is fire. This chakra has also been called the center of power.

    Svadhisthana One's Own Self / Sacral Chakra. –this chakra corresponds to the sex glands. It governs vitality and strength. It is associated with food, sexuality and reproduction, its color is orange and its element is water. This chakra has also been called the center of sensation. Other spellings include Swardhisthana.

    Muladhara Basic / Root Chakra– this chakra is located as the base of the spine and corresponds to the adrenal glands. It governs kundalini. It is associated with survival instincts and the connection to mother Earth, its color is red and its element is earth. This chakra has also been called the center of security.

Chalice– in Wiccan and Pagan traditions the chalice is a cup used in ritual to represent the Goddess, the high priestess and the element of water. In Roman Catholicism and other Christian denominations the chalice is used to hold sacramental wine during Eucharist or Holy Communion. It is also associated with cleansing, healing and scrying.

Chance– unpredictable, random influences on events.

Chanting– is the constant repetition of words, mantras or other sounds in a rhythmic manner, usually with the use of drums or other rhythmic instruments, to induce an altered state of consciousness. Almost all religions use some form of chanting. The act of praying with rosary beads is a form of chanting found in Buddhism, Islam, Hinduism and Christianity. According to Vedic scriptures, chanting the name of God is a way to increase spiritual progress. According to Edgar Cayce, chanting is a way to transform vibrations and energize the chakras.

Charging– in magical practices, charging is the act of transmitting energy or empowering an herb, stone or other object with one's own energetic vibrations for magical purposes and spiritual healing.

Charm– from the Latin carmen which means "ritual utterance, "incantation" or "song", a charm is a magically empowered verse or text which is recited or worn to ward off danger, evil or illness or to bring good luck. Charms can be used for both good and evil but they are more commonly good. Also see Magical Amulets.

Christianity– is one of the major religions of the world, Christianity is based on the Old and New Testaments and on the teachings of Jesus of Nazareth (Christ or Anointed One of God). It teaches above all that "God is Love"; that God is omnipotent and rules over all that is in heaven and earth, righteous in judgment over good and evil, and beyond time, space and change. Christianity includes the Catholic, Protestant and Eastern Orthodox Churches. The original doctrines included the belief in reincarnation but these references were deleted by the Emperor Constantine in the 2nd Council of Nicea in Constantinople in the 6th Century for political reasons. The essential beliefs of modern Christianity are: the authority of The Bible; the existence of a triune God; that man is a physical and spiritual being; that Jesus Christ was sent to save mankind and the Church is God's ordained institution. The main Christian festivals are: Ash Wednesday is the first day of Lent when traditionally blessed ashes in the form of the cross are placed on the foreheads of the faithful as a reminder "That Thou Art Dust, and To Dust Thou Shalt Return"; Christmas meaning "Christ's Mass" marks and celebrates the birth of Jesus. The date chosen by the early Christian Church to celebrate the birth of Jesus was made to coincide with the winter solstice which was a widely spread Pagan celebration honoring the Sun God; Easter celebrates the resurrection of Jesus from the dead, Easter always falls on the first Sunday after the vernal equinox; Holy Week is the week before Easter and it commemorates the events in the last days of Christ's life. It begins on Palm Sunday and ends on Easter Monday, it includes: Palm Sunday (also called Passion Sunday), the entrance of Jesus into Jerusalem; Holy Thursday (also called Maundy Thursday), last supper and the betrayal of Jesus by Judas; Good Friday (also called Holy Friday), the arrest, trial, crucifixion, death and burial of Jesus Christ; and Holy Saturday, the Sabbath on which Jesus rested in the grave; and Pentecost is the festival where Christians celebrate the gift of the Holy Spirit. It is regarded as the birthday of the Christian church.

Clairvoyance– or divination by psychic vision is described as the ability to obtain information on, or visualize persons or events at other locations or times using methods or abilities other than normal mundane senses; by psychic means rather than the physical senses. The practice of clairvoyance may or may not include the use of crystal balls, mirrors or other magically empowered objects or methods. It can also be described as thought transference between people on a subconscious level. Clairvoyance can be divided into three main categories:

> Clairaudience– meaning "clear hearing" is described as the ability to "hear" spirit voices or sounds that are beyond reach of the common person;

> Clairvoyance–meaning "clear vision" is described as the ability to "see" and through this obtain information of places, objects or events that take place in another location; and

> Clairsentience– meaning "clear sensing" is described as the ability to "sense" psychic manifestations or good or bad vibrations or disturbances in the atmosphere.

> Consecrate– the process of empowering or declaring a person or thing sacred through religious or magical ritual dedication, usually for a specific magical or religious purpose.

> Concentration– concentration is the ability to completely focus the mind on one thing without being distracted.

Contemplation– is meditation where the goal is to experience God directly.

Conscious Mind– the mental faculty of being aware of existing; the conscious mind is the state of waking awareness and understanding of the surrounding environment and personal feelings, sensations and thoughts.

Correspondence– in Wiccan traditions a correspondence is an item or tool used in ritual magic for a corresponding purpose, such as a white candle for spirituality or green decorations for healing.

Glossary

Cosmology– is the study of the universe as a whole. The term cosmology is used to denote a theory of the nature of the universe and how it came to being. The Western cosmology, or Judeo-Christian cosmology, postulates a specific moment of creation by a pre-existent Deity. Qabbalistic cosmology, suggests a condensation of the universe out of an eternal field of unmanifestation.

Coven– is a group of Wiccans or Pagans who meet for religious and magical purposes. Coven means "gathering" and in Wiccan traditions a coven is a group of Wiccans with three to thirteen people under the leadership of the high priestess, sometimes sharing her authority with the high priest.

Creative Visualization– also called Guided Imagery, creative visualization is a technique involving the use of positive thoughts and images to manifest life changes in matter in the physical world.
Cross– One of the oldest and most recognized symbols, seen in the traditions of the Aztecs, Buddhists, Babylonians, Hindus and many other cultures. The four points of the cross usually symbolized Earth, Air, Fire and Water. Principle symbol of the Christian faith, the cross represents the crucifixion of Jesus Christ.

Crystal Ball– the crystal ball is a sphere usually composed of glass or crystal used for crystal gazing and scrying.

Crystal Gazing– is an ancient method of scrying for divination purposes using crystals or crystal balls where the concentration of the eyes is focused on the reflective surface of the crystal and the mind is quieted to produce altered states of consciousness. Crystal gazing is also called Crystallomancy.

Crystal Therapy– also called Crystal Healing, Crystal Therapy is an ancient method of physical and spiritual healing by laying-on-of-stones, crystals or gems on the body, over the chakras or other energy centers or affected areas. The placement may be by color to stimulate the chakras by their nature or by the placement by the properties of the stone or crystal. When the chakra system is activated and balanced the physical body can heal itself. Crystals and stones are also placed in sacred geometric patterns to change the level of awareness and vibrations.

Crystals– throughout history almost every culture has considered that crystals have special powers. According to Aldous Huxley precious stones and crystals remind us of the glittering vistas of the inner worlds. Even today mediums and psychics use crystals as a means for concentration to obtain higher levels of awareness. Crystals are also used in physical and psychic healing by directly placing them on the skin over the chakras.

Curse– a willful and conscious mental emission of negative energy towards a person, object or place. An evil formula used magically with the intent to harm or cause misfortune, illness or death to a person, or the act of reciting a form or charm with intended evil. Curse is also called hex.

Dagger– is a short, acutely pointed knife with a flat triangular blade and a cylindrical grip and usually are double edged. Daggers are used in ritual magic as one of the principal working tools. Daggers represent the element of air and are used to invoke and command the powers of that element.

Demon– originally demons were spirits, good or bad, human or other. In Greek lore, demons were benevolent spirits, Angels or familiars. The term is now used to describe an evil or malevolent spirit, or a supernatural being, devil or fiend. In religions as well as mythology, demons play the role of evil versus good. They are said to possess people or places with evil influences. The Vedas describe a variety of evil beings that harm people and work against the Gods. The Bible refers to demons as "unclean spirits" and "fallen angels". Traditional Christian demonology says that some demons can be equated with the seven deadly sins: Asmodeus (lechery), Beelzebub (gluttony), Belphegor (sloth), Leviathan (envy), Lucifer (pride), Mammon (avarice) and Satan (anger). The practice of expelling demons is called exorcism.

Destiny– may be understood as a predetermined future based on the belief that the universe has a predetermined natural order. Destiny may be seen as changeable by human will or as a fixed sequence of events that remains unchangeable.

Devas–in Persian mythology, Devas are Fairies or that appear as small spheres of light and are found especially around lakes and forests.

> Devas– from Sanskrit, Devas means "celestial beings" or "shining ones" in Buddhism and Hinduism Devas are described as three different types of exalted beings or divinities; mortals who live on a higher realm than other mortals, enlightened beings and Brahaman appearing as a personal God. Other spellings include Daeva. Also see Supernatural and Spiritual Beings.

> Devas– Theosophy, Occultism and Wicca define Devas as a hierarchy of Spirits of Nature or beings on a different sphere of evolution, closely related to the human evolution and who help rule the universe. They were described by Charles Leadbeater as a Kingdom of mighty spirits, comprised by many different kinds in many different degrees of evolution, and by Madame Blavatsky as progressed entities from previous planetary periods.

> Devas– In Zoroastrianism, Devas are malevolent spirits.

Discarnate– without a physical body, incorporeal.

Divination– from the Latin divinatio which means "the ability of foreseeing", divination is the discovery or insight into hidden knowledge of events, past, present or future through a specific method or technique or the foretelling future events or hidden knowledge by Occult means. Forms of divination have been found in all civilizations, both ancient and modern, popular divination methods include the I Ching, the Tarot, Astrology, runes and crystal gazing and dream Interpretation among many others. The Golden Dawn says that the practice of divination stimulates the faculties of imagination, intuition and clairvoyance, and defines it as a "Method for determining the outcome of life events, used as a means for developing intuition of the inner psychic sense".

Divination Tools– are used for divination. Some divining Tools include: Crystal Ball, Dowsing Rod, I Ching, Magic Mirror, Ouija Board, Pendulum, Runes, Shewstone, Speculum and Tarot.

Dowse– to dowse is to search for objects or substances such as, water, precious minerals, lost treasures, archaeological remains or even bodies buried underground, using a dowsing tool such as a

Glossary

divining rod or a pendulum, either directly over the ground or over a map. Dowsing is one of the most widely accepted esoteric arts and is also called Doodlebugging and Water Witching. Dowsing is also known as Radiesthesia.

Dowsing Rod– is a staff, wand, branch or stick used to dowse for water, treasures or precious minerals underground. The Dowsing Rod is also called a divining rod.

Druidism– is a religious faith, doctrine, philosophy and priesthood developed by the ancient Celtic people from Gaul and the British Isles around the 2nd Century B.C.E. until around the 2nd Century C.E. They professed in the immortality of the soul and reincarnation and also practiced astrology and natural magic. Goddesses were considered of great importance and they believed in the trinity concept, God/Goddess/Holy Spirit. The Druids celebrated the same festivals as the Wiccans and Pagans do today, such as Oimelc(Imbolc), Beltane, Lughnassadh (Lunasa) and Samhain as well as the Sabats and the phases of the Moon. These celebrations were usually held in the clearings of forests. There were three main divisions within the order: Bards, who were poets, musicians and storytellers, the "keepers of tradition", and who also dealt with divination and prophesy; Druid Priests, who were also teachers, advisors, theologians, astronomers, astrologers, scientists, counselors and judges (Brehons); and Ovates, also called Faithi meaning "seers", who were prophets, seers, philosophers and healers and dealt with death and regeneration.

Dwarfs– See Elementals.

Earth Religions– is religion or philosophy where the individuals strive to be in harmony with and worship all forms of life. Earth Religion may also include the worship of Fertility Gods and Goddesses. Some of the best known forms of Earth Religions include: Buddhism, Druidism, Paganism, Pantheism, Shamanism and Wicca.

Elementals– also known as Elemental Spirits, the Elementals are described as a class of beings belonging to the nature of one of the elements and inhabiting the astral realms. With lower vibrational rates than humans do, they are rarely seen by persons who do not have psychic or clairvoyant abilities. Elementals are believed to possess only one of the attributes of man, the one that belongs to their element, and are not on the same line of evolution as humans are. Elementals are said not to take much notice of human acts unless strong feelings or emotions are involved; responding positively to loving thoughts but when openly provoked becoming mischievous.

> Elementals of Earth– called Gnomes, which from the Greek gnoma meaning knowledge or one who knows, are the Nature spirits who care for the Earth's treasures and minerals. They are also known as; Goblins, Hobgoblins, Dwarfs and Trolls.

> Elementals of Fire– called Salamanders, which comes from the Greek salambe which means fireplace. These Fire Spirits can be seen in and around hearths, fireplaces, fires, candles, etc. They show the least interest in human beings but can help clearing psychic and psychologi

cal obstacles. They are also known as Fire Drakes.

Elementals of Air called Sylphs– comes from the Greek silphe meaning butterfly or winged one. These beings are powerful and mysterious they can be an unlimited source of inspiration, knowledge and ideas. They are also known as Zephyrs and Mountain Fairies.

Elementals of Water– called Undines, which comes from the Latin are also known as, meaning wave or creature of the wave. They produce or inspire the essence of plant life and abundant growth and are closely associated with the healing of plants, animals and humans. They are also known as Fairies, Nymphs, Mermen and Mermaids.

Elements– there are four physical magical elements: Earth, Air, Fire and Water and an ethereal element akasha or fifth element. These are regarded as realms of existence or kingdoms of nature.

Air– is a combination of heat and moisture, it is considered, masculine, active, ethereal and intellectual; the element of transformation of the mind and body and intellect.

Earth– A combination of cold and dryness, it is considered feminine, passive, stable, grounded and solid; the foundation of physical being and sensory perception.

Fire– A combination of heat and dryness, it is considered masculine, active, spontaneous, energetic and vitalizing; the power of self determined form, and will.

Water– A combination of cold and moisture, it is considered feminine, passive, creative, receptive and regenerative; the spiritual principle of dissolution and transformation and emotions.

Akasha– (or fifth element) or is the element that binds these elements together being the Element of Spirit. Also see Akasha.

Empowering– Empowering can be described as the ability to transfer personal energy or power into; herbs, stones, amulets or other objects for use in magic.

Esoteric– Secret or occult knowledge understood by, or meant only for, a select group with special training, information or interests, to be revealed only to those initiated, as opposed to exoteric or knowledge for anyone.

Etheric Body– Described by Charles Leadbeater as the vehicle of vitality and life principle, which he said, is perpetually circulating through our bodies. The etheric body is also described in Occultism as the invisible vehicle of the soul. It is the source of all physical vitality; the body which absorbs the universal energy or life-force and is an exact copy of the physical body, cell for cell. The etheric body is also called the etheric double.

Exorcism– Elaborate religious or magical rituals, usually performed by a priest, shaman or adept, in which evil spirits, ghosts, poltergeists or demons are driven out or expelled from a body, object or place through the ritual utterance of chants and incantations. The ancient Egyptians, Greeks and

Glossary

Babylonians had specifically trained priests for exorcisms. Jewish and Christian traditions also describe exorcisms. The Bible includes a number of references to exorcisms and the New Testament describes occasions when Jesus Christ expelled evil spirits by prayer and the power of his command.

Fairies See Elementals.

Faith– is the belief, trust and confidence in the divine truth, existence of God or other realities or states that are not proven with current scientific methods. According to the Dalai Lama "Faith is not simply admiration, but something that arises from a deep understanding of the teachings…". Samael Aun Weor said "Those who have true faith do not need to believe". Stuart Chase said "For those who believe, no proof is necessary. For those who don't believe, no proof is possible".

Faith Healing– also called spiritual healing refers to non medical cures treated with prayer, suggestion and spiritual therapy.

Fasting– is the act of willingly abstaining from ingesting food and in sometimes drink for a period of time for spiritual or religious purposes. Fasting is mentioned in The Bible, Book of Mormon, the Qur'an, the Mahabharata and the Upanishads, among many others.

Fate– From the Latin factum meaning "prophetic declaration" or "oracle", fate is defined as the force (of God) outside of man's control which determines events as they occur.

Fire Drakes See Elementals.

Fumigation– A thorough spiritual cleansing of a room, building or area by burning incense or mixtures of dried herbs. Fumigations are commonly used to cleanse an area for a ritual, to rid a place of bad vibrations, malicious thought forms or evil entities.

Gaia– The theory postulated by Professor James Lovelock proposing that the biosphere and the lithosphere combined with the atmosphere form a single integrated system, a self-regulating organism and a living entity Gaia, from the Greek Gaea Goddess of Earth, as the name given to describe the soul of the Earth.

Gazing– is the process of staring into or at an object with the purpose of having a vision or inducing an altered state of consciousness.

Geomancy– also called earth magic, geomancy is an ancient method of divination by means of the element of Earth.

Ghost– is usually that of the apparition of the soul of a dead person or animal, or a nonmaterial disembodied spirit appearing either in a foggy form or in much detail and solidity. Ghosts usually seem to appear in places that were meaningful to them in life, whether it be the place where they died or another, such as their home, even though this can be very far from the place where the soul met its death. Many agree that when a soul has what it considers unfinished business it remains earthbound until such a time that it decides to continue its journey towards the light. There are also cases of souls who do not know they are dead, or have extraordinary ties to previous incarnations. These cases are especially common when a person dies a violent death, such as murder, accident or being killed in a war.

Gnomes– from the Greek gnoma meaning knowledge or one who knows, are the Nature spirits who care for the Earth's treasures and minerals. They are also known as; Goblins, Hobgoblins, Dwarfs and Trolls See Elementals.

Gnosis– from the Greek word gnostikos, (one who has gnosis, or "secret knowledge"), Gnosis means "knowledge".

Gnosticism– Oriental mysticism and philosophical and religious movement that influenced the Mediterranean from the 1st Century B.C.E. to the 3rd Century C.E. which takes elements from Occultism, magic, Astrology and the Qabbalah as well as from Egyptian, Indian and Christian religions. The two major branches are Jewish Gnosticism also called Sethian Gnosticism and Christian Gnosticism also called Vanentinian Gnosticism. Both share the belief of the redeeming power of esoteric spiritual knowledge acquired through divine revelation and seem to have been influenced by Zoroastrianism. The discovery of the Dead Sea Scrolls in 1945 has provided a basis for new interpretations of Gnostic influence and beliefs.

Goblins See Elementals.

Godform– an archetypal image of a God or Goddess created for ritual purposes by visualization on the astral planes.

Gods– in Occultism, Gods are powerful immortal beings in the heavenly hierarchies, having power over lesser spirits and Angels, they are also known as Deities.

Golden Dawn– formally known as the Hermetic Order of the Golden Dawn, this Occult Order was founded in 1888 by S.L. MacGregor Mathers, William Wynn Wescott and William R. Woodman. It was based heavily on manuscripts of ritual Qabbalah and Enochian magical formulae found by Dr. Wescott and decoded with help from Mathers. The Golden Dawn is dedicated to the Spiritual, Philosophical and Psychic evolution of mankind through the study and practice of; Qabbalah, Divination, Astrology, Spiritual Alchemy, Scrying, Egyptian and Enochian magic and ceremonial magic.

Guardian Angel– Christians believe that a Guardian Angel is assigned at birth to a person and from then on this Angel guides them throughout their physical and spiritual life. The Occultists believe

Glossary

this and that it is possible to communicate with this Angel. There is a 15th Century manuscript called The Book of the Sacred Magic of Abramelin the Mage, translated by S. L. MacGregor Mathers which describes a ritual that promises 'knowledge and conversation of the Holy Guardian Angel'. The Guardian Angel is also a term for the Spirit Guides.

Guardian Spirit– the belief in Guardian Spirits is widely diffused and they are frequently described as having an animal form which can shape-shift into a human form. This Guardian Spirit is said to protect individuals as well as tribes and sometimes provides magical powers.

Hallucination– a false perception of a sensory modality due to the absence of external stimulus, as opposed to an illusion which is a misperception of external stimulus. Hallucinations may be visual, gustatory, tactile, olfactory, auditory or proprioceptive and can include such alterations of perception as hearing flowers sing or seeing music

Haunting– a haunting is the phenomena of paranormal activities within a certain place. Paranormal disturbances are usually attributed to the spirits of the dead or ghosts. The phenomena may include moving objects, strange noises, lights, cold spots, unpleasant smells, and the appearance of ghostly figures. Most Hauntings are attributed to discarnate spirits of those who have suffered some sort of violent death or to a place where violent acts occurred such as a battlefield.

Heathen– originally heathen was the term used to describe people who lived outside of cities, a person of the heath. Now the term is associated with Pagans.

Heaven– is generally used to describe the dwelling place of God, Gods, Angels and other spiritual beings, although different religions interpret the concept in different ways. According to the Old Testament Heaven is the abode of Yahweh, later described as the destination of the deceased righteous who would be resurrected to live with God. Jewish mystics regard the Heavens as contained in the seven spheres of the firmament. Christianity describes Heaven as the destination of the believers and followers of Christ. Islam preaches that Heaven is a place of joy to which the faithful Muslims to according to the will of Allah and also recognizes the existence of the seven Heavens of the firmament.

Hell– is usually used to describe the abode of evil spirits and dammed souls in after-death punishment. Hell is the absence of God. The concept of hell as a place or a state of being that separates the good souls from the evil souls is found in most religions. Judaism describes hell as an infernal place of punishment for the wicked. Christianity views hell as the fiery domain of the devil and fallen Angels; a place of eternal damnation for those who lived a life of sin and died unrepentant. Hinduism describes hell as a stage in the progress of the soul where it must live until the evil accumulated during it life has been exhausted. Modern views of hell are mostly derived from Dante's Inferno, a part of The Divine Comedy, where Dante describes in detail, its different levels and punishments for every sin.

Herb– is a plant or tree that has specific properties and specific uses in medicine, food, religion and magic.

Herbal Magic– can be defined as a process or art that harnesses and directs the natural energies of herbs for magical or healing purposes.

Hex See Curse.

Hinduism– Religion and philosophy based on the teachings of the Indian Vedas, Upanishads and Bhagavad-Gita (Holy Books) and the doctrines of karma and reincarnation. Hinduism differs from other religions in that it doesn't have a single founder and has evolved from many different religions for over 3,000 years. A few the main mystic teachings of Hinduism are the belief in karma and the practice of Yoga, and its ultimate goal is mystical transcendence to escape from the world of maya (illusion) through the union with Brahma, the divine. The main Deities of Hinduism are Brahma, the Creator, Vishnu, the Savior and Shiva, the Destroyer/Restorer, but there arealso many other Gods, spirits and devils. Hindu festivals vary by area.

Hobgoblin See Elementals.

I Ching– also known as the Book of Changes and the Holy Book of Mutations, the I Ching is an ancient Chinese system of profound philosophy and method of divination. Both the Confucians and the Taoists claim the I Ching as theirs, but traditionally the work has been attributed to Wen Wang (sage and father of the Chou dynasty). The basic principle of the I Ching is the subdivision of phenomena into the negative and positive forces or yin and yang. It is based on 64 symbolic hexagrams which are broken down into triagrams. There are 8 basic triagrams each named for a natural phenomenon. The book of I Ching is then consulted by casting lots of hexagrams six times to determine the appropriate hexagram. The oracle then reads the current state of yin and yang. Other spellings include Yi Ching and Pinyin Yi Jing.

Illumination– to understand, realize or comprehend the meaning of the union with the divine. Illumination can be described as a complete understanding of the divine plan of spiritual evolution. This illumination then frees the soul from all karma and the need for reincarnation.

Imagination– ccording to Occultism imagination is the "creative faculty of the human mind". When we use our imagination we create forms and images on the astral planes, the more concentration and imagination used in conjunction with the will, will create a more dense and or powerful form or image. Many things have been said about the imagination. Albert Einstein said "Imagination is more important than knowledge. Knowledge is limited. Imagination encircles the world." Paracelsus said "Man has a visible and invisible workshop. The visible one is his body; the invisible one is his imagination." It is said that the spirit is the master, imagination is the tool and the body is the means to material realization. Imagination has also been described as the powers of the higher soul.

Incantation– a mantra, phrase or text, chanted, spoken or intoned as part of religious or spiritual rituals. Incantations are often used to banish evil spirits and to summon good ones.

Initiation– Initiation means "to begin", "to start something new". Described in Occultism and Theosophy as a ritual or period of instruction in which a new member or neophyte is admitted or initiated

Glossary

into an Organization, Society or Order. According to the one tradition, "Initiation is the preparation for immortality". On a personal level initiation is basically an individual transformation involving a transition from one level of awareness to another higher more spiritual level.

Inspiration– has been defined as a psychic state in which a person becomes susceptible to spiritual and creative influences and becomes an instrument for through-flowing ideas.

Intuition– is defined as a direct perception or inner knowing of a truth, independent of a conscious reasoning process. A feeling or sensation, sometimes described as an inner voice that communicates something of importance. Knowledge that arrives spontaneously, without conscious thought.

Invisibility– in Occultism and other magical traditions, invisibility is the magically empowered act of fading from the physical or exterior environment in such a manner as to create the illusion to others that the person is no longer present or by leading them to forget that they have seen the person. This process is also called the "Shroud of Concealment".

Invocation– is the act of invoking or calling upon a specific spiritual entity Deity, Elemental, Angel, spirit or other entity for protection, inspiration or aid, or to request their appearance. Also described as potent formula, prayer or ritual used to invoke a deity or to establish communication with higher spiritual entibies.

Islam– Muslim monotheist religion founded by the Prophet Muhammad in the 7th Century B.C.E. Allah is the sole God, and is described in the sacred scriptures or Qur'an. Muhammad was given the message of Islam by the Angel Gabriel. The term Islam means "to surrender" and expresses the fundamental religious ideal that the believer accepts to "surrender to the will of Allah". It also teaches that the path to spiritual enlightenment is open to all. Islam is also calledMohammedism. The main Islamic festivals are: Eid ul-Fitr is a huge celebration at the end of Ramadan which is the thirty day fast and Eid-ul-Adha is to remember the time when Abraham was to sacrifice his own son to prove his obedience to God.

Judaism– is the religion and culture of the Jewish people, Judaism was founded by Abraham and Moses 3,500 years ago. The Tanakh (Old Testament) is the main religious text, and along with the Torah and the Talmud describe the commandments of God and determine the basic beliefs and values to live by as well as religious statements and concepts. For thousands of years, up until the mid eighteen hundreds, Judaism included the concept of Gilgul, or reincarnation, concept which is still held by the contemporary Orthodox and Chasidic communities. The main festivals are:

Purim– (Festival of Lots) is a one-day festival takes place four weeks before Passover and usually falls in late February or early March. It recalls the story of Esther, a Queen who foiled a plot by one of her advisors, Haman, to kill all the Jews;

Pesach– (Passover) takes place around March/April, and commemorates Moses freeing the Israelites from their enslavement under the Pharaoh in Egypt. This festival lasts for eight days and during that time no 'leavened' food may be consumed;

Shavuot– (Pentecost) takes places seven weeks after Passover (usually around late May or early June) and it commemorates Moses being given the ten commandments by God after the Exodus from Egypt. This festival lasts for two days;

Rosh Hashanah– (Jewish New Year) takes place around September/October, and is considered to be one of the most important holidays in the Jewish calendar. As well as a time for celebration Rosh Hashanah is also a time for reflection and repentance for sins committed in the previous year;

Yom Kippur– (Day Of Atonement) is the day on which the fates of the Jews are sealed for the following year. This High Holy day is considered the most solemn and serious day in the Jewish calendar, and it involves 25 hours of fasting and praying for forgiveness for sins and afflicting oneself as punishment for those committed in the past year;

Succot (Tabernacles) is an eight day festival which begins five days after the end of Yom Kippur and commemorates the booths the Israelites constructed and lived in after their exodus from Egypt;

Simchat Torah– (Rejoicing Of The Law) celebrates the end of the reading of the Torah, in synagogue - and the fact that it can now be re-read from the beginning. It is considered one of the happiest festivals in the Jewish calendar;

Chanukah– (Festival of Lights) is an eight-day festival, celebrated in December. The story of Chanukah goes back to when Jews were forbidden to follow their faith and many were made to convert or were killed for not converting. That's when some Jews called the Maccabees formed an army and revolted against the Greeks and won, albeit at a very high price because their temple and way of life was almost destroyed. These men cleaned up the temple and attempted restore the faith by lighting the Menorah, with only enough oil for one day. A miracle is then said to have happened when the Menorah continued to remain lit for seven days on only one day's supply of oil. Also see Religions, jewishpeople.com, jewishvirtuallibrary.org and religioustolerance.com.

Koran– See Qur'an.

Kundalini– is the Sanskrit meaning "serpent of power" or "serpent of fire", kundalini is described as the dormant spiritual or cosmic energy stored in the root chakra which, when adequately aroused through meditation, rituals or yoga techniques, rises through channels called the ida and the pingala to the other chakras until it reaches the crown chakra where it produces spiritual enlightenment and activates the psychic abilities.

Law of Attraction   The law of attraction is a New Age theory that proposes that we attract what we think of and says that no one should dwell on negative thoughts because the law of attraction will attract negative things. On the contrary to attract positive things into one's life, one should strive to think positively, with thoughts of love and gratitude to attract good things into one's life.

Glossary

Libation– A libation is a very ancient universal ritual pouring of a beverage as an offering to a God or poured on the ground itself as an offering to the Earth or the God who represents the Earth. Even today in places such as Chile and Peru a small amount of one's drink is poured on the ground before toasting and drinking to honor Pachamama (Mother Earth).

Lightworker– Lightworker refers to people who spiritually help others though meditation, prayer, teaching, healing, speaking and unconditional love regardless of their spiritual traditions and religious backgrounds. Many people believe that the choice to become a lightworker was made before incarnating here on Earth.

Magic Circle– in Wiccan and Occult traditions the magic circle is a sacred space or sphere of personal energy which is projected by the magician to protect him or herself and the environment during a ritual against negative forces or evil influences. The magic circle or sphere may be physically drawn on the floor or envisioned on the astral planes, either way it symbolically extends above and below ground, the ground being the middle of the sphere. The magic circle is the place where Gods and Goddesses are invoked and rituals are performed.

Magic Mirror– is a tool used in scrying. A magic mirror may be simply a mirror or a black mirror for basic scrying or elaborately decorated and ritually consecrated mirrors for more complex or ceremonial forms of scrying.

Magical Amulets– are passive magical empowered objects, used to deflect negative energy and carried to ward off evil, illness or misfortune, and to bring good fortune and health.

Magical Correspondences– refers to days, moon phases, colors, herbs, angels, oils or objects that are ritually chosen and used to match or "correspond" to the intent of the ritual.

Magical Name– also known as magical motto and craft name, the magical name is a name or phrase chosen by the magician for personal use in a Brotherhood, Lodge or Occult Order. The original purpose of the name was for anonymity but it is currently used to disassociate oneself from the material world during rituals or magical work.

Magical Tools– also called Ritual Tools are active tools used in ritual or ceremonial magic.

Magician– from the Sanskrit word maha, meaning "great", a magician is a person well versed in the secret or esoteric knowledge or the occult sciences and who practices and teaches magic.

Manifestation– refers to the belief that we can, by force of will, desire and focusing energy, make something come true or "manifest" on the physical level. An apport is an example of manifestation.

Materialization– is a term used in Occultism and Theosophy to describe the temporary psychic phenomena of a spirit clothing itself with a material form or using the astral body to solidify temporarily. This can either be done by using the electromagnetic or etheric energy field (ectoplasm) of the medium during a séance, or by act of will, gathering and condensing surrounding etheric energy to produce the materialization.

Meditation– is the mental effort of calming and quieting the mind and relaxing the body to hear the inner voice or higher self. Continued or extended contemplation or spiritual introspection to achieve altered states of consciousness or community with the divine. Edgar Cayce defined meditation as "man listening for God's voice" versus prayer which he said was "man talking to God". There are two main techniques for meditation, heightened concentration where the individual gives their undivided attention to a single thought or idea in a trance like state where the external awareness dims, and the second technique, used mostly in Buddhism, involves a passive examination of all ideas and thoughts taking care to not cling to any idea or thought but to passively letting that idea or thought pass.

Medium– according to Occultism a medium is person who has the ability to enter a state of trance and suspend rational consciousness or who is sensitive to vibrations from the spirit plane and may become the conscious or unconscious channel for manifestations of discarnate entities and receive and convey messages from other planes of existence. Mediums are also called Trance Channelers.

Mental Plane   See Planes of Existence.

Mermen/Mermaids See Elementals.

Mountain/Fairies See Elementals.

Mystery– is from the Greek word mystos meaning "keep silent", mystery is used to describe the doctrine of the schools of magic. Mystery has also been defined as a religious truth beyond human comprehension that can only be understood by divine revelation.

Mysticism– is a system of beliefs in intuitive spiritual revelations for the purpose of union with the divine. This mystical union is achieved through intuition, faith, insight and spiritual awareness. It is also described as a spiritual search for inner truth and wisdom for the purpose of union with the Divine. Mysticism is any doctrine, philosophy or belief system that relates to the spiritual side of the world. The basis of mysticism is that the world is a spiritual place and this is the only reality.

Myth– is a traditional or legendary story usually passed down by word of mouth, that ostensibly relates actual events to explain some practice, belief, or natural phenomenon, and which is especially associated with religious and magical rites and beliefs.

Natural Magic– is magic that deals with the occult virtues or magical energies and spiritual powers of herbs, plants, gems, metals and others. In Western magical traditions natural magic is one of two types of magic, the other being ceremonial magic.

Nature Worship– is the expression of human feelings of awe, gratitude and dependence in the powers of nature. In most ancient cultures, Gods where related to powers of nature.

Glossary

Neophyte– is from the Greek neophytos meaning "newly planted", a neophyte is a student of Occultism or Theosophy who may or may not have been formally initiated into an Order, Brotherhood, Occult Society or Fraternity. A neophyte is also described as a candidate for initiation into the Mysteries.

Nymphs   See Elementals.

Obsession– according to Occultists, obsession is described as a cutting off of the higher will from the lower or conscious will, which is induced by evil thoughts or extreme fear from the spiritual consciousness. This in turn ends up in the withdrawal of a soul from its sphere of sensation and its replacement or complete domination by another soul, human or other. When this is done on purpose the method employed is to flatter the lower will until access to the sphere of sensation is established and then applying strain on the lower will until it is weakened allowing the passage of the force behind the obsession.

Occult– is from the Latin occulere, occult means "to hide" or "to cover up". Occult wisdom means secret wisdom or knowledge that should be kept hidden, not be revealed to the non-initiated. Occult knowledge has also been defined as divine wisdom that can only be communicated or acknowledged from within.

Occult Orders– is also known as Fraternities, Societies, Schools, Orders, Organizations or Brotherhoods, Occult Orders are schools wherein a secret knowledge unknown to the common man may be learned. Admission to these orders requires initiation where tests and rituals take place as a general rule and where oaths of secrecy and silence are made.

Occult Powers   See Psychic Abilities.

Occultism– is defined as an extension of psychology and science, the study of the occult has, throughout human history occurred in all societies. It is the study and practice of that which is hidden or secret, pertaining to magic, esoteric studies, the higher powers of the mind and the manipulation of energies which are invisible and normally imperceptible. It has also described as a branch of knowledge which is hidden from the many and reserved for the few, a wisdom that is kept secret so as to be kept pure.

Offering– is an offering is a ritual gift or sacrifice to a God, spirit or supernatural being. Offerings have been made for religious and magical purposes in most cultures throughout the history of the world.

Omen– is something (such as an event, phenomenon or sign) perceived or interpreted to be a portent of a good or evil that will influence an event or circumstances in the future. Ancient cultures observed the flight of birds, eclipses, meteors, comets, the movement of clouds and storms and the paths or actions of certain sacred animals as Omens.

Oracle– is from the Latin orare meaning "to speak" or "to pray", an oracle is divine communication or divination obtained through a medium or prophet who was associated with a specific place. The Greeks and Romans dedicated shrines to oracles where people went to consult priests/priestesses or prophets/prophetesses. Some of the most famous sites are the Oracle of Zeus at Olympia, the Oracle of Apollo at Delphi and the Oracle of Zeus at Donona although there are dozens of others. The Egyptians and Hebrews understood oracles from different perspectives, the Egyptians by observing motion of images and the Hebrews by reviewing dreams and observing sacred objects.

Out of Body Experience See Astral Projection.

Paganism– is from Latin paganus, meaning "civilian" or "country dweller", Paganism is a blanket term currently used to connote a broad set of western spiritual or religious beliefs and practices of natural or polytheistic religions such as Wicca and Shamanism.

Paradise– is from the old Persian pairedaeza, meaning "enclosure" originally referred to an enclosed garden or a park. Currently the term is used as a synonym for Eden or Heaven.

Paranormal– is a term that is used to describe any phenomenon which does not have a logical explanation according to the laws of science and nature as we currently understand them.

Parapsychology– is the investigation and study of paranormal phenomenon that relates to the human mind, such as psychic abilities which include: extrasensory perception, clairvoyance, precognition, psychokinesis, telepathy as well as other psychic phenomena.

Parasite– in Occultism a parasite is any entity or being that lives on the psychic or spiritual energy of another entity or being.

Pendulum– is a weight suspended from a chain or string used for dowsing, radiesthesia and divination. The material for the pendulum itself may include crystals, metals and even roots of herbs or wood. The interpretation of the movements of the pendulum is called pallomancy or radiesthesia.

Pentagram– is considered divine and magical, the pentagram is a geometric figure and powerful symbol with five lines and five points, in the shape of a star. It is used by Occultists to invoke spirits; the star pointed upwards for benevolent spirits. Frequently referred to in Occultism and Wicca, the pentagram is attributed to the five elements of fire, water, air, earth and spirit (or akasha). It is a symbol for perfection and beauty, associated with the Goddess and symbolic of the sacred feminine. The pentagram is also called the Star of the Magi, the Blazing Star and the Wizard's Foot. Other spellings include pentacle and pentalpha.

Pentacle– is a magic diagram of a five pointed star, or pentagram surrounded by a circle, pentacles can be inscribed on metal, wood or other material used to create a talisman. The pentacle is also a symbol that refers to the element Earth and the initiates understanding of the Universe. Wiccans consider the pentacle to be a prime magical symbol and use it as a talisman for protection and power.

Glossary

Planes of Existence– is also called Planes of Manifestation, are explained as the seven spiritual planes through which we, as divine sparks of God evolve. The planes have different levels or layers of vibrations, the higher up the more pure vibrations and proximity to Angelic or Divine realms, and the lower planes closer to the physical or manifest plane of existence. The planes are described by Occultists as the following:

> First Plane– is the Physical or Material Plane (starting with the smallest and darkest), is the physical world and what we perceive through our "normal physical" senses. There is an "in between" plane called the Etheric Plane which lies between the Physical and the Astral Plane;
>
> Second Plane– is the Lower Astral, Psychic Plane or Plane of Illusion, is described as an in termediate level of reality beyond the visible material and physical. The world of dreams, psychic manifestations and thought forms;
>
> Third Plane– is the Upper Astral and is the plane of emotions;
>
> Fourth Plane the Lower Mental and is the plane of concrete thought and memory;
>
> Fifth Plane– is the Upper Mental and is the plane of abstract mind;
>
> Sixth Plane– is the Lower Spiritual and is the plane of concrete spirit;
>
> Seventh Plane– is the Upper Spiritual and is the plane of pure spirit or Abstract Spirit, the first phase of manifestation drawing its substance and energy directly from the Great Un manifest. Upon this plane All are One and One is All

Poltergeist– comes from German and means "noisy ghost". Poltergeists are said to be annoying discarnate entities who manifest their presence by rapping on walls, hiding or breaking objects, and in general being a nuisance. There are also said to be cases in which poltergeists attach themselves to people rather than places. And there are cases, originally attributed to poltergeists in which the psychic disturbances are due to externalization of psychic energy from emotionally distressed children or adolescents, excluding the presence of poltergeists.

Positive Thinking– in this Quantum New Age reality, positive thinking is a way of re-conditioning the mind and re-wiring the brain towards positive spiritual and physical goals, self-improvement and health.

Prayer– is an appeal, petition, confession, contrition, supplication, thanksgiving or a loving thought aimed at a specific Deity. A prayer may be a feeling or sensation of devout spiritual communion with God. They may be formal or spontaneous, spoken or silent, based on religious texts or inspired by heart and mind, and may be practiced individually or in groups. Prayers also describe a formula or sequence of words used for praying.

Precognition– is the present perception of future events through extrasensory or psychic means. It has been described as the ability to "for-sense" rather than "for-see" events.

Prediction– is to foretell future events by previous knowledge or shrewd inference from facts of experience, or the ability to foretell, forecast or see future events without the implication of underlying knowledge.

Premonition– are intuitive feelings such as a sense of dread, warning of future events, usually negative in nature such as accidents and natural disasters. Premonition is also called Presentiment.

Prophecy– is described as a vision or revelation of events that will happen in the future and the act of divining or foretelling future events. Prophecies may be achieved through personal insights or visions, by Divine inspiration or by using exterior divination methods such as astrology, oracles or scrying.

Presence– is the perception or feeling that the soul or essence of a person, animal, spirit or discarnate entity is in the vicinity, but is not physically there.

Preternatural– is used to describe any natural phenomenon which does not have a logical explanation according to the laws of science and nature as we currently understand them.

Psychic Abilities– is the ability to receive information without the use of the physical five senses.

Psychic Attack– is a form of malicious action against someone done by a person or persons with occult knowledge. Psychic attacks take place on the lower Astral Plane and come through to the Physical Plane by means of suggestion aimed at the victim. These types or attacks are very rare due to the mental effort involved required to produce results at this level.

Psychic Centers See Chakras.

Psychic Energy– is the energy created in the atmosphere surrounding us by the emotions and feelings of people. Positive psychic energy or good vibrations are generated by feelings of love, sympathy, happiness, laughter and other positive emotions, while negative psychic energy or negative vibrations are generated by feelings of hatred, jealousy, greed and other harmful emotions.

Psychic Healing– is an esoteric technique which involves the channeling of spiritual energy or psychic power through a healer into a patient. The religious aspect of psychic healings involves personal or group prayer.

Psychic Vampire– is also called an astral vampire, a psychic vampire is an entity who preys on the life force or spiritual energy of another, knowingly or not. These psychic vampires can be incarnate or discarnate.

Purification– is to rid a person, place or object from undesired vibrations, sticky thought forms or disrupting psychic energy. To make pure, clean and free from physical or spiritual contaminants or pollutants or to purge of sin or guilt.

Glossary

Qabalah– is Jewish esoteric doctrine meaning "received tradition". It is a system of religious philosophy and esoteric theosophy. The Qabalah was supposedly taught by God himself to a select company of angels. These in turn passed down to Adam, who passed it down to Noah, who passed it down to Abraham and so on. Also spelled; Cabala, Kaballah and Kabalah among others. Among its central doctrines is that the soul is immortal and that everything emanates from the Deity. Held by the experts or initiates to penetrate the mysteries of the universe.

Qur'an– Muslim Holy Book that holds a collection of the revelations and sacred scriptures that were given by God to Muhammad delivered by the Archangel Gabriel. The Qur'an which comes from the Arabic qaraa meaning "to read", is divided into 114 chapters or suras, and is the foundation of Islamic law, religion, culture and politics. The main doctrines laid down in the Qur'an are that only one God and one true religion exist; and that all will undergo a final judgment, with the just being rewarded and the sinners punished. Other spellings include Koran and Coran.

Rapport– in Occultism and Wicca a rapport is a mystical link between two or more individuals on a conscious or unconscious level. Rapports may also happen between humans and elementals.

Reincarnation– is to be reborn in a new body or the doctrine and spiritual law of cause and effect that holds that each soul lives through many lifetimes, gradually evolving spiritually, gaining skills and knowledge until it is no longer necessary to incarnate on earth as a human being. During the process of incarnating life after life, the soul gains experience, learns and hopefully produces good karma. Between lives the soul rests, on other planes of existence, referred to as Heaven by many, while it prepares itself for its next incursion in a human existente.

Religion– is various systems and institutions of faith and worship to a God or Gods.

Resonance– refers to affinity, empathy and attraction which will cause conditions to be brought together and vibrate in tune.

Revelation(s)– are messages to humans from the Godhead or Divine Will, received through dreams, visions, mystical insights, altered states of consciousness, oracles, and divination among others.

Ripple Effect– is the result of our own thoughts and thought patterns and those of everyone else on the unconscious or astral level that in turn reflects back and affects our collective unconsciousness on a spiritual – evolutional level.

Runes– are called the Viking Runes and Runic Alphabet, the runes are described as symbols in an ancient Nordic and Germanic method of divination and which consist of 25 basic runic symbols, usually made of ceramic or wood. According to the legend, Odhin hung from the World Tree for nine days and nights and lost one of his eyes to obtain the knowledge of the runes. Runes are also described as poems or sayings with mystical meanings or for casting spells. Runes are also used for divination.

Sacred– is set apart or dedicated to religious use; regarded as Holy, extraordinary or unique.

Salamanders– is from the Greek salambe which means fireplace. These Fire Spirits can be seen in and around hearths, fireplaces, fires, candles, etc. They show the least interest in human beings but can help clearing psychic and psychological obstacles. They are also known as Fire Drakes. See Elementals.

Scrying– is a method of divination or clairvoyance that requires the contemplation of a shiny surface such as a mirror or a bowl of water; crystal gazing is a method for scrying. Scrying is a means to aid concentration and induce trance states that allow the spiritual or psychic visions to be perceived. The Golden Dawn defines scrying as "originally related to crystal gazing, but now refers to the development of inner vision." Other spellings include skrying.

Self-Healing– all healing is self-healing. It is the process of physically, spiritually or mentally recovering from an injury or trauma. The best self-healing is achieved through understanding and applying such techniques as deep relaxation, breathing, meditation, visualization, guided imagery and self-hypnosis.

Self-Initiation– is the process by which an individual who either will not or cannot follow a formal group initiation does so on their own, usually following the same rituals and procedures of a written form of initiation.

Sensitive– is a person who can sense positive or negative energies from people or places or who shows psychic abilities such as telepathy and clairvoyance.

Shaman– is often called a Witch Doctor or Medicine Man was originally a Buddhist spiritual leader and healer among the Tartars in Siberia. The term now is used all over the world to describe a religious healer, priest, mystic, medium, specialist or intermediary (often called a Witch Doctor or Medicine Man) who, among other duties, interacts or acts as a medium with the spirit or astral world usually through trance visions, dreams or through ritual chanting, drums and the use of hallucinogenic drugs for the purpose of healing and divination. Other duties and abilities may include communal sacrifices, escorting the souls of the dead to the other world and even astral projection and shape- shifting.

Sixth Sense– is used to describe the psychic abilities (or faculties of extrasensory perceptions) that according to occultists are latent in everyone.

Smudging– in Native American, wiccan and other pagan traditions smudging is cleansing an area with the smoke of burning herbs to rid it of negative vibrations and evil spirits. In North America sage is traditionally burned for spiritual cleaning and to clear areas from evil spirits. This is done by burning sage in an abalone shell and dispersing the smoke with a feather (or feather wand).

Glossary

Soul– in religion and philosophy, the soul is the personal part of an entity, the individual essence or immaterial aspect of human beings sometimes considered to be synonymous with the mind or higher self. In Theology, the soul is described as the middle portion of the three-fold constitution of man that relates between physical side and the spirit, as in body, soul and spirit which survives physical death. It is also described as the vital principle or breath of life. Both the ancient Egyptians and Chinese conceived of the soul as dual. The Egyptians describe the ka, meaning "breath", which survives death but remains near the body and the ba (or spiritual side) that continues onto the land of the dead. The Chinese described a lower sensitive soul that disappears at death and a higher principal called hun with survivesphysical death. Pythagoras said that the soul was of divine origin and that it existed before and after death. Plato and Socrates accepted the soul as the immortal part of the body. Muslims and Christians believe that the soul comes into existence at the birth of the body.

Spell– is a magically empowered verse or text. A spell is a word, phrase or group of words ritually used to empower a magical procedure or words spoken in a set formula with magical purpose.

Spirit– is defined in occultism, Theosophy and theology as the divine spark in each human being, the spirit is the non physical, invisible form of all entities and is the inherent actuating element in life. The principal of conscious life: the vital principal or force in all entities, animating the physical vehicle or body and mediating between the vehicle and the soul. A spirit in general terms refers to all discarnate entities, angels, guides or gods.

Spirit Guides– are defined in general terms as discarnate entities or non physical beings, spirit guides, also called guardian Angels and channeled spirit guides, are said to be spirits of departed loved ones or beings of a higher evolution that guide or assist humankind on a spiritual level. According to occult beliefs, between incarnations we are called upon to perform as a spirit guide to a loved one incarnated.

Spiritual Cleansing– is the process of removing negative vibrations from an object, person or place using positive psychic energy and natural magic.

Spiritual Evolution– in occultism, mysticism and Theosophy, spiritual evolution refers to the evolution of human consciousness though physical experiences and many lives, maintaining that as spiritual beings were are evolving on a spiritual level.

Spirituality– has traditionally been associated with religion, deities and afterlife, it actually relates to the nature of the spirit including existentialism and introspection developed through spiritual practices such as contemplation, meditation and prayer.

Supernatural– is contrary to or above and beyond the known laws of science and nature as we currently understand them.

Superstition– is unreasonable or irrational belief based on ignorance and sometimes on fear in something not justified by reason or evidence.

Supplication– is called petitioning, supplication is a form of prayer where a person asks a god or other power to give them something, either for themselves or others. Also see Contemplation, Spiritual Techniques, and Prayer.

Supraconsciousness– is described as the stage of development of consciousness where are metaphysical and psychic abilities are readily accessible, ei astral projection, clairvoyance, precognition and telepathy, among others.

Sylphs– are from the Greek silphe meaning butterfly or winged one. These beings are powerful and mysterious they can be an unlimited source of inspiration, knowledge and ideas. They are also known as Zephyrs and Mountain Fairies. See Elementals.

Sympathetic
Magic   Magic that is based on two principles, that "like produces like", meaning that objects resembling each other share a certain occult affinity and that persons or things that have been in contact with continue to have effects upon one and another at a distance even after they have been separated and no longer have direct influence on each other.

T

Talisman– is a form of magically empowered, charged or consecrated object (amulet) usually carried for health, protection or luck and frequently bearing an engraved character or magical sign. The Golden Dawn defines Talismans as "a dead or inert substance galvanized into life by magically charging it with a specific form of energy." Talismans are active in principal where amulets are passive. Talismans are found in all magical traditions.

Tarot– an ncient divination method and the most popular divination method in modern Occultism, the Tarot uses a 78 card deck, subdivided into 22 major arcana consisting of 22 major trumps and 56 minor arcana and further divided into four suits: wands, clubs, pentacles and cups. Each card has a specific meaning and every time the cards are thrown they tell a different story. The cards of the major arcana refer to spiritual matters and current tendencies in the person's life. In the minor arcana, wands deal mostly with business matters and career, cups with love, swords with conflict, and coins with money and material comfort. In the last Century occultists have revived the diverse traditions of divination and magic using the Tarot and state that through practice and concentration the intuitive abilities are developed and the stories get clearer and easier to discern.

Telepathy– is from the Greek words tele meaning "distant" and patheia meaning "feeling", telepathy is described as communications between minds by psychic means, or transference of thoughts, feelings or images between people on a subconscious level, and without using the normal sensory channels of communication.

Theosophy– comes from the Greek theos, meaning "God", and sophia, meaning "wisdom", and is usually translated as "divine wisdom". Theosophy, also called the Wisdom Religion is a religious philosophy with mystical concerns that has its foundation in the premise that God must be experienced directly in order to be known and understood. The deepest source of theosophical views has been Indian thought, especially through the Vedas, the Upanishads and the Bhagavad-Gita. Both the old and modern theosophical writers agree that a deeper spiritual reality exists and that direct contact with that reality is achieved through intuition, meditation, revelation, or other mystical experiences. It is held that knowledge of divine wisdom gives access to the mysteries of nature and humankind's

Glossary

deeper being and understanding. There is also an emphasis on esoteric doctrine and the difference between an inner, or esoteric, teaching and an outer, or exoteric, teaching. Theosophy is the secret doctrine on which occult and esoteric teachings are based.

Therapeutic– relates to the treatment or cure of a disorder or disease, something that may benefit the health of an individual and can refer to spiritual as well as physical.

Thought– in occultism a thought is described as the force projected when the lower will expresses an idea through reasoning and the higher will illuminates and solidifies it.

Thought Forms– in occultism, thought forms are the energetic objects, shapes and forms assumed by thoughts and emotions expressed on the astral planes, visible to psychics, clairvoyants and astral travelers. Thought forms may be formed intentionally or unintentionally. When formed intentionally and reinforced through ritual visualization, they may take shape and image on the physical plane. All thought forms exist for a limited time, unintentional thought forms exist for a relatively small amount of time while purposely created thought forms can last longer, depending on how much mental energy and thought is invested in them.

Trance States– are altered state of consciousness with loss of normal awareness in which the mind is susceptible to suggestion, trance states may be spontaneous, self-induced or induced through hypnotism or other altered states of consciousness. Mediums may use trance states to reach other planes of existence or vibrational frequencies and communicate with discarnate entities or access the Akashic Records. Psychics use trance induced states for scrying and other forms of divination, and others use altered states of consciousness for Astral Projection.

Transcendental– means going beyond the limits of experience, beyond all common classifications and categories of being, transcendental is also described as that which rises above matter and is free from the physical influences of the material world and emphasizes the intuitive and spiritual about the material and empirical.

Transition– is often applied to death, because death is seen only as a transition from one plane or dimension to another.

Transmutation– is the process of changing a substance, nature or state to another substance, nature or state. It also refers to the changing of something base into something higher, more pure. In a physical sense transmutation is the conversion of one chemical element into another and in a spiritual sense transmutation refers to changing a state of mind or emotion into an expression of the same, such as transforming sexual/instinctive energies into intellectual and spiritual ones.

Trolls   See Elementals.

Unction– also called Anointing, Unction is a ceremonial or sacramental application of oil, blessed water or wine for magical or religious purposes; commonly found at baptisms, initiations and death rites among other types of rituals and ceremonies. Christians use the sign of the cross when anointing and Wiccans and others use the pentagram.

Undines– is from the Latin are also known as, meaning wave or creature of the wave. They produce or inspire the essence of plant life and abundant growth and are closely associated with the healing of plants, animals and humans. They are also known as Fairies, Nymphs, Mermen and Mermaids. See Elementals.

Vedas– is from Sanskrit, meaning "knowledge", the Vedas are the entire body of the most sacred and ancient (one of the oldest if not the oldest) written Hindu texts. The Vedas are derived from the Upanishads and its four main texts: Brhadaranyaka, Chandogya, Taittiriya, and Katha. And all of these derived from the famous poetic dialogue, the Bhagavad-Gita. These sacred texts deal mostly with mantras, spells, chants and rituals.

Vibrations– in occultism, vibrations are described as electromagnetic energy or psychic waves.

Vision– is an experience in which a person, thing, event or sequence of events appears vividly in the mind. Vision also refers to the act or ability of anticipating future events, usually in great retail.

Visualization– is the process of forming and holding mental images in the conscious mind with intense clarity. Most magical systems use this technique in rituals.

Voodoo– is the Polytheistic Religion of Haiti that is also practiced in Brazil, Cuba, Trinidad and parts of the southern United States, Voodoo derives from ancient African cult worships based on Theology, magic and Roman Catholicism. The term Voodoo derives from the word vodun, which means "spirit" or "God". Voodoo cults worship a high God, Bon Dieu and the souls of dead people, which are the Rada, or good ones and the Petro, or bad ones and other spirits or saints called Loa. The Loa are usually identified or paralleled with Roman Catholic Saints. Followers of Vooodoo believe that the soul is twofold, having a Gros Bon Ange (big guardian) and the Ti Bon Ange (little guardian). They believe that the Ti Bon Ange leaves the body during sleep and when in a state of trance during rituals. The rituals are lead by a priest calledHoungan, or by a priestess, called Mambo who act as shamans, healers and spiritual guides to the living. They are known as expert magicians in white magic. On the darker side Voodoo, there are also priests called Bocors who deal with black magic.

Voodoo Doll– is a doll constructed of wax, wood, corn or cloth meant to represent a specific person in sympathetic magic, sometimes these dolls may include hair or nail clippings from the person. Also see Poppet, Sympathetic Magic and voodooshop.com.

Glossary

Wand– in magical and occult traditions the wand is the most popular and traditional magical instrument. Described at length in the Key of Solomon and other medieval texts, many, many traditions use wands in their rituals. Wands consist of a straight, thin hand-held, slim baton made of wood, ivory, metal or other material. Wands are used to direct magical energy and represent the masculine, active and positive power of nature.

Warding– in Wicca and other traditions warding is a magical act performed to protect, prevent access or ward off a person, place or thing.

Wicca– is also known as The Craft, the Old Religion and Witchcraft, Wicca is a benevolent, nature oriented religion and magical system which believes in the Goddess as their principal and triple deity; Maiden, Mother and Crone together with the Horned God, her male counterpart and High Priest. Their belief system has no central doctrines but most Wiccans include the beliefs of reincarnation, karma, and the reverence of nature. Their main motto is "And it harm none, do what thou wilt". The Wiccans organize themselves into covens with upto 13 persons each. There are several different branches of Wicca which include Alexandrian Wicca, Dianic Wicca, Gardenerian Wicca, and the Georgian Tradition, among many others such as Druidic Witchcraft, Faery (fairy) Wicca and Celtic Wicca.

Witch– is a person (male or female) who professes the Wicca religion and/or practices witchcraft, when used in the correct terminology. Unfortunately the terms witch and witchcraft have been misconstrued to describe evil beings or practices since the burning times of the Middle Ages, when the entire Wicca religion and traditional herbal healing, (and almost anything else out of the ordinary) came under attack by the Inquisition.

Witchcraft See Wicca.

Worship– is the expression of love, devotion and reverence accorded to a sacred object, Saint, Angel or Deity. This expression can be personal or a ritual ceremonial experience of many people.

Yoga– literally means a binding together of psychic power for spiritual development. It is a complete science developed thousands of years ago in India. Yoga is one of the six Darshans of Hindu Philosophy. The main purpose of all yoga is to raise the spiritual awareness by reaching a state consciousness that will activate the chakras. The Upanishads and the Bhagavad-Gita are two well known Hindu books on the disciplines of yoga. As with all other Darshans, the goal of yoga is that of spiritual enlightenment. There are many different schools of yoga which use different methods to reach the same goal, which is to train the body and mind.

Zephyrs See Elementals.

Spell Book

Introduction

The Spell Book, also known as "The Book of Shadows", "Black Book" or "Grimoire" has been an important source of information through out history for Occultists and for those who wrote, learned from or inherited one. More than a mere register of spells and potions for love, prosperity, protection and others, the Spell Book also represents traditions, instructions, intuitions, dreams, inspirations, theories and personal discoveries. Gathering this information is very useful because it provides us a reference tool which can be an effective resource for our spiritual and magical development. In the process of creating our own magic we can also learn from those rituals and spells which have been successful as well as of those that were not.

Creating a Spell Book can be as simple as using a personal diary or notebook, or, as elaborate and colorful as tastes our fancy. There are Spell Books that are made from leather decorated with gems and shells and engraved with startling calligraphy. The imagination is the only limit.

It is convenient write *in all detail* the events that occur during the ritual. Do not forget to write down those "feelings or sensations"; retrospectively, they tend to be very revealing. It is also very useful to write down anything unusual that happens, being totally honest with oneself, (and always looking for the logical explanation).

An example of a Spell Book that is given on the next page is a mere suggestion of what could be a diary of rituals. This should be a very personal register and should conform to the tastes and needs of each person.

Register of a Ritual

    Date
    Day of the Week
    Lunar Phase
    Time
    Principal Color
    Sign or Planet

Objective

Preparation/ Ingredients

Bath

Incenses

Oils

Candles: Offering
    Astrological
    Altar
    Day (Week)

Gems and/or Metals

Talismans

Spell Book

Texts

Sensations

Conclusions

About the Author

Heather (Eaton) Mulholland was born in San Francisco, California in 1964. She lived her first few years in the Bay Area, after which her family moved to Terra Haute, Indiana and Cincinnati, Ohio briefly before joining the Peace Corps and moving to Chile where she spent the following 30 years. In 2003 she returned to the Bay Area to be near her children and grandson. Recently married after a whirlwind romance, she now lives happily ever after.

Heather was raised by scientists in an atheist environment. In her 30's she suffered a serious foot injury which left her in a wheelchair for several months. Having been an avid reader her whole life she turned to more spiritual interests and started writing. She has written several books.

Colophon

Titles set in Celticmd
Test in Cambria
Using Adobe Indesign CC

History of the Fonts

"I found a Celtic typestyle in a book of Celtic art and scanned it. Then I imported it into Corel 3.0 and cleanedit up to export as a .PFB. It is primarily a drop-cap style and so with out lower-case letters it appeared quite ineffectual, so, I took the lower case from Celtic,the .PFB, with FontMonger v 1.07, and incorporated those. I then fudged several keysinto forming the rest of typeface; and VOILA!, CelticMD was created. I have a stronginterest in my Celtic heritage and will be using this font in a national newsletterrelating to Celtic and Scottish history and clann events." From the author of Font

The Cambria Font Family was designed for on-screen reading and to look good when printed at small sizes. Cambria is part of the new Windows ClearType font collection. The Cambria fonts have excellent legibility and readability characteristics. Cambria replaces Times New Roman as a Windows Vista and Microsoft Office default serif font.

www.onespiritpress.com
Onespiritpress@gmail.com

www.ingramcontent.com/pod-product-compliance
Lightning Source LLC
Chambersburg PA
CBHW081209230426
43666CB00015B/2687